PENGUIN BOOKS

CAT VS. CAT

Pam Johnson-Bennett, CCBC, is the bestselling author of eight books on cat behavior. She starred in the Animal Planet UK series *Psycho Kitty*, and is one of the most popular and sought-after cat behavior experts in the world. She is considered a pioneer in the field of cat behavior consulting and has been a major influence on many practicing in the field today. Pam began making house calls to work with clients on cat behavior problems in 1982 and had her first book published in 1990. Since then, she has led the way as an inspiration and mentor to many in the cat behavior profession. Her books have been used as texts for professional behavior courses.

Pam was vice president of the International Association of Animal Behavior Consultants and founded the IAABC Cat Division, where she served as chair for eight years. Pam has served on multiple advisory boards, including the American Humane Association's Advisory Committee on Animal Behavior and Training, and was also a member of the American Humane Association's Cat Health and Welfare Forum. She served on the Advisory Board for Tree House Humane Society and has also worked with the Winn Feline Foundation.

Pam's book *Think Like a Cat* and its groundbreaking approach to cat behavior has been featured and profiled worldwide since it was first published in 2000. An updated and expanded *Think Like a Cat* was released in 2011 and remains one of the bestselling cat training books. Her books are considered the "cat bibles" when it comes to understanding felines and what makes them tick. Her training methods have improved the lives of thousands of cats through her books, work with clients and shelters, worldwide lectures, and media appearances.

Pam and her family live in Tennessee, along with Pearl, her rescued cat, and Griffin, a rescued dog. Both Pearl and Griffin are pretty sure they were the ones doing the rescuing, though.

Cat vs. Cat

Keeping Peace When You Have
More Than One Cat

COMPLETELY REVISED AND UPDATED

Pam Johnson-Bennett

Certified Cat Behavior Consultant

PENGUIN BOOKS

PENGUIN BOOKS

An imprint of Penguin Random House LLC
penguinrandomhouse.com

First published in Penguin Books 2004
This revised edition published in 2020

LIBRARY OF CONGRESS CATALOGING-IN-PUBLICATION DATA
Names: Johnson-Bennett, Pam, 1954– author.
Title: Cat vs. cat: keeping peace when you have more than one cat /
Pam Johnson-Bennett, CCBC, Feline Behaviorist.
Other titles: Cat versus cat
Description: Updated and expanded edition. |
New York: Penguin Books, 2020. | Includes index.
Identifiers: LCCN 2019058197 (print) | LCCN 2019058198 (ebook) |
ISBN 9780143135586 (trade paperback) | ISBN 9780525507239 (ebook)
Subjects: LCSH: Cats—Behavior. | Cats—Psychology.
Classification: LCC SF446.5 .J355 2020 (print) | LCC SF446.5 (ebook) |
DDC 636.8—dc23
LC record available at https://lccn.loc.gov/2019058197
LC ebook record available at https://lccn.loc.gov/2019058198

Printed in the United States of America

Set in Dante MT Std
Designed by Sabrina Bowers

*This book is for all who have opened their hearts
to the cats who were labeled unadoptable, unfixable,
and unlovable. You are my heroes.*

Acknowledgments

So many cats have allowed me into their world, whether they were cats I've met through my behavior work or the ones who simply showed up at my door. Every day, cats give me a renewed appreciation for their beauty, loyalty, grace, intelligence, and endless patience with humans.

Thank you to all the veterinarians who have welcomed me into their community from the beginning of my career. I am grateful for our longtime friendships and for how generous you are with your time. I am in awe of the love and dedication you have for all the animals in your care.

To the cat parents I have had the honor of working with since I did my very first house call in 1982, thank you for the trust you placed in me, especially in those early years when this profession seemed very odd to almost everyone I met. Still, you followed my recommendations, showed patience when I missed the mark, and continued to make life better for your cats. Thank you for being willing to *think like a cat*.

Thank you to my agent and longtime friend Linda Roghaar for your never-ending support and wisdom. Thank you to Wendy Wolf, my editor, for making me look much smarter than I really am. Thank you to my family at Penguin for creating such beautiful books.

Thank you, Marilyn Krieger, for years of close friendship and for sharing in my passion to make life better for cats. Special thanks to two incredible friends in my life, Mary Beth Nicholson and Chris Chichuk. I love you.

Thank you, Don Wright, for your friendship, support, and amazing talent. I am so grateful for all you do and constantly surprised at your ability to achieve the impossible.

Thank you to Scott, Grace, and Jack. I love you all so much. You have endured my crazy travel schedule and the weird comments from people about what I do for a living. You never complain about late dinners or the endless cat stories I babble on about. Thank you for loving cats as much as I do.

Thank you to Albie, Ethel, Olive, Mary, Bebe, Rona, Lucy, Abigail, and Buster. You were the best teachers.

Contents

Introduction   xi

1 The Feline Social Structure   1

2 Decoding: Understanding Cat Communication   13

3 Turf 101: Understanding Territory   40

4 New Introductions   60

5 Enriching the Environment   97

6 Managing Mealtime in a Multicat Home   141

7 How to Maintain a Happy Multicat Litter Box Environment   160

8 Scratching the Surface: Training Cats to Scratch Where
You Want Them To   200

9 Keeping the Lid on Aggression   212

10 Managing Stress   244

11 Aging and Illness in a Multicat Home   261

12 Professional Help   279

Appendix   285

Index   289

Introduction

Cats. Oh, how we love them. They rule our hearts, quite a few of them rule our homes, and they certainly have ruled the internet for years. It's easy to fall in love with these exquisite, loving, and intelligent creatures.

Once you've shared your life with a cat, it's easy to want to increase your cat family to two, three, or more. There are so many joys in living with more than one cat. But life with multiple cats has its share of challenges as well. While *any* cat can experience a behavior problem, the likelihood of one occurring certainly can become amplified in a multicat home. In some cases, it can be difficult just trying to figure out which cat is causing the problem.

We love cats so much, but we don't always understand their social structure. I have made countless house calls to multicat homes and have spent a great deal of time with confused pet parents who had the best intentions but now feel overwhelmed by the problems within their feline family. Relationship issues between the cats can be tricky. All too often, cat parents don't know enough about what happens when cats are asked to live together, so they don't understand how to create an environment that fosters peaceful coexistence. When there's more than one cat in a home, they often have less personal space and more overlapping territory, both of which can cause them much stress. Overcrowding can create anxiety and turn a happy home into a war zone. Cats give us so much, and we have a responsibility to create an environment in which everyone can feel happy, stimulated, safe, and secure.

This book will teach you how to avoid behavior problems when you've got more than one cat, and will also help if you're unfortunately stuck in the middle of a crisis right now. Keep reminding yourself of one fundamental rule: You want to give the cats a reason to *like* each other. If you're a first-time cat parent or considering becoming one, I recommend you also read my book *Think Like a Cat*, to get a good foundation in the basics of care, behavior, and training.

Cat vs. Cat will provide you with valuable insight into how cats communicate both with humans and with other cats. When you learn the *why* behind behaviors, you'll better understand what cats need from you, their environment, and each other. When *Cat vs. Cat* was published in 2004, it was the first book dedicated to the joys and challenges of living with multiple cats. This newly updated and vastly expanded version draws from the latest research and data on behavior; every day we learn more and more about what goes on inside the heads of these wonderful animals, and that information will help you bring out the best in your cat family.

If you're a seasoned cat parent, this book will help you sharpen your detective skills and solve current problems. You'll be able to take a step back to examine your multicat home in a more productive way, then map out a behavior plan. Whether your situation just needs a little tweaking or a major overhaul, you'll find techniques in this book to get you and your cats back on track.

I must bring up one issue before you delve into these chapters, though. You must spay and neuter your cats. Intact cats cannot coexist peacefully. Intact males will spray and fight. If allowed outdoors, intact males will roam, fight, and indiscriminately mate. Unspayed females will *call* repeatedly, attract unwanted cats into your yard, and constantly try to escape out the door. Intact animals are also at a higher risk of developing certain types of cancers. Cats who are not spayed or neutered are ruled by their hormones and are impossible to maintain peacefully in a multicat home. So that's your first step, if you haven't done so already.

If you're currently a cat parent and are considering adding to your cat family, this book will guide you through the introduction so you can avoid many of the mistakes cat parents make without even realizing it. If you already have a multicat environment and things have gone south, don't worry. It's never too late to turn things around if you're willing to do the work.

Finally, with the increased popularity of the cat behavior field, there is a lot of bad advice out there. My goal with this updated and expanded version of *Cat vs. Cat* is to give you accurate, commonsense, compassionate, and easy-to-understand techniques so you can help your cats live in harmony.

Cat
vs.
Cat

The Feline Social Structure

You may look at your multicat household as one happy family; you love your cats equally and feel there shouldn't be any reason for fighting or squabbling. In reality, though, your cats don't view each other as equals, nor should they. Whether you have two cats or twenty, there is a bit of a pecking order. It may bother you to think that a few cats might have higher status than others, but some form of a hierarchy is necessary in feline society. In a free-roaming environment, it prevents overcrowding of the colony and gives cats a sense of order and security.

It used to be that cats weren't thought of as being social animals, especially when compared to their canine counterparts. Even today, many people imagine that their cats are solitary, even antisocial, but they're misinterpreting what they see. Cats are solitary hunters, and they're looking out for themselves. They capture only prey large enough for one meal. Watching them on the prowl, many people incorrectly label them as solitary animals in all aspects of their lives.

Another behavior that adds to cats' mistakenly labeled reputation as asocial is their territorial instinct and their attitude toward newcomers. We recognize dogs as social creatures—pack animals—because existing canine households will often easily accept a new puppy. When cat parents think of adding another cat, visions of hissing, scratching, fights, and, in general, disaster come to mind. This hardly inspires one to label cats as *social*. But it can work, so long as you go about it in a way that makes sense to the cats involved. It's important to understand and then work out territorial issues before putting two cats together; if you do, they can become friends and develop a long-term relationship. Cats can readily adapt to living in groups, and although they may still maintain some preferred personal areas, many enjoy companionship and benefit from group living. It just takes a little finesse.

The social structure is complex and easy to misunderstand. It's built around resource availability. The need for food and other resources often outweighs the desire to fight. Cats will coexist in closer proximity to one another near a common food source or shelter. Even in those situations, most cats may avoid each other and "live alone" in a group. Between the independent ferals and the dependent indoor cats you'll find free-roaming cats: ferals who interact minimally, and owned cats who have access to the outdoors.

The most common social relationship is between a female cat and her kittens. With indoor cats, kittens are generally separated from the mother too early by people wanting to adopt them out (kittens should be kept with the mother and littermates for twelve weeks). In free-roaming environments, kittens usually stay with the mother longer. Female kittens, once they leave the mother, will generally stay within the same area, whereas males will travel farther.

In feral colonies, far from being antisocial, related females are often so closely bonded that they may nurse each other's kittens as well as help raise them. This benefits the mothers who are not as strong, so all the kittens have a better chance at survival. Females commonly move their kittens often if they fear attacks from males or outside predators. Females will also band together to help defend against aggressive males who pose a threat, or any other potential danger to their kittens. In free-roaming cats, long-term bonds aren't formed between mating partners. There's nothing romantic about sex in the feline world. It's all about survival.

In multicat homes you'll see a spectrum of different social behaviors; the cats may only tolerate one another, or some cats may form very close bonds. Much of this will depend on how well the cats were socialized as kittens, how they were introduced to each other, their distinct personalities, their allotted spaces and their understanding of the territorial divisions, and how the cat parent has set up resource availability and has handled squabbles.

In a cat colony, unfamiliar cats are typically driven away, but if a cat keeps returning, he may work his way in and eventually be accepted. This is a slow process and mirrors the way a new cat entering an established multicat household may be accepted. Just as in the outdoor cat colony, the introduction of a new cat into your home must be gradual in order to increase the odds of acceptance.

Avoiding conflict is a major concern in a feral colony and also in your multicat home. It's important to pay attention so you can minimize the fighting/aggression period and also make sure all your cats are safe and don't harm one another as they're being introduced. Cats are very sensitive to feeling threatened, which may not only result in an obvious display of aggression but may cause cats to withdraw and remain chronically stressed. Ongoing stress or conflict can lead to illness. The body isn't designed to stay in the stress response (fight/flight) long-term.

In a multicat home, just as in an outdoor colony, cats form unique relationships with each other. Certain cats may develop close bonds. They may frequently engage in allogrooming, rubbing, sleeping close together, tail-up greetings, and tail entwining. When cats are closely bonded, it's not unusual to see one act as a pillow for the other when sleeping. With other cats in the group, there may be friendly relationships but not as close.

Often, one cat may lick the head of another cat as an invitation to play. This might be welcomed and result in a game of chase or play wrestling, but sometimes it's ill timed and results in a swat to the nose of the initiator. This is how the cats begin to learn each other's play signals.

When two familiar cats approach each other in a friendly environment or in an area where there are no turf disputes, they will start with nose-to-nose sniffing, head rubbing, and possibly licking the face and ears. Anal sniffing follows. If the cats are not so friendly, then the exchange will end at nose sniffing.

When your cat jumps in your lap, goes nose-to-nose with you, and then turns to present his backside, you may have considered this distasteful, but it's very polite in terms of feline social etiquette, and you should feel complimented (though you don't have to respond in kind!). Another often misinterpreted behavior is when a cat lounges with his back toward you. What he's really saying in both situations is that he trusts you. Scratching is appreciated then.

STATUS AND HIERARCHY

Although there is a general hierarchy in your cat household, it's not a pecking order forever set in stone. The hierarchy is dynamic and subtly shifts and moves. When a hierarchy is well established, the security and familiarity of knowing where they stand allows the cats to coexist peacefully. But in some households the delicate hierarchy remains in balance only by a whisker. One or two cats may rule the roost, usually simultaneously but with turf areas worked out so they don't step on each other's paws, so to speak. Subtle shifts in status can occur, depending on who is in the room and what events are taking place.

Think of the hierarchy as the rungs on a ladder. The highest-ranking cat sits on top. In a perfect world, each new cat added to the household would take his place at the next highest available rung. Oh, if only it could be that simple, there wouldn't be so many battles. Unfortunately, though, a new cat may be more assertive and might attempt to knock another cat off an attractive rung. As you can imagine, that never sits well with the existing cat community, and suddenly the rungs on the ladder get a bit shaky. If you're going from one cat to two, your resident cat may willingly step aside from the top rung (it's easy to be top cat when there are no other cats in the house). He may feel more comfortable taking a lower status if the new cat is more confident.

The rungs of an actual ladder are evenly spaced, but the rungs on the feline hierarchy ladder aren't. Some cats may be relatively close in status, so their rungs may just be a whisker's width apart. Other cats may be separated by very wide gaps. This unevenness in the spaces is one reason why the hierarchy may hit bumps in the road. The competition between two cats close in rank may routinely ignite the anxiety of one, and they will be more likely to engage in physical confrontation. A middle-ranking cat may repeatedly pick on a very low-ranking cat, especially if he has been the target of the cats above him. Since he doesn't feel confident enough to stand up to the more senior cats, he turns his frustrations on a cat beneath him.

A major role of being the higher-ranking cat is to ensure priority when it comes to resources such as the food bowl, litter box, favorite resting areas, etc. Of course, it's not always guaranteed that the higher-ranking cat will gain that priority access if one or more subordinate cats decide to challenge. Just as in the human world, life doesn't always go according to plan.

There are traditional signals and behaviors that help communicate subordinate status and higher-ranking position. Some are so subtle you may easily miss them. For example, a subordinate cat will often look away and avoid direct eye contact with the higher-ranking cat. He will also turn his body more sideways when the other cat is near; he may crouch and attempt to appear nonthreatening. It's normal to see a subordinate cat give way on a path to allow the higher-ranking cat to pass.

A higher-ranking cat may use direct stares, straighten and stiffen his legs, and have his body forward facing.

Status in each group-living environment is unique, based on the personalities of each cat and how they work out their time-sharing in the environment. Your neighbor's multicat household may have more issues than your household even though you may have more cats. Every situation has its own set of circumstances.

The hierarchy within a multicat household may appear flexible in that one cat may rule a certain room, while another cat may claim dibs on another location, such as the kitchen, where the food bowls are located. When it comes to any kind of hierarchy, don't think in terms of an overall dominant or alpha cat and don't think of the rungs of the ladder as being stiff and unmovable. The arrangement cats work out has more to do with how they do their territorial negotiations and their choices of what resources/territories matter to each of them.

Scrutiny of your environment can provide clues about the relationships between your cats and their status. For example, height can play a role in status. I'm not referring to how tall a cat may be, but rather the ability to access and control higher elevations in the home. The cat who controls the elevated locations in a room—tabletops, tops of bookshelves, or dedicated cat-climbing furniture—may likely develop the higher status. The higher perch provides the cat with the ability to oversee his area and demonstrates his status to subordinates. It may also help reduce conflict, because the cat may choose to go to his perch to show indifference and status rather than engage in active aggression.

The physical position of the cats as they enter a room may also provide clues as to who is in charge in that area or at that time. For example, two cats enter the room and one walks toward the middle of the space while the other walks along the perimeter. The one occupying the center of the room may give a direct stare to the perimeter cat. The perimeter cat avoids direct eye contact. The center cat most likely has control of that room.

In a tense environment, cats who are less prone to anxiety tend to be higher ranking. This stands to reason, because when the group faces a stressful situation, it needs leaders who are calmer and more able to react appropriately for the benefit of the colony. A higher-ranking cat in your household may not necessarily be the one who displays the most aggression, but the calmest cat of the bunch.

Cats close in status are more likely to engage in an actual physical confrontation. These cats may be on the middle rungs of the status ladder. A clearly higher-ranking cat may show indifference and walk away from a tense situation or groom himself. Acting indifferent can appear more intimidating. It works to his advantage not to display weakness.

Higher-ranking cats may posture instead of entering into actual aggressive confrontations. Posturing is an important precursor to any potentially aggressive encounter. Guarding choice areas is a common example. A high-ranking cat may block the pathway to the litter box or food bowl or might stay in the litter box longer and be the first one to use it after it has been cleaned.

Higher-ranking cats frequently claim the prime areas of a territory. For some cats that may be the cat parent's bed. For others, it could be the soft chair by the fireplace or the window that overlooks the outdoor bird feeder.

Sometimes, when a number of cats share a territory, you'll find one who becomes a pariah. This is the lowest-ranking cat, who stays far away from the others. The pariah lives on the perimeter of the territory, walks low to the ground, and will usually growl when in the vicinity of another cat. You may find him slinking to the feeding station to grab leftovers long after the other cats have eaten. It's important to provide safe retreats for the lowest-ranking cat and places where he can access resources without fear of attack.

How a cat interacts with you doesn't influence his rank in the feline group. A higher-ranking cat, however, may display some of the same status-related behavior toward a human as he would another cat—he might stare you in the eye, rub against your leg or arm, and then back away as a challenge or exhibit mouthing (the cat puts his teeth on you but doesn't apply any pressure).

What determines a cat's place in the hierarchy? There are many factors, such as age, size, confidence, sexual maturity, social maturity, number of cats, whether the cat had littermates and how they interacted, health, the availability of food—the list goes on. It's dynamic and complex.

EARLY SOCIALIZATION

Socialization of young kittens is very important. It can make a big difference in how they respond to humans as they mature, as well as how they respond to other cats. Frequent, gentle handling by more than one person can help the kittens become less fearful adults. Kittens should be touched gently, starting at two weeks of age. The critical socialization period is between two and seven weeks, but it's still beneficial as late as fourteen weeks. It's during this time that this kind of handling and exposure to new experiences can help decrease fear, increase confidence, and increase friendliness toward humans and other animals. Socialization done during kittenhood can have benefits that last throughout a cat's life.

But don't jump the gun here. During the first two weeks, the kittens need to nurse, sleep, and stay warm by being snuggled close to mom. This is an important time for mother and kittens to bond and establish a routine. If cat parents interfere prior to two weeks, the mother might become distressed and move her nest. For the mother, this early time is essential for her to feel secure and calm about the safety of her nest.

Pam's CatWise Tip

Even after the socialization period, it's still very beneficial to continue the socialization process because learning is always taking place.

Kittens should ideally stay with the mother and littermates for twelve weeks. Kittens that are weaned and able to successfully eliminate in a litter box may appear ready for adoption as early as six to eight weeks, but there are many social and psychological advantages to keeping them together until they're twelve weeks old. Kittens taken away too early or raised without littermates don't learn some very critical social skills. They may overreact (that is, bite too hard) during play or social interactions. That extra time with mom and siblings helps kittens accept other cats in the environment more easily and interact more appropriately with them.

Littermates start engaging in social play with one another at around three weeks of age, when the kittens can move around more easily. Each week the social play gets more refined as the kittens become adept at balance and coordination. As the kittens get older, they engage in less social play and in more object play. By twelve weeks of age, their play patterns may begin to resemble fighting more than playing. More hissing and crying may be heard during wrestling, and more serious posturing is visible.

TENSE SITUATIONS

There are various situations that will cause rumbling throughout your multicat household. Events such as the addition or loss of a cat or human family member, moving to a new home, illness in the feline family, and cats reaching sexual maturity are the types of upheavals cat parents realize are most likely to affect cats. There are also some not-so-obvious reasons for a sudden shakeup. One event many cat parents aren't aware of is *social maturity*. This occurs between two and four years of age and is not to be confused with *sexual maturity*, which occurs around six to seven months. Almost all cat parents know a kitten officially becomes an adult at the age of one year, but the cat still has more maturing to do in the social department. Much like human adolescence, the period when they start to reach social maturity is the prime time for cats to jockey for social position. This may cause subtle and not-so-subtle shifting in a formerly peaceful cat family. This can be a time when a cat feels more confident and views an opportunity to elevate his status.

Illness also plays a role in hierarchy that you may not be prepared for. A sick cat may lose his current position and become subordinate to some or all the healthy ones, regardless of previous status.

CAN YOU HAVE TOO MANY CATS?

There is a situation where a bump in the road turns into a brick wall, and that is when you simply have too many cats. This isn't a subject cat parents like to discuss and many can become very defensive about it. It's imperative to recognize a healthy limit to the size of your family, taking into consideration the various demands on you, your home, and the different personalities of the cats already in the home. Although cats require less space than dogs, there is only so much physical territory to go around. You won't be doing your cats a favor if they're forced to live in uncomfortably close quarters in a constantly hostile environment.

A question I am often asked is, "How many is too many cats?" People are usually looking for me to give a fixed number, such as five, fifteen, or more than twenty. The truth is, for some people, two cats are too many based on things very specific to their living conditions. The answer is unique to each person. You must look at the following:

- Your own living conditions, including the size of your home
- Your current cat family and their personalities
- Your financial situation
- Your physical and emotional abilities
- Your schedule and the existing demands on your time
- Your reasons for wanting to acquire multiple cats
- Your family members' opinions and concerns
- Legal restrictions

Carefully consider the cost of keeping multiple cats and whether you can afford it. In addition to the cost of food, there are ongoing veterinary expenses. Your responsibility as a cat parent doesn't end with saving a cat from the side of the road—you are also responsible for making sure the cat's medical needs are met. While many cat parents are lucky enough to have only the yearly expenses of routine vaccinations and checkups, others aren't so fortunate and may end up with one or more cats who require special food, prescriptions, ongoing monitoring, or even extensive diagnostic tests or surgery. Veterinary medicine has grown by leaps and bounds, and it's amazing what can be done to keep our precious cats living longer, but those advances may come with a hefty price tag.

Decoding: Understanding Cat Communication

Cats are masters at communication. While we humans rely on verbal communication, cats use multiple methods.

Cats are territorial animals who choose to avoid conflict whenever possible, so maximizing communication skills can mean the difference between injury and safety, and, in some cases, life and death. The more skilled you are at being able to interpret what your cats are communicating to one another, the better able you'll be at heading off potential intercat feuds. Even if you live with only a single cat, the more you know what she's communicating to you, the stronger the bond between you. If you get scratched or bitten quite often, you may be misreading a cat's cues. Understand feline communication and the signals your cats are sending out and you'll end up with fewer scars.

The problem with feline communication is that all too often humans don't pay enough attention to it. People look at certain cat behaviors through a human filter. Cat parents make many inaccurate assumptions about what cats are communicating by their behaviors, based on the human's level of frustration, expectation of what a cat should be doing, and lack of knowledge regarding what really triggers behavior. Many people are also far more familiar with dog behavior and communication, so when a cat doesn't respond the way a dog would, cat parents get confused and disappointed. Cats aren't fur-covered children and they aren't dogs. Too often, though, cats are brought into the family with the expectation that they will act and communicate in the way the human family members want them to. If you take the time to really look at all the ways your cats communicate with you and with one another, you'll see your frustration filter start to dissolve. You'll develop a new appreciation for how complex, efficient, and beautiful the feline *language* really is and the essential role it plays in a cat's survival. More awareness of how cats communicate can strengthen or repair the bond you share.

Between how *you* communicate and how *your cats* communicate, you'll find there's a bridge. You and your cats can find it and happily meet on it. Let's get started by teaching you about the marvelous world of cat communication.

SCENT COMMUNICATION

Scent is big in a cat's world. Really big. It's basically a cat's version of an ID card. With our very inadequate noses, we don't have the capacity to fully appreciate how much information is transmitted through scent. Here's a fact that will help put it in perspective. Cats have 200 million scent receptors in their nasal cavity. Humans have 5 million receptors. With that many scent receptors, there aren't many odors that get missed by a cat. Would you even want 200 million scent receptors? I know I wouldn't.

Cats smell scents and they create them in many ways. Cats have scent glands on their paw pads, cheeks, forehead, chin, lips, flanks, and tail, and there are also glands on either side of the rectum, and all of them leave a scent trail. The scent produced by the anal glands are used to mark feces as it emerges. From our point of view, it certainly doesn't seem as if cat poop needs any more odor, but it's important to remember that just about everything belonging to a cat gets a personalized *stamp*. Then, of course, there's the scent associated with urine-marking. Again, it's all about personalization. When it comes to communication by scent, cats pretty much have it covered from head to tail.

Pam's CatWise Feline Fact

The color of a cat's nose is determined by genetics. Sometimes the nose color fades as the cat ages. Nose color may also fade during cold winter months.

How Scent Is Used

Scent glands release chemicals known as pheromones. These scent-packed pheromones help cats share information without having to risk physical confrontation.

Scent is used for identification of members in a colony or multi-cat environment, to announce reproductive availability, to gain information about unfamiliar cats in the vicinity, and is also a form of covert or subtle aggression. Scent is important for bonding, familiarity, self-soothing, and territory identification.

The way that cats deposit scents, and which glands they use, provides information about what they're feeling at the time. Scent glands located around the head are associated with bonding and familiarity. Facial pheromones are known as the friendly pheromones. A cat may rub her cheek along an object she considers part of her territory. She may also cheek rub or head bunt cat

companions or human family members as a social bonding behavior. These behaviors reflect a sense of security, familiarity,
and affection.

The paw pad scent glands come into play when a cat scratches
objects. The claws leave a visual mark, but the pheromones leave
a scent mark so that others know who left the mark, and also create a comforting, familiar smell.

The back-end pheromones, such as the ones released when a
cat spray-marks, are used for transmitting reproductive status, or
for territory marking, covert aggression, and other high-intensity,
stressful situations.

The Importance of Group Scent

In addition to your cat's amazing ability to use her scent receptors
to evaluate things in her environment and detect prey or other
predators, scent is also an essential method of personal identification. Scent is a major way cats identify one another. When a cat
comes across the scent of an unfamiliar cat, the scent evidence
can provide the cat doing the sniffing with many facts, such as
the sex of the cat who left the scent, as well as its status, whether
the cat is in heat, and how recently the scent was deposited.

In group living, cats create a communal scent. Each cat has her
own unique scent, and it's by combining scents that a communal
scent identity is created. Rubbing, allogrooming, and bunting are
all part of the process. In addition to the affection and social bonding aspect, the group scent created by the above behaviors also
plays a role in keeping peace in the colony or household between
cats who are not so friendly. The group scent-marking lets cats
know who's "in" already, and helps them identify their feline
friends more quickly.

Group scent-marking is also how cats help recognize one another as they come and go throughout the day and night. An

indoor/outdoor cat who returns from roaming is greeted with lots of sniffing so colony members can be reassured that this feline wanderer is a familiar member.

The Vomeronasal Organ

As if their normal sense of smell weren't remarkable enough, cats come equipped with a special "scent analyzer" known as the Jacobson's organ, or vomeronasal organ. Located in the roof of the mouth, it's used for analyzing pheromones, especially those found in urine.

The scent is collected in the mouth and then the tongue transfers it up to the ducts located just behind the front teeth. These ducts lead into the nasal cavity. You can tell when a cat is engaging the vomeronasal organ because her mouth will be partially open with the upper lip curled. The expression, which resembles a grimace, is known as the flehmen response.

All cats have this special organ and can use it whenever a scent requires extra analysis, but it's used most often by intact males when they come across the urine of a female in heat.

Rubbing

Cats rub against each other as part of social bonding. It's an affectionate gesture and helps mix scents. Often, cats who are higher in status get flank rubbed by subordinate cats. When your cat flank rubs against your legs, it's her way of showing affection and acknowledging your higher status.

When you return home, one or more of your cats may engage in flank rubbing you and cheek rubbing to show affection and to help you regain the familiar, comforting "colony" scent again.

Lip and cheek rubbing are also common behaviors performed against inanimate objects for marking purposes. The rubbing creates familiar scent signposts. Your cat may also rub her lips against you as well as a sign of affection and familiarity.

Pam's CatWise Tip for Greeting an Unfamiliar Cat

When meeting a cat who does not know you, extend your index finger and let her approach for a sniff. This is similar to nose-to-nose sniffing that cats do. Don't reach to pet the cat, just leave your finger extended. After the cat does a scent investigation, she may then rub the side of her mouth along your finger or even rub her head or the side of her body. This is her way of letting you know she's at ease with you. At that point, you can offer to pet her. Don't pet until she has finished her scent investigation, and don't pet her if she backs up and stares at you.

Even if the cat doesn't want to engage beyond the finger sniff or touch this first time, you're building trust. Next time, she may engage a little more. Trust building requires patience, but it's worth it as you watch a cat take those baby steps toward interacting with you.

Bunting Behavior

Often described as headbutting, the correct term is actually *bunting*. Cat-to-cat head bunting is usually reserved for those who already have established a friendly relationship. Cats typically display this affectionate bunting behavior toward cat companions, dog friends, and humans. When a cat head bunts, pheromones are deposited. Cats only head bunt familiar animals and people and not inanimate objects.

Some cats lower their heads and engage in very gentle bunting, but there are those cats who seem to prefer a full-on forehead collision. Regardless of the intensity of the forehead contact, rest assured it is truly a sign of affection and not just a way to leave a scent.

Bunting may also be used for attention-seeking purposes. When a cat bunts you with her forehead and tucks her head down, lowering it to the side, she may be asking to be petted or scratched. If she does this with another cat, she may be requesting to be groomed. This is also a behavior effectively deployed in the wee hours of the morning when a cat feels your alarm clock must not have been set the night before. They want to ensure you aren't late for breakfast . . . well, actually it's their breakfast that concerns them, but let's not get picky.

Spray-Marking

If you live in a multicat environment and you haven't had to deal with a cat who urine-marks, you're very lucky. The higher the cat density in your home, the greater the chances you will have to deal with this behavior at some point. Spraying occurs with both male and female cats, even if they've been spayed or neutered, and it is a very effective form of communication; cats use it to mark territory, to warn, when feeling threatened, to announce their arrival, to engage in dispute without physical confrontation, and to announce reproductive availability. Spraying is also performed to help a cat reinforce ownership of a location by creating a urine signpost.

When a cat sprays it's not just plain urine. Scent chemicals are released with the urine to provide the all-important personal identification information. The standing position cats assume for spraying is intentional in order to direct the spray so it hits an object at approximate nose height. This makes it very hard for other cats to miss.

This is an unpleasant dialogue from a cat parent's perspective, especially when it involves indoor cats, but you (or your couch) don't have to be a helpless target. You can greatly reduce the chances of a spray-marking situation from ever developing. To get more detailed insight into spray-marking and for the behavior techniques to help correct the behavior, refer to chapter 7. Spray-marking is often misunderstood, and as a result, the ways of addressing it can be counterproductive. Learn the underlying reasons for the behavior and how to effectively correct it.

MIDDENING

Seen more in outdoor cats, middening is a visual and scent-marking behavior. A cat will defecate in an open area and not do any of the follow-up covering behavior. With normal defecation, a cat would look for a more hidden area, dig a shallow hole, defecate, and then cover. With middening, the location choice will be a conspicuous one. The feces, once deposited, will be able to be seen from a distance. Cats typically use middening to mark hunting paths or territorial boundaries.

Pam's CatWise Feline Fact

Not all cats cover their waste. Covering behavior can be influenced by whether it was taught by the mother cat.

With indoor cats, one may use middening to mark a path such as the hallway leading to a preferred litter box. If you do see fecal deposits, don't assume it's middening, though, because there's a much better chance the behavior is due to a medical or physical issue or is related to unappealing litter box conditions. If there's a marking issue happening in your multicat home, chances are that spraying is the preferred method used by the cat.

SCRATCHING

Scratching serves multiple functions that are highly beneficial to a cat. For communication purposes, scratching does double duty by providing both a visual and a scent mark.

When a cat reaches up and scratches, she leaves a visual mark with her claws, but as she presses against the object, pheromones are released from scent glands on her paw pads.

The importance of the visual mark is that it can be seen from a distance. This feline signpost helps reduce unwanted encounters with unfamiliar feline intruders who may see the mark and then avoid entering the territory. The visual mark also serves as a familiar welcome home sign for the cat who did the scratching as she wanders about.

The scent mark provides information-packed pheromones for any cat who ventures close enough.

The benefits of scratching go beyond marking. For more information on the role this behavior plays in a cat's physical and emotional life, refer to chapter 8.

BODY LANGUAGE

Posture

Body posture can generally be classified into two categories: distance increasing and distance reducing. Basically, a cat's body posture is saying *Not right now* or *It's okay to come closer*. Interestingly, the posture can quickly change based on the cat's comfort level. It might start out saying it's okay to come closer but switch to *That's far enough*.

A cat in an offensive, aggressive state walks on tiptoe with a lowered head, whiskers forward, ears erect but rotated sideways, claws visible, pupils constricted. Subordinate cats may crouch, avoid eye contact, or flee the immediate area. If a rival cat approaches, the two may try to stare each other down like slow-motion gunslingers. They may walk slightly past each other and then the aggressor may pounce. The defensive cat may roll over into a belly-up position to engage all weapons. A confident, offensive cat approaches head-on with a direct stare. A shy, fearful, or subordinate cat presents a profile and avoids direct stares.

Below are some general descriptions of body postures to help you better interpret what your cats may be trying to communicate:

Crouching—Defense or fear, and also as preparation to pounce. The tail will usually be tucked closely around the body. This protects the tail and makes the cat appear smaller and less threatening to the opponent. A fearful cat will press her ears back and down. An extremely fearful cat may drool. If terrified, she may even urinate or defecate. On the other hand, crouching is also part of the hunting posture (some cats will even do this when "hunting" their favorite toy).

Legs held straight with hindquarters slightly elevated—Offense. The cat's hind legs are longer than the front, so this stiff-legged posture is easy. It also helps the cat look taller and more imposing.

Belly up—This posture means different things depending on the circumstances. As the ultimate defensive posture, it allows the cat to engage her teeth and all four sets of claws should she have to fight an opponent. In this case the posture is a warning that lets the opponents know that should they agree to back down, no interaction will take place. On the other hand, a sleeping or relaxed cat may also stretch out on her back, exposing her belly, where it is most vulnerable. This is a sign of total relaxation but may trigger a defensive reaction if you pet the cat's stomach or if another cat approaches. The degree of the defensive reaction depends on the individual cat. If your relaxed and happy cat exposes her belly to you, don't tempt fate by trying to rub her tummy. Instead, appreciate this extraordinary sign of trust and vulnerability. Respond to this gesture of trust by not putting your cat in the position of suddenly feeling defensive.

Kittens may display the belly-up position when soliciting play. You must observe accompanying signals to be sure. If the kitten's ears are forward, then she's in play mode. If the ears are rotated back, then her belly-up position is defensive. If the kitten is asking for playtime, then she may meow or trill, but if she's defending herself she may hiss. If you pay close attention to the circumstances, you'll be able to interpret and evaluate the situation and respond accordingly.

Many people, because of their familiarity with how dogs roll onto their backs and solicit belly rubs, assume cats are communicating the same thing. This assumption often results in scratches and maybe a bite to the hand.

Side-to-side rolling—A play solicitation and a friendly greeting. Cats frequently roll when enjoying catnip. The rolling may also be accompanied by a belly-up position. Some cats roll when greeting a cat of higher status. Females in heat will also roll.

Arched back with piloerection of hair—This "Halloween cat" posture is a defensive display when the cat feels threatened. It communicates that the cat is ready to do whatever is necessary in reaction to an opponent's next move. From the arched-back position, the cat may switch to offensive or defensive aggression. It's the cat's way of warning the opponent to think twice about the next move.

Kittens may display this posture during social play. They may go up on tiptoe and do a comical crablike walk while soliciting another kitten to play.

Brief arched back when stretching—After a long nap, a cat may engage in stretching by briefly arching her back and then stretching out her front legs and elongating her spine. This is usually accompanied by a big yawn. This very brief arched-back position with no sign of piloerection is just used for maximum stretch to unkink muscles.

Elevator butt—I know it's not a very delicate description, but this posture really does resemble a cat's hindquarters going up elevator style. When you stroke your cat down her back, she may go into elevator butt position by keeping her front end low and raising up her hind quarters. It's a very common position meant as a friendly gesture and an invitation to continue scratching or petting her. Although the cat raising her butt to you may seem a little insulting, it's actually a very positive response to the fact that you've hit just the right spot when petting her. Typically, that spot is at the base of her tail. Not all cats enjoy being scratched or petted along the spine or at the tail base. If one or more of your cats do enjoy it, you've probably witnessed that elevator going up on many occasions.

The hind end raising up in an intact female cat has a very different meaning though. That position, known as lordosis, is how the female shows the male she's ready for mating. With intact cats in lordosis, the tail position will be different than ordinary elevator butt. The tail will be off to the side in preparation for entry by the male. The female may also tread with her hind feet. If your intact cat is displaying true lordosis, it means she's in estrus, so it's very important to make sure you keep her indoors. When in estrus, females are noticeably more affectionate and vocal. You'll probably be presented with the lordosis position just about every time you pet her. If you do have an unspayed female, talk to your veterinarian about the right time to have her spayed.

Meat loaf—A relaxed cat may rest by tucking her paws underneath her and loosely wrapping her tail around. This posture may serve as a signal to others that claws are safely put away and the cat poses no threat. The position truly resembles a meat loaf, so it's a very fitting name.

Turning her back—When two familiar and friendly cats greet each other they do a little nose-to-nose sniffing and then engage in a little flank sniffing or even flank rubbing. One of the cats will probably then turn around to present her backside for some anal sniffing. For a cat to present her anal area for sniffing is considered very polite. Unappealing to us, but polite in cat circles.

If your cat turns around and presents her backside to you, she's displaying proper feline manners. What should your response be? Just offer an affectionate gesture by petting her along the back or wherever she prefers most.

When your cat settles down next to you or next to a cat companion, instead of looking at you or her feline friend, she may sit or curl up with her back facing toward you (or her buddy). This posture is another sign of trust. The cat knows it's totally safe to turn her back so she can oversee what's going on in the room that might require her attention, such as an opponent cat or, if she's lucky, a mouse or other prey.

Kneading

Kneading behavior, also known as the milk tread, is a holdover from when cats were kittens. It originates when kittens nurse on the mother. Kittens instinctively flex and release their paws to stimulate lactation and start the milk flow. Even after weaning and long after they have become adults, many cats continue the kneading behavior. With adult cats, kneading is often triggered when on a soft surface or on the lap of a familiar human.

While kneading, the cat will often have her eyes partially

closed and may even look like she is in kitty dreamland. Many cats purr while kneading and some even begin to drool as they let their jaws become so relaxed.

Kneading is just one of the many ways cats communicate contentment and affection.

Pam's CatWise Feline Fact

Scent starts to play a vital role immediately after kittens are born. Even though they're born blind and deaf, the kittens already have a sense of smell. Once they locate a nipple for nursing, it gets scent-marked by the scent glands in their paw pads. Each time they nurse, they return to their scent-claimed nipple.

Eyes

Every feature of a cat's eyes is designed to assist her as a hunter. Cats' pupils are vertical and slit shaped, compared with a human's round-shaped pupils. The pupils are designed to respond to quick movements. This is something very beneficial, since cats hunt fast-moving prey.

Of the cat's overall visual field, 90 degrees is binocular. This means both eyes see the same image, a vital function for accurate distance calculation when prey is spotted.

Cats do have color vision, but it's limited due to the number of cones they have. They can see blues and greens but not reds. Rods are needed for seeing in low light; cones are used for color determination. For cats, though, color is not that important. What matters to a cat is the ability to detect movement and location accurately. So even though a cat's low-light vision becomes primarily black and white, she sees images in sharp detail compared with human vision. For a hunter who spends a lot of time searching for prey in low-light conditions, that's what matters most.

In addition to the pupils dilating or constricting in response to light conditions, a cat's pupils can change based on level of interest, fear, or aggression. Dilated pupils may indicate excitement. You may see your cat's eyes quickly dilate when you move an interactive toy across her visual field. Constricted pupils can indicate agitation or aggression.

Half-closed eyes indicate relaxation and can also be a sign of affection. A slow blink from a cat can be viewed as a *cat kiss*. If your cat gives you a slow-blink cat kiss, try returning the kiss by offering a slow blink yourself.

Since a cat's pupils dilate or constrict based on light conditions but also due to different emotional states, it can be easy for a cat parent to misinterpret what is being communicated. Always take the overall environment into consideration. It's essential to note that pupil size can also vary due to illness or injury.

Between cats, a direct, unblinking stare is a way to establish status and can be used as a challenge. A higher-ranking cat is comfortable staring directly at other cats. Subordinate cats avert their eyes and avoid direct stares. This signal between cats can be easy for cat parents to miss. In a multicat household, a direct, unblinking stare from a higher-ranking cat standing near a resource can be enough to warn other cats not to venture forward.

Pam's CatWise Etiquette Tip

Prolonged staring may be viewed as an aggressive threat. When you look at your cat, use soft gazes and never stare.

Ears

Even though a cat's ear function is focused on hearing and balance, you can interpret some moods and level of reactivity based on positioning.

Cats have funnel-shaped ears that can move independently of each other. This ability helps a cat precisely pinpoint the location of a sound. When hunting, this precision can mean the difference between a successful capture or a failed hunt. For mothers, the ability to accurately pinpoint a kitten's location is crucial when a youngster gets lost or is in distress.

The ears have thirty-two muscles and can independently rotate 180 degrees. Since cats are prey themselves as well as predators, the ability to rotate their ears so widely can help them detect a potential threat approaching from behind.

Cats can hear high-pitched sounds much better than humans can. As with their other specialized equipment, this ability to hear the squeak of prey is necessary for successful hunting.

When the cat's ears are facing forward and ever-so-slightly rotated to the side, it usually indicates relaxation. If something interests her, the ears will prick up even more forward facing. Even while napping, the ears are forward facing, ready to receive.

If something causes the cat to become uneasy or fearful, the ears will move sideways. The more fearful the cat becomes, the more she'll flatten her ears. Many people refer to this sideways ear position as *airplane ears*.

Ears that are flattened against the head indicate an aggressive posture. The cat flattens the ears to protect them from potential injury should a battle become inevitable. The flattened ears also are a very visible signal to others of an overt aggressive posture.

Flattened ears don't always mean fear or aggression. The reason one or both ears may be held sideways could be due to an underlying medical condition such as an ear infection, mites, or an injury. If a cat is holding her ears in an unusual position and the circumstances don't seem to warrant it, or if the cat paws at an ear or repeatedly flicks it, a veterinary exam is needed.

Pam's CatWise Caution

It can be very confusing to try to interpret what a cat is feeling and communicating if you look at only one aspect. You must take everything into consideration—eyes, ears, whiskers, body posture, vocalization (if any), and the current environment.

The Tail

A cat's tail is multifunctional. One very important role is its contribution to the cat's sense of balance. It serves as a natural counterweight for abrupt turns during high-speed runs. It helps keep the cat balanced when walking on a narrow surface, such as a tree branch or fence top. It also helps a cat when jumping.

A tail is an effective communication device. Its position or movement can act as a mood indicator. Tail positions are used to communicate to other cats. The position also allows a cat to be very visible (tail held high) or under the radar. You can learn a lot about what your cats are feeling by watching tail positions.

Here are a few tail positions and what they may be communicating:

Upright tail—A cat who walks with her tail in an upright position is typically displaying a feeling of confidence and comfort in her surroundings. It's almost as if the tail were a flag in the air indicating a willingness to be noticed and to engage in social interaction. If one of your cats walks toward you and you notice she also gives a little flick with the tip of her upright tail, consider that a friendly greeting. Make sure you don't pass her by without offering some response in return.

The question mark—An upright tail that has a little hook or curve at the top is an indication of a desire to interact as the cat approaches. She may also give a slight flick of the tail.

Slight horizontal (half-mast)—This can be a neutral signal, depending on circumstances. A relaxed cat may walk through her territory with her tail held in a slightly horizontal position. It's important to take all signals into consideration when evaluating whether this is relaxation or not. If at ease, the cat will have a relaxed body posture and the tail will not appear stiff. It can also be displayed if the cat is being a bit careful while exploring an area. When stalking prey, the cat will also lower the tail to remain less visible and to position herself for the pounce.

Unhappy horizontal—A tail held low as the cat walks or stands can indicate she is a very unhappy camper. This tail position is to be taken seriously because it could indicate aggression if you approach or try to initiate any interaction. A cat who is fearful and doesn't want to be noticed will also walk around with a lowered tail. Her body will be positioned low to the ground as well, as she navigates around a room to retreat to safety.

Tucked tail—If a cat holds her tail between her legs or tucked under her body, she is extremely fearful. Something in her immediate environment is making her feel threatened.

Puffed-up or bristled tail—This indicates a cat is afraid and feels threatened. Cats really prefer to take the option of retreating rather than fighting, but when in a threatening situation, they often puff themselves up to look larger and more menacing than their opponents. When puffed up, the tail resembles a bottle brush.

Arched tail—The tail will also be puffed up when arched. The cat perceives a threat and is prepared to do battle. This display can be a sign of either defensive or offensive aggression. She will also arch her back and stand very straight-legged to maximize size. Her hope is that the opponent will think better of attacking and choose to back down, but she'll fight if needed. With young kittens who are just learning how to interact, you may see this puffed-up tail posture as they play with one another, but without any hissing or signs of aggression.

Wrapped tail—Similar to the tucked tail, the cat is frightened, and by wrapping her tail around her body she is trying to appear smaller, less threatening, and almost invisible. A wrapped tail is also for minimizing injury should she get attacked, in contrast to a relaxed cat in meat-loaf position, where the tail may be loosely wrapped around her body.

The spray quiver—Cats about to spray-mark will back up to an object and the upright tail will begin to quiver. Body posture will also include treading with front paws. Cats who are spray-marking usually close their eyes or have them half closed. And yes, female cats do spray, in case you were wondering. (We'll cover that in chapter 7.)

The anticipation quiver—If the cat is happy or excited, the upright tail will quiver just as if the cat is spray-marking, only no urine will be deposited. This mock spray quiver is one displayed when a cat is anticipating something positive such as a meal or a treat. You'll also know it's a happy quiver and not a spray-marking quiver because the cat's eyes will remain open; in fact, she'll probably be looking at you since you're the source of whatever yummy treat she thinks she's going to receive.

In a tense situation, however, less confident cats may take the spraying posture without spraying because they may be too scared of the response.

Twitching tail—This is often seen when the cat is watching prey. The twitching may be her way of trying to contain her excitement. The more intense the excitement, the faster the twitching. The movement may initially start as a little swish and then accelerate into outright twitching.

Lashing or thumping tail—Whether it's slow or fast, this is an indication of irritation. You may be petting your cat and she reaches her tolerance level or maybe you're brushing her and she's trying to tell you she has had enough. Lashing may almost look like the wagging tail you see with dogs, but make no mistake about it—your cat is not happy when the tail is lashing back and forth that way. The cat is giving you a very clear signal to back off. The cat may also thump the tail as well as lash it. The more agitated the cat, the faster the tail goes.

Dual wrap or entwining—This one is my favorite. Two cats may entwine their tails, and this display is a sign of bonding and affection. This is the equivalent of humans holding hands. You may notice a cat even does this with you when she stretches out next to you. Pay attention to whether her tail casually drapes across your arm or leg. Consider it a sign of affection.

Whiskers

Whiskers serve multiple functions and are very sensitive. Whiskers are thicker than the cat's normal hair. They're actually touch receptors, deeply rooted and rich in nerve endings. Whiskers are the tactile information gatherers for a cat. Muzzle, eye, and paw whiskers all have separate functions.

Whiskers can detect changes in air currents, which helps a cat navigate in darkened conditions so she can avoid bumping into objects and detect any movement from potential prey. Whiskers are so highly sensitive they can detect not only the direction of air flow but the speed of the air.

The muzzle whiskers are also an aid when a cat tries to determine if she can fit through a small opening. In theory, the muzzle whiskers should extend to the width of the cat's body. If the whiskers fit without getting bent, then the cat should fit. If the cat is overweight, however, that method becomes useless.

There are four rows of whiskers on each side of the muzzle. The top two rows can move independently from the bottom two. When hunting, the muzzle whiskers help to determine movement and position of prey so the cat can potentially execute a perfectly accurate killing bite.

Whiskers above the eyes trigger an eye blink if a cat is walking through brush or around branches.

Carpal whiskers, located at the wrist, are valuable when capturing prey. When the cat has prey under her paw, the carpal whiskers will detect movement. Additionally, since a cat's close-up vision isn't as good as her distance vision, the carpal whiskers help to determine how the prey is positioned so the cat can deliver a more precise killing bite.

Whiskers can also give insight into what a cat is feeling. When whiskers are relaxed, the cat is probably comfortable and at ease. If she's frightened or preparing for a fight, the whiskers are flattened against the face to limit damage to them. When hunting or on the alert, whiskers will be forward facing to detect prey or gather information regarding air movement and direction. They may also fan out to capture as much information as possible. When a cat's whiskers are very much forward facing, it can indicate extreme interest, that a threat is very nearby, or that prey is about to get ambushed.

VOCALIZATION

Meow

When it comes to cat-to-cat communication, adult cats rarely meow to one another. Kittens seem to do most of the meowing when they need something or have gotten themselves into trouble. The meows of kittens are mostly directed to the mother cat.

As the cat leaves kittenhood behind, meowing becomes less effective than other forms of communication, such as visual and scent. These other methods are generally more effective at navigating conflict and sending a message at a safe distance.

When cats vocalize to one another, they tend to be more high intensity, such as growls, hisses, pain shrieks, and howls. Of course, there's the purr—that magical combination of sound and vibration that cats use in a variety of situations. More on that later.

Vocalization will often be used in hostile standoffs with other cats to accentuate body postures. Yowling and growling add the exclamation point to a tense impasse. Intact males will also yowl when a female in heat is nearby, and females can also be very vocal when they want to be let outside to search for a potential mate.

Meows Are Most Effective Toward Humans

As adults, cats seem to quickly learn that meowing is the best form of communication with the human family members. In many cases, it doesn't take long to train humans to give in and provide whatever is being requested through repeated meowing. Whether the food bowl should be refilled or a door needs to be opened, humans learn quickly.

If you don't like how much your cat meows her appeals, pay attention to whether you're guilty of reinforcing the behavior.

When you respond to unwanted meowing, you're fundamentally rewarding the cat for it.

Meow Warning Signs

If a cat displays a change in her normal vocalization, it could indicate a potential underlying medical issue. Some older cats may begin increased meowing or even yowling. With older cats experiencing age-related cognitive issues, the vocalization may be more common at night, when the house is dark and quiet. If you notice a change in the amount of vocalization or a change in the sound of a cat's voice, it's time for a visit to the veterinarian.

Here are some other ways cats communicate through vocalization:

Purr—It's the sound that makes you smile and think all is happy in a cat's world. That gentle sound relaxes and even mystifies you. Some facts about purring may surprise you, though. The purr serves more than one purpose. Many people think cats only purr when happy or content, but that's not always the case.

How the cat's purr happens has always fascinated people and there have been multiple theories over the years. The theory now thought to be most credible is that it's created by the laryngeal and diaphragmatic muscles in combination with a neural oscillator. A message from the brain gets sent to the laryngeal muscles, causing them to vibrate. Their movement controls how much air passes through them.

Purring occurs when a cat inhales and exhales. In some cases, the purr is so quiet and low, you may feel it more than hear it.

When a cat is about to give birth, she often purrs during labor, which may be to self-soothe and for pain control. Endorphins are released when cats purr, which can help in pain management. Once the kittens are born, the mother's purr is crucial to their survival. Kittens are born blind and deaf, but they do feel vibrations. It's the mother's vibrating purr that leads them to her body for nursing and critical warmth, since they're unable to regulate their own body temperature yet. This warm and reassuring feeling of being snuggled close to mom and receiving meals on demand certainly may explain the contentment aspect of the purr.

In an adult cat, the purr communicates several different emotional states. The one humans are most familiar with is that a purring cat is happy, but cats also purr for reasons not associated with contentment.

The cat's purr has been compared to the human smile. People smile for a variety of reasons. People smile when happy, nervous, unsure, or when trying to make someone else feel comfortable. It's that way with the purr as well. Cats may purr when happy, but they also use it for self-soothing or to soothe a potential adversary when they feel escape is not an option. They also purr when nervous, sick, in pain, or even when close to death. This may be due to the release of endorphins.

Many cats really know how to maximize the purr to their advantage. A study done at the University of Sussex in the UK identified that cats have developed a specialized purr referred to as a "soliciting purr." The specialized purr includes cries at similar frequencies as the cries of a human baby. It appears cats can dial up the high frequency in order to get their food requests met.

Purring is also believed to be used for healing. Purrs vibrate at 25Hz to 150Hz, which is the frequency that helps physical healing and bone mending. Purring during resting might also be a form of feline physical therapy for bone strength, since the frequency is in the range that increases bone density.

Pam's CatWise Feline Fact

Cats can make up to one hundred different vocalizations. Dogs have about ten vocalizations.

Mew—A sound used for identification and location purposes between cats.

Grunt—The first vocalization of newborn kittens.

Moan—A mournful, lonely, and long sound that some cats make before vomiting or hairball regurgitation. Some older cats may moan during the night if they become disoriented or confused by the sudden quiet of the household. Some cats also moan when sitting at the front door begging to be let out or in.

Chirp—A sound the cat might make when she sees something desirable that she's about to receive. It's usually a meal or a treat but can also be a wanted interaction with a cat parent. Mothers may also use this sound with their kittens.

Trill—A sound similar to a chirp but a little more musical in sound. It's a happy vocalization.

Growl—This is a low-pitched sound produced with an open mouth and can be offensive or defensive. It's one of the cat's verbal warning sounds.

Spit—A sudden, short, airy, popping sound that usually follows or precedes a hiss. Cats tend to spit when something takes them by surprise.

Pam's CatWise Etiquette Tip

The proper way to pick up a cat is to place one hand beneath the cat's bottom in order to support the weight and prevent the hind legs from dangling. Place your other hand under the cat's chest so she can rest her front paws on your arm. Hold her close to your body, but don't make her feel confined. Never scruff a cat as a way of transport as it's very stressful, can be painful, and may cause injury.

Hiss—A snakelike sound created when the cat forces a burst of air through her arched tongue. When a cat hisses, any animal or human directly in front of her can feel the force of air.

Hissing is a defensive action and it indicates the cat is feeling immediately threatened. It's basically a verbal warning to a potential challenger. The hiss is letting the opponent know that aggression will follow if needed. A hissing cat is fearful but will engage in battle if escape is not available.

The hissing sound may be created to mimic that of a snake. Mimicry is a common behavior in the animal world for the sake of survival. Some animals vocally or visually mimic predators in the hope of avoiding detection as prey.

Murmur—A soft sound made with a closed mouth that usually accompanies purring or is given as a greeting.

Squeak—A raspy, high-pitched sound usually made when the cat anticipates meal preparation. Also used during play.

Shriek—A harsh, high-pitched sound given out when in pain or during intense aggressive encounters.

Snarl—An intimidating expression where the upper lip curls, exposing the teeth. This may or may not be accompanied by a growl.

Chattering—This behavior looks and sounds as if the cat is talking to herself. The behavior typically occurs when the cat spots prey. With an indoor cat, she will most likely be sitting at the window and start chattering when a bird lands in the yard or a squirrel scurries by. A bit of tail twitching usually accompanies chattering.

There are several theories as to why cats chatter. There are some who believe it's likely connected to frustration at not being able to get to prey. It's also believed to be a reflex action in anticipation of delivering the killing bite to prey. Perhaps it's how the cat practices her technique. Another theory is that the cat is trying to control her excitement. Finally, if those theories don't satisfy you, the last theory is that the cat is mimicking the sound of prey, most likely a bird. So, until cats give us confirmation of which is the right theory, chattering will remain a feline mystery.

Turf 101: Understanding Territory

In a free-roaming, outdoor environment, a cat's area is divided into different sections. The outermost area where the cat roams and patrols for food is referred to as the home range, and it may overlap other cats' home ranges as well. Adult males tend to have a larger home range than females, and during mating season an intact male's home range will increase temporarily as he seeks to mate. In the home range, a cat is more likely to flee than engage in conflict.

Inward from the home range is the cat's more exclusive territory. This is the area a cat will defend against intruders. For indoor cats, the home range and territory are obviously smaller, and they overlap or are combined into one due to the physical space limitations. A cat may permit another familiar social cat friend to enter his territory up to a certain point, and may allow another even closer, depending on their bond.

The innermost part of the territory is the cat's personal or critical space. This is where moms raise their young and where cats sleep, eat, and play.

TIME-SHARING

I'm referring to territory time-sharing, not overpriced vacation condos. Cats are experts at developing time-share schedules, and this is foremost in how most multicat homes share limited space. One cat may occupy a certain room or sleep on a piece of furniture at a particular time of day, and then another cat claims it during the next shift. This isn't just a coincidence but rather a delicate balance of peace through avoidance. Trouble occurs when one cat elects to occupy an area at the off schedule. A prudent cat defers to the other cat who normally resides there at that time, but every now and then someone doesn't play by the rules. Not all objects will be open for time-share negotiations. Certain favorite spots or rooms, though not occupied by the individual cat twenty-four hours a day, are not used by other cats, either. Some cats do not time-share at all; they own their preferred undisputed area all the time.

When you stop to think about how judiciously some cats work out time-sharing arrangements, you can begin to appreciate how upsetting it must be when furniture is rearranged, certain pieces are removed, a new cat is added, or you make a move to a new home.

VERTICAL LIFE

If you're thinking like a human, you view your home as one territory. Whether it has one room or twenty, it's still basically *your* territory. If you're thinking like a cat, you can see your home as numerous territories on many different levels, geographic and psychological, and negotiating them is a central part of maintaining cat family harmony.

Here's a way to visualize the importance of levels and elevated locations. Elevation can signal status or rank or can provide refuge. Imagine the living room in your home without any furniture—just the carpet, walls, and windows. If you put your cats in there, they might head for opposite corners because there's only one level. The higher-ranking cats wouldn't have areas of elevation, and everyone might become stressed and unsure about where they were supposed to be. Now imagine putting one chair in there. Immediately, one cat might rub on it and perhaps hop up on it. Another cat might hide beneath or behind the chair. If it's a big, upholstered armchair, you might even find one cat perches on the high back and one on the arm. One cat might get cozy in the seat of the chair. Just by adding this one chair you have increased property through elevation and helped the cats maintain any already-established status. Now imagine adding a table, another chair, a bookcase, a cat tree, and so forth. With every piece of furniture, you add more cat space. What was once a one-level, open, vulnerable area is now a more secure, comfortable environment where cats can interact with or avoid one another, a place where cats have the choice to remain hidden or be out in the open.

Look around your home with all the furniture in it. You probably see higher-ranking cats in the highest areas and the more timid or lower-ranking cats choosing hidden areas. There might be a cat claiming the top of the refrigerator because that may be the highest elevated location in a room. In the bedroom, there may be a cat resting on the top of a dresser or just camped out right in the center of your bed, while in that same bedroom, there may be one cat hiding under the bed or behind the shoe boxes in the closet. Cats often make use of as much vertical space and levels (low, medium, high) as they can access.

If you don't allow your cats on any of the furniture or if you haven't supplied elevated cat furniture, this may be one reason why there could be unease between the cats—they aren't able to establish areas. They don't own any property.

Pam's CatWise Feline Fact

Sometimes a timid or fearful cat will also use an elevated perch because it provides safety from being ambushed.

HOW TO INCREASE TERRITORY

If you've ever been to a cat sanctuary, group cat room in a shelter, or even a cat café, you may have marveled at how several cats could live together. Look closely and you'll see assorted elevated levels, open areas, and hidden spots. There are shelves, perches, and cat trees at varying heights. You'll see that when set up correctly, the room provides the choice for engagement and avoidance.

Look around your home and you probably will see unused vertical space that could be converted into areas for cat access. As a multicat parent, ample personal cat space becomes more of an issue. Unless you plan on breaking down a wall and building onto your home, your best option is to make use of that vacant vertical real estate.

When it comes to increasing vertical territory, you can get as elaborate or as basic as you'd like, depending on your taste and budget. From a cat's point of view, vertical areas just need to be

- safe,
- comfortable,
- easy to ascend and descend, and
- well located.

Cat Trees

One of the quickest and easiest ways to increase vertical space is by adding multiperched cat trees. If you get a tree with multiple perches, a couple of cats can share a relatively close space and still maintain a comfortable distance. Two cats who normally might not sit side by side on a windowsill to watch the birds may peacefully share the tree because of the different levels of perches. Multiple perches will also make it easier for less mobile cats to ascend to the higher perch without having to make a giant and potentially painful leap.

A cat tree is a good way to help a timid cat choose to stay in a room when company visits. When I was working on rehabbing a feral cat, all she wanted to do was hide whenever I entered the room. I had created a sanctuary room for her with various hiding options. When I wasn't in the room, however, she loved being in the cat tree. To help her feel more hidden and secure, I bought some silk tree branches from my local craft store and wired them to the cat tree. I strategically placed the branches so my cat Bebe could lounge on the perches yet feel hidden. Bebe began to feel more secure about staying in the cat tree when I entered the room. Instead of hiding behind furniture or in a box, she was able to watch me from between the leaves of the branches. It was at this point that she became interested in the interactive toys I would bring in or the yummy food I placed on the floor.

You can find cat trees at any pet supply store and online. They're so popular you'll surely be able to find one that fits your budget and sense of aesthetics. There are companies that will custom design trees for you based on your specifications for height, number and style of perches, and even type and color of carpet.

When shopping for trees, make sure the perches are wide and comfortable. Some companies design trees that are visually appealing to the cat parent but not the least bit comfortable for cats.

Be sure the perches are wide enough to accommodate the size of the cat. Some trees have square, flat perches and others have curved, U-shaped ones. I find the cats tend to prefer the curved ones, which may give a cat an added feeling of security since no body parts hang off and become vulnerable to getting swiped at by another cat on a lower perch. The U-shaped perches also help the cat feel as if he can lean his back against something. This may give him an additional sense of being protected from the rear. U-shaped perches provide a bit more cover for a cat so he can duck down and peer over the side if watching a bird at the window, or if he just needs that extra bit of concealment for security. On the other hand, some cats prefer stretching flat out. For those cats, wide, flat perches work best.

Some cat trees also do double duty as scratching posts. You can find trees with support posts wrapped in sisal, the scratching texture favored by many cats. You can also find support posts in bare wood or even bark. Some of the larger trees with more support posts can have assorted coverings so you can satisfy the sisal scratcher as well as the bare-wood scratcher in your feline family.

Trees come as freestanding or mountable to the ceiling. The freestanding trees tend to have wider, more comfortable perches and are easier to relocate. The taller the tree, the heavier and wider the base should be. If the tree seems the least bit top-heavy, don't even consider buying it because one good leap from a cat could topple the thing over. Even if the tree doesn't fall over but only wobbles, that instability can deter cats from returning to it.

If you love DIY projects, consider making a tree for your cat. There are several online instructions and YouTube videos detailing how to construct a homemade tree.

When it comes to where to place cat trees, don't be tempted to stick them in empty, unused corners. Place them where your cats will enjoy and use them, like with a window view. Cat trees may not be the most attractive pieces of furniture in the house, but if you're going to make the investment in them, place them in cat-friendly locations, like near a warm radiator but not near noisy equipment or anyplace where a cat might feel stressed or unsure. If you want your cats to hang out with you, place trees in rooms in which you spend the most time.

When you first bring a cat tree into the house, you can rub some catnip on the support posts as a nice introduction for your cats. If your cats get upset by new furniture, lay a T-shirt or towel containing your scent over each perch for a day so they take on a comforting scent. Unless you're trying to provide a tree for a specific cat, it's best to use an article that has your scent as opposed to your cats' scents because you don't know who is going to claim which branch of the tree.

When you first start shopping for cat trees, you may get hit with sticker shock. Some high-end trees can be very expensive. Don't despair, because there's a wide range of prices, depending upon how extravagant you want to get. It'll be a complete waste of money to buy an inexpensive tree if the cats won't use it because the perches are too small or the tree isn't stable. On the other hand, if budget is a concern, choose a simple, well-built tree without fancy extras. Even though a strong, sturdy tree may cost more than you expected, a well-made one will last for many years. One of the cat trees in our home is more than twenty-five years old and is still functional and strong. That tree was a good investment.

If you have kittens, don't be tempted to buy a cat condo in place of a tree. Cat condos are relatively small, round, and carpet covered. Some have upper and lower compartments. Kittens will soon outgrow it and it won't serve as a vertical tree. If you want to buy one for the kittens to play in and sleep on while they're small, that's fine, but it's not a replacement for a sturdy cat tree designed for climbing and elevation.

Window Perches

In rooms where you don't have space for a cat tree, or if you're limited by budget, window perches are another way to add vertical territory. Many perches don't require permanent installation and can be attached to windowsills or frames through tension mounting and/or hand-tightening screws without damaging your walls. That's great news for apartment dwellers.

Window perches come in assorted coverings. Some have removable covers that can be machine washed. A few perches have heating elements as well, so cats can stay warm and cozy. This is a nice option if you have drafty windows or if you have older cats who need more warmth. Make sure there are always unheated perches nearby in case a cat gets too warm.

Perches come in various shapes and styles. Some are padded, flat-board styles, and others are designed like hammocks. When shopping, keep your cats' preferences in mind based on the types of places you've seen them sleep in your home. Some cats like the cozy comfort of sinking into a hammock, but others may feel too vulnerable and prefer something with more solid support.

Even if you have cat trees it's a good idea to have window perches as well because they create a middle level. Perches are also portable, so they're very useful if you must set up a sanctuary room temporarily or move one to accommodate location preferences.

Cat Shelves, Cat Walkways, and Cat Skyways

Cat shelves and walkways are fun options for adding vertical space. Strategically placed shelves allow multiple cats to have their own raised locations. Walkways provide elevated travel around a room.

Some of the shelves can be flat and combined with a few U-shaped perches. Flat ones can be used for resting but also for moving from perch to perch. There are many design and layout options based on the size of your cats, their mobility, and the layout of the room.

Before you buy or make shelves, walkway, or skyways, plan out what kind of arrangement would be best. Do you want just a few alternating perches? A walkway where cats can go completely around the room? Walkways that lead to a skyway closer to the ceiling? How will the cats ascend and descend? Do research online to see how others have designed vertical space and then adapt it to fit the needs of your cat family.

Start by installing some perches close to the floor or start mounted stairways low enough to make it easy for cats to begin their climb. It's also important to have more than one entrance/exit–ramp option so cats never get trapped on a perch by an adversary cat who uses the opportunity to climb up there for an ambush. You never want to create an elevated dead end where a cat has no escape option from an approaching rival.

Choose perches, walkways, and skyways that are wide, for added comfort and safety. They should also be covered in nonslip material for extra grip.

In addition to shelves and ramps being used for transit, there should also be rest areas. Create cozy elevated spots that are perfect for napping. These could be hammock-style perches or shelves covered with soft material.

Many companies make wonderful cat shelves, stairs, and walkways. Just be sure installation is secure and can safely hold the weight of your heaviest cats.

When planning the placement of the shelves or perches, make sure they're correctly spaced so a cat can securely move from one to another without having to leap.

Depending on where you live, you may be able to find a company that custom designs and installs vertical cat space so you don't have to do any of the carpentry work yourself.

If you own your own home and really want to dial up the fun

factor, consider cutting entrances and exits in the walls between rooms so cats can take the skyway from one room right into the next. Look online and you'll find many images from cat parents who have created very inventive versions of skyways and room openings.

When installing shelving and skyways, make sure they aren't so out of human reach that you can't retrieve your cat in case of an emergency. I've seen some extremely imaginative cat skyways that go across very high ceilings and I wonder how in the world a cat parent could get a cat down from there in an urgent situation.

Don't forget about maintenance and cleaning when you build vertical territory. Routinely check each component to make sure nothing needs repair and that all shelves and walkways are still firmly attached.

Vertical territory needs to be cleaned as well, because hairballs can happen anywhere. You also don't want cats napping on dusty shelves.

Pam's CatWise Reminder

THE BENEFITS OF VERTICAL CAT SPACE
- Increased territory
- Added fun
- More visual warning time for a cat to see who's approaching
- Easier to prevent a surprise attack from behind
- A way for a cat to peacefully display status without a confrontation
- A safe retreat out of reach of small children or the family dog
- A great place to watch wildlife from the window
- Climbing and exercise
- The consistent and familiar scent of the cat group

HIDING PLACES

One aspect of providing security in a cat's environment that's sometimes overlooked is the importance of hiding places. Many people view a cat needing a hideaway as a negative, but it's a beneficial option. Having the ability to hide is a valuable coping mechanism. It gives the cat time to calm down and assess the immediate situation while having the reassurance of feeling invisible.

In a hiding place, a cat has the choice to ultimately venture out, engage, or stay put. Having that choice is powerful. Without the option to hide, the cat may remain stressed, frightened, or otherwise at a higher level of arousal.

Your timid or subordinate cats may seek out hiding places. For cats who like to hide, it's good to have options for them in every room. Hideaways can be anything from a box, a paper bag on its side, a high-sided bed, covered bed, or cat cave. The main thing is that it provides a place out of view in which the cat will feel invisible and more secure knowing no one can sneak up behind him. Place the hideaways in areas that are out of the main flow of foot traffic but in socially active rooms, and make sure the occupant in the hideaway has an escape route, if needed. For example, place the hideaway in a spot where the cat can choose to leave the room without having to navigate around several people. For very timid cats, place the opening of the hideaway at a slight angle so no one in the room will be looking directly at the cat inside it. This may help him feel less threatened and may entice him to stay in the room rather than bolt for another room. If he does choose to leave, though, just let him go. The important point here is that you're giving the cat a choice.

Some cats may prefer elevated hiding places. Pay attention to the preferences of each cat so you'll know if you need to provide both low-level, mid-level, or high-level hideaways. For an elevated hideaway you can place a cat cave or covered bed on a perch of the cat tree or even set the bed on a piece of furniture.

Pam's CatWise Reminder

Cats are small animals and they don't need lots of room in order to coexist peacefully. Even if you live in a small apartment, you can have well-adjusted and contented cats. It's all about planning and using the right techniques.

Pam's CatWise Safety Tip

When you live in a multicat environment, it's critical to do a cat count before leaving the house or going to bed. A cat can easily sneak out the door, dart into a closet, or jump into a drawer without being noticed. While tidying up in a multicat home it's easy to overlook somebody, so it's good to develop the routine of a cat count to make sure everyone is present and accounted for.

CAT TUNNELS

These are ideal for playing in and as secure passageways for frightened cats. For playtime, a tunnel is a perfect place for a cat to hide as he waits to pounce on a toy during your interactive play sessions. Cats love hidden areas where they will be invisible to potential prey. Tunnels are also excellent during social play between cats.

For the frightened cat, a tunnel can provide a sheltered way to get from one side of the room to another. When I set up a sanctuary room for a cat, I often create a few tunnels: one from a hiding place to the litter box and one to the food bowl. The tunnel doesn't have to go right up to the litter box or food bowl; it mainly just needs to cover the center of the room, because that's where the cat will feel most vulnerable and exposed. This may encourage a frightened cat to feel secure enough to start venturing around the room.

You can be as extravagant and imaginative as you want when it comes to tunnels. You can buy soft-sided cat tunnels that connect to make them long and winding, or you can make several short tunnels.

Another option is to make your own tunnels out of boxes or paper bags so they can be customized for specific areas of your home. Cut out the bottoms and tape the ends together. If using paper bags, roll a cuff a couple of times over on each end to prevent the bags from collapsing. When you make a tunnel, cut out one or two escape holes along the sides, depending on the length of the tunnel. This way, if two cats enter the tunnel from opposite directions, they won't meet each other head-on, and one cat can escape out of the hole to avoid a feline train wreck.

If the paper bags you are using have handles, cut them off before creating a tunnel. Never give your cats a bag that has handles attached because of the risk of strangulation.

Pam's CatWise Reminder

- Increase vertical territory on multiple levels.
- Provide hiding places.
- Use cat tunnels.
- Offer choice so cats have the option to go where they feel most secure.
- Observe and respect how your cats divide up their territories.

PREFERRED AREAS AND RESOURCE AVAILABILITY

Once territories and home ranges are established (hopefully without too much incident), it's important to understand and identify each cat's preferred area as well as neutral areas/pathways, socially significant locations, and areas of confrontation. Because of the environmental limitations, these personal areas are smaller than they might be in the vast outdoors and must overlap.

Once you have an idea of where each cat feels the most comfortable, look at how you've set up resources, including number and location. An easy way to get an overall perspective of your cats' indoor environment is to draw a simple floor plan. Do this for each floor of your home. Now mark where each cat tends to prefer staying. Also label locations of resources, including the following:

- Food bowls
- Water bowls
- Pet beds

- Cat trees
- Perches
- Litter boxes
- Scratching posts
- Favorite napping areas
- Favorite furniture pieces

Next, identify areas where skirmishes and challenges typically occur. Use colored pencils or pens to label and color-code to make it easier to identify each cat and the various aspects of your floor plan. When I create this type of floor plan with my clients it becomes much easier for them to see preferred areas and how the current resource setup may contribute to tension and antagonism.

Look at your floor plan and reevaluate resource availability. A main component of a cat group's social structure functioning peacefully involves not having to battle for resources. The other key is the ability to avoid having to cross into unwelcoming territory in order to access a resource.

Have you created an environment where the cats must share a food bowl or share too few litter boxes? Perhaps you have enough litter boxes but you've located them all in one room or one area of the house. A common mistake I often see cat parents make is to assume all the cats will be comfortable sharing. Just because you bought one gigantic litter box large enough to accommodate six cats doesn't mean they all feel at ease being in that one location. This type of mistake is often made with the feeding station as well. Putting down one big food bowl for everyone to share can be an invitation for intimidation and stress.

Set up your environment to reduce competition and minimize situations that prompt anxiety and concern. Place litter boxes throughout the house so one cat doesn't have to leave his preferred area and walk through another cat's turf when nature calls. The litter box setup and how to deal with litter box problems is covered in detail in chapter 7.

The feeding station is another area that can cause anxiety. Depending on how well your cats get along and the size of your cat family, the ideal setup may be as simple as individual bowls in one location, or you may have to establish multiple feeding stations in various rooms. Cats aren't social eaters, so it puts unnecessary stress on them if they must eat side by side or stick their heads together into one large bowl. Mealtime should be in a place where a cat feels safe and relaxed. How to create mealtime peace is covered in detail in chapter 6.

Proper resource placement can be the secret to maintaining harmony. Be more thoughtful about each cat's preferred area and you'll probably see fewer standoffs in the hallway and staredowns at the food bowl.

Set up your environment so each cat has the choice of whether to engage or avoid. Offering choice is a powerful element in avoiding behavior problems whether you have a large feline family or just one single cat.

Pam's CatWise Reminder

Place some hideaways in rooms that are socially significant in the household—the bedroom, where you watch TV, or where you entertain. This may embolden fearful or timid cats enough to stay in the room without having to commit to being totally visible or vulnerable.

MOVING IN FROM THE GREAT OUTDOORS

If some or all your cats have outdoor access, and you want to make the transition to having them all indoors all the time, it's not as hard as you think. And I think it is worth the extra effort.

The outdoor environment is not a safe place for a cat. There are many dangers out there, including cars, disease, poisoning (accidental or intentional), injury or death from cat fights or other animal attacks, parasites, and getting lost or getting stolen. Keep your cats indoors and you'll know they're safe. They can still enjoy indoor versions of all the good qualities of outdoor life through environmental enrichment.

Additionally, from a behavior standpoint, outdoor access can sometimes elevate tension back inside because a cat may come back aroused by the scents of unfamiliar cats in his territory or maybe from having had a physical encounter. The outdoor environment is unpredictable, and giving your cats access to it can bring unknown and unwelcomed stress into your home.

Even though your indoor/outdoor cats may have all spent time in the house together, there will be a change when everyone stays indoors permanently because their territories will be reduced. The cats will likely go through a period of renegotiating territorial boundaries and working out new time-share schedules. To help with this, look around to see where you can increase vertical space with added cat trees, shelves, perches, or skyways. This is also the time to up the fun factor in terms of making sure everyone gets ample play sessions and activities to keep them occupied so they don't focus on one another. You can find lots of ideas to increase environmental enrichment in chapter 5.

If the previously indoor/outdoor cats were outside for much of the day, you'll now have more litter box usage inside. You may have to increase your scooping schedule and increase the number of litter boxes as well as box locations.

Be forewarned that at least one of the cats will not view this indoor transition as a good thing. You can pretty much count on one cat sitting by the door and meowing in his most insistent tone. He'll look over at you with confusion, wondering whether you've lost your mind or maybe you just can't hear him—so he'll meow even louder. Be strong and don't let him out. If you crumble, you'll be setting yourself up for failure, because the next time he wants out he'll meow and cry, knowing that it worked the last time.

To make a successful transition for all of you, you can't just start keeping cats indoors without making sure you have increased the appeal of indoor life through environmental enrichment. What cats love about outdoor life is the stimulation of discovery, hunting, interesting scents, climbing, and finding sunny places to nap. You can provide all that indoors through environmental enrichment. Don't worry, I'm not going to suggest you bring in live prey, but through interactive playtime and incorporating puzzle feeders (see chapter 6), your cats will get all the joy of hunting without any of the risks or disappointment due to the mouse that got away.

Outdoor Enclosures

If you insist on maintaining outdoor access for your cat family, the safest way is to construct an outdoor cat enclosure, commonly referred to as a catio. They have become very popular as a safe way to let cats enjoy fresh air, sunshine, and interesting scents.

For many multicat households, an outdoor enclosure is also a way to increase territory and ease tensions. Check online for ideas and you'll see some very creative and elaborate enclosures. Of course, you don't have to turn this into an expensive work of art. Cats don't care if something is fancy; it just needs to be functional.

You can construct your own enclosure or have a company

install one for you. Safety is first and foremost, so ensure the enclosure is escape-proof. Cats also need the option of being able to go back into the house on their own, so the enclosure should be securely connected to the home with an entrance/exit option.

Never leave cats in the outdoor enclosure overnight or when you aren't home to supervise.

Enclosure shelving and walkways need the same safety considerations as indoor ones. Don't set up dead-end shelves where a cat can get ambushed.

In an outdoor enclosure, cats are at risk of parasites, so keep up on flea and tick prevention. Sunburn and heatstroke are also a concern in summer, so provide lots of fresh water and areas of shade and don't let cats out in the enclosure during the hottest part of the day.

Pam's CatWise Caution

DANGERS OF OUTDOOR LIFE
- Shorter life span
- Poisoning risk (sometimes intentional)
- Risk of injury or death from cat fights
- Risk of attack from dogs and larger predators
- Increased risk of disease
- Internal and external parasites
- Risk of injury or death from vehicles
- Risk of getting lost or stolen
- Risk of being the victim of animal cruelty
- Exposure to questionable or spoiled food
- Weather-related issues (sunburn, paw pad burns, frostbite, hypothermia, hyperthermia, heatstroke)
- You won't know where your cat is at a time when he may need you most.

Even though your cats won't be able to roam outside the enclosure doesn't mean other outdoor cats can't come around. Watch for unfamiliar cats who may come into the yard, especially if they see, hear, or smell your cats. If this becomes a problem, you may not be able to have your cats in the enclosure unless you're there to supervise.

Set up a security camera so you can watch your cats while they're in the enclosure. Even though you'll be home to routinely check on them, the security camera is an extra safety feature. Most cameras have apps for your smartphone so you can quickly do a cat count if they're in the enclosure and you're in the kitchen preparing dinner.

New Introductions

HOW TO INTRODUCE A NEW CAT
TO A RESIDENT CAT

Cats are social but also territorial, so introductions require finesse and patience. Even though a new cat introduction will take work on your part, it's a small amount of time given what the reward will be—cats who hopefully learn to coexist peacefully and, in many cases, form close relationships.

While there are many people who may brag about how they just tossed the cats in together and let them work it out for themselves, I'm here to tell you that's absolutely the worst thing you can do. Never force the issue, and don't expect them to figure it out on their own. The indoor environment has physical limitations that don't exist in an outdoor cat colony, so forcing cats to work it out themselves can be a traumatic experience and can set them up to forever dislike one another or to develop an agonistic relationship. It's also a method that goes against everything that makes sense in the feline social structure. Finally, it's incredibly cruel.

Unlike most dogs, cats aren't quickly receptive to newcomers.

Don't make the mistake of not preparing ahead of time and realizing there's a problem only after the fur is flying. You don't want the introduction process to consist of doing damage control. It doesn't matter if you're adding a second cat to your household or your seventh cat; there is no introduction shortcut. Do it right the first time and you'll save yourself and your cats much grief.

AN IMPORTANT CONSIDERATION

Before you start this whole process, weigh the different factors in adding another cat to the household. Don't assume your solitary cat is lonely unless you've evaluated the situation. Some cats are quite content being the only feline in the home. Will this be a benefit or detriment to your current feline family? Do you feel the cats will have adequate territory? Are you able to dedicate the time and patience required to do an introduction? Even when a new cat takes you by surprise, such as in a rescue situation, you should still set up a game plan that will cause the least amount of stress on everyone concerned with a result that will be beneficial to all. Perhaps the cat you rescued would be better off in another home. Based on what you know about your resident cats' personalities, ages, and health, is adding another cat going to improve the quality of their lives?

If you're already dealing with any sort of litter box problem, get it resolved before you add further stress to the situation by introducing another cat. If there's any behavior issue happening in your home now, it may only become bigger with the arrival of another cat. Take time to examine your current situation and make an informed decision about whether this will be good or not.

Not every cat wants a cat buddy. If you live with just one cat now, you can do the most careful introduction, but it still isn't a guarantee that the new cat you picked for your resident cat will be a compatible match. Not every cat craves company.

A LITTLE MEALTIME PREP WORK IN ADVANCE

If you currently free-feed (that is, you leave dry food available all the time), this is the time to transition to scheduled feeding. Do this before you bring in a new cat. Food is a powerful training tool, and in order to use it to your advantage it can't be readily available twenty-four hours a day. Scheduled feeding is a more natural way of eating in the cat's world anyway. Prey isn't hanging around all day, ready for the picking. To learn more about scheduled mealtime, refer to chapter 6.

CHOOSING A SECOND CAT

Try to make a compatible match to increase the chances of a successful introduction and a mutually beneficial relationship. Think about the cat you already have at home and the personality she has.

If your resident cat loves to chill out most of the day or nap in the sun, look for another cat who also loves that low-level activity. Don't try to find a high-energy cat, thinking she will get your resident cat to be more active. All the new cat will do is annoy your current one.

If you have a cat with limited mobility, avoid adopting a cat who is very energetic. On the other hand, if your resident cat is extremely active or assertive, you wouldn't want to pair her with a timid cat. Try to match complementary personalities.

Adopt an adult cat instead of a kitten and you'll already have a good idea about her personality. This may help you make a better match. Also, don't adopt a kitten as a cat companion for a geriatric cat because that can put too much stress on the resident cat. A kitten doesn't have a strong sense of territory and will want to play with everyone all the time. That can be too much stress to put on an older cat, especially if there are already any health concerns being dealt with. I've seen situations where cat parents get a rambunctious little kitten for a geriatric cat with the hope that the little newcomer will spark the older cat to enjoy life more, or they get the kitten to help soften the anticipated grief they fear is coming soon when the older cat passes away. The health and well-being of the geriatric cat needs to be the priority.

MAKE A GAME PLAN AHEAD OF TIME

In a colony setting, it's not unusual for a cat who is not a member to remain on the fringes until others begin to become familiar with her scent and realize she is not a threat. She will leave and return and eventually work her way into the territory. There's no standard time frame for this in the cat's rule book. That's how you need to view a new cat introduction as well. Don't be obsessed with trying to move the process along quickly. An introduction is not about you—it's about the cats and the pace at which they are most comfortable.

For an introduction to go smoothly, the cats need to be able to

- easily avoid one another,
- establish their own secure areas,
- not have to compete for resources,
- associate one another with positive experiences,
- work out neutral zones,
- get to know one another at their own pace, and
- have the choice of how much and how close they want their interactions to be.

THE SANCTUARY ROOM

When you bring a cat into a new home, it's necessary that she have her own sanctuary room. The newcomer needs a quiet, safe area where she can get her bearings, and the resident cat doesn't need to come face-to-face with the "intruder" in an unwanted way. The sanctuary room isn't optional—it's a must. If there's no possible way to give the newcomer her own safe space, then you need to rethink whether adopting another cat is a good idea.

The sanctuary room gives the newcomer an opportunity to get familiar with the scents of her new home. It also gives her time to get to know you and begin the trust-building process. For a rescued cat who has been through physical or emotional trauma, a sanctuary room enables her to make the transition in a calm, comforting way.

Pam's CatWise Tip

A sanctuary room can be any room in your home that has a door. The cat doesn't need a lot of space right now—she needs safety and security. A bathroom is not ideal but will do in a pinch. If you live in a studio apartment, it may be your only option.

Prepare the Sanctuary Room for the New Arrival

The room shouldn't be empty. There's nothing more frightening for a cat than not having places to hide. In addition to the furniture already in the room, set up hiding places so the cat doesn't just dive under the bed or in a closet. Boxes are simple and effective hiding places. Put one or two on their sides and line them with towels or T-shirts that contain your scent. If the cat is very timid, use boxes or paper bags as tunnels, as described in the previous chapter. Tunnels in the middle of the room that lead to various resources can help a timid cat begin to venture out from under the bed and feel more secure walking to the food bowl or litter box.

When you set up the items in the sanctuary room, such as the litter box, scratching post, bed, and toys, they should be new or ones that came with the newcomer. Don't use items that belong to your resident cat. The new cat will already be dealing with lots of new scents without having these valuable resources smell potentially unwelcoming. It's also important to your resident cat not to lose any resources. This is not the time for a cherished scratching post, familiar litter box, or bed to suddenly disappear.

Place the food and water bowls on one side of the room and the litter box on the opposite wall. The litter box shouldn't be located close to the food because cats don't eliminate where they eat. No matter how small the sanctuary, make sure you've separated the food from the litter box as much as possible.

The litter box should be uncovered. If you're bringing in an adult cat and she had a previous home, use the same type of litter she's accustomed to and then gradually transition to the kind of litter you use with the rest of your cats by mixing a small amount of the new litter into her current brand, slowly increasing the amount over the course of several days.

Cat-Proof the Sanctuary Room

Look around the sanctuary room and do all necessary safeguarding. Secure dangling electrical cords, remove delicate objects from shelves, and make sure lamps aren't top-heavy. Use cord shorten-ers for the cords on blinds and shades. If the newcomer is a kitten, coat electrical cords with a bitter antichew product.

Plug in a night-light so a timid cat can move comfortably around in a low-light setting and so you won't have to flick on a bright light when you enter the room to check on her. She can see in the dark, but you can't. You can also install a dimmer switch to control the amount of lighting in the room. Low lighting is espe-cially helpful when it comes to getting a frightened or aggressive cat to calm down and relax.

The Sanctuary Room Scratching Post

The sanctuary room will need to have its own scratching op-tions. This is not only important so the cat can condition her claws and stretch her muscles, but it's comforting for a newcomer entering unfamiliar territory to be able to see her claw marks and recognize her own scent. If you adopt a kitten, the scratching post will help her get a good head start on appropriate training.

Use a tall, vertical post covered in sisal and get a horizontal scratching pad. For the pad, you can get an inexpensive corrugated cardboard scratcher. Since you probably won't know whether the newcomer prefers horizontal or vertical scratching, or both, you'll be covering your bases and protecting your furniture.

Don't Forget About Toys

You'll need some toys for the new cat to enjoy during solo play as well as one or two types of interactive toys for your play sessions together. The interactive toy will be an important tool for build-ing trust so you can keep your distance while the cat learns to associate you with positive experiences. Interactive playtime tech-niques can be found in chapter 5.

For solo toys, get a few furry mice and some Mylar crinkle balls. Choose toys that are light and will have movement when batted. Choose appropriate toys for the cat's size and personality. Don't get huge, intimidating toys for a kitten or frightened cat. Catnip-filled toys are appealing, but use them sparingly (see chapter 5 for a fuller discussion of catnip).

Since the new cat will spend a good amount of time in the sanctuary room, create more activities for her beyond just normal solo playtime toys. Create puzzle feeders to give her a reward-based activity. Learn more about food-dispensing toys in chapter 6.

Important Extras

Elevation—Cats love and benefit from having elevated locations. Add a window perch or a cat tree to the room. At the very least, put a cat bed on top of a box or piece of furniture. If there's a window in the room, place the elevated perch or piece of furniture there so the cat will have a sunny place to watch wildlife.

Music—Classical music is frequently played in shelters to help reduce stress in the cats. Play a classical radio station or stream some quiet music for the newcomer. The music will also serve as a bit of a buffer if there's any meowing or other feline grumbling happening on the other side of the door.

Pheromone help—There are commercial pheromone products available that may help in creating familiarity in a new environment. These synthetic pheromones mimic the calming pheromones that cats release to identify locations as safe and familiar. Some of my clients think the synthetic pheromone products work great and other clients report no difference at all. If it's in the budget, it's worth a try to add a pheromone product to your toolbox, but they are not a replacement for the behavior work that will need to be done.

PREINTRODUCTION VETERINARY CHECKUPS

Your veterinarian should see the newcomer before you bring her into your home. She should get all needed tests and vaccinations and be dewormed if those things haven't already been done. Make sure your resident cat is up-to-date on vaccinations. If you don't vaccinate some or all of your indoor cats due to age or medical concerns, don't bring an unfamiliar cat into the environment without first getting guidance from your veterinarian.

BEGIN THE INTRODUCTION PROCESS

The big day has finally arrived. Bring the cat (in her carrier) into the home and go right into the sanctuary room, which you will have already set up. If the cat is an adult, open the carrier and let her decide whether she wants to come out right away or not. If she's reluctant to come out, don't try to dump her out of the carrier. Just let her make the choice of where she wants to be.

If the newcomer is a kitten, she'll likely bolt right out of the carrier. She will also likely need time with you as she checks out her temporary accommodations. Play with her or engage however she needs. When she's ready for a nap and has settled in, you can leave the sanctuary room and see how your resident cat is doing. If you just immediately leave a kitten alone in the sanctuary room, she may start crying or meowing and that won't sit well with your resident cat. If there's a family member or friend available, the extra help would be great to keep a meowing kitten busy.

If the cat is frightened and doesn't want to interact with you, then just leave the room and let her venture out and explore the sanctuary room in her own time without an audience. If she does come out right away and wants to spend time with you, then interact with her in the way in which she is most comfortable. She may want to be in your lap, or she may just want to check out the interesting and unfamiliar scents you carry.

When you put the newcomer in the sanctuary room, try not to let any resident cats hang out on the other side of the door, meowing or hissing. That will only make the newcomer feel trapped. An extra hand entertaining or distracting the residents will help.

When you leave the sanctuary room, don't overdo the emotion with your resident cat or she'll really begin to worry that something very big and bad has happened. Instead, be casual and normal in your behavior. A good plan is to entice your resident cat into an interactive play session on the other side of the house.

To make things a little less threatening to your resident cat, leave a robe or towel in the sanctuary room during the initial stages. This way, you can hold the newcomer without getting an overwhelming amount of her scent on you. Be sure to wash your hands afterward as well. Even though your resident cat will surely be able to detect the smallest amount of the newcomer's scent on you, there's no need to present an in-your-face olfactory insult.

In addition to doing interactive play sessions with your resident cat, do sessions with the newcomer as well. If the newcomer is a kitten, the playtime will help her bond with you and help her work off some of that endless kitten energy. If the newcomer is an adult, especially if she's frightened, the interaction will help her stay within her comfort zone while playing. This is a great way to begin bonding and trust building.

There are a couple of important aspects to the introduction that you need to keep in mind. First, the process should be done *one sense at a time*. Also, you want to *give the cats a reason to like each other*. Mere separation is only half the plan. You can keep cats separated for months, but if you don't help them form positive associations with each other when they do meet, the introduction will likely fail.

The cats will first use scent before they see or touch each other. Scent will play a big role in the introduction and your cats' noses will really be working overtime. Restrict the process to one sense at a time (smelling without seeing) and emotions stand a much better chance of staying in relative control.

Pam's CatWise Reminder

Patience is key during new cat introductions. Let the cats set the pace.

Once the newcomer is in the sanctuary room, you may need to leave things at this stage for a while before progressing. Your resident cat may already be upset over the fact that someone's on the other side of the door. You need to let her get used to this and give the newcomer time to get situated. Use your best judgment concerning the time to start actively introducing the cats following the step-by-step plan outlined below. You know your resident cat better than anyone else, so you should be able to tell when it's okay to proceed. For the most part, your resident cat should be performing normal daily activities such as using the litter box and eating, and if you have multiple resident cats, there shouldn't be any redirected aggression. In the sanctuary room, make sure the newcomer is comfortable with her surroundings and isn't spending all her time in hiding before taking the next step.

Every cat is an individual, and every cat parent's circumstances are different. Some cats can breeze through this process in a matter of days, and others may take weeks. Don't be discouraged if your introduction gets stalled before it even gets under way.

And if you went to the shelter to get one new cat and came home with two, the process is essentially the same. Just keep an eye out and make sure they get equal time and territories to establish.

STEP ONE: SCENT

The sock exchange—The first sense to introduce is scent. My sock-exchange technique will help the newcomer and resident to begin to get to know each other in a very safe, controlled way. Pheromones are personal scent chemicals that tell a lot about a cat to others. This sharing of information of the friendly facial pheromones is a great first *How do you do?*

Take a few pairs of clean socks that have been washed without added fabric softener. Put one sock on your hand and rub your resident cat gently along the cheek to collect some of the facial pheromones. If you have multiple resident cats, start with just one cat and pick the one who is calm, sociable, and may be the most likely to be receptive to the newcomer. This cat will act as the ambassador and will be the one who goes through the introduction process first. If you try to introduce a large multicat household to a newcomer, it will certainly overwhelm the poor little cat. Start with the cat who seems the easiest and then you can work up to the others.

Once you've collected the scent on one sock, go into the sanctuary room and, with another clean sock, rub the newcomer around the face if she's comfortable enough to allow it. Leave the resident's sock in the newcomer's room and take the newcomer's sock into the main part of your home. If the newcomer is frightened or you feel rubbing her cheeks will damage any trust building you've started, then just place a couple of clean socks on her bedding or around the room to collect scents passively.

The sock exchange can also help you determine how upset or calm a cat may be. If a cat goes crazy and starts hissing, growling, and attacking the sock, chances are this will not be a record-breaking introduction in terms of speed. If the cat sniffs the sock and shows only mild interest, that's a good sign. Even if a cat does show a strong negative reaction to the sock, don't be discouraged. Introductions are tough in the beginning, but that's not necessarily an indication of how the cats will ultimately get along. It's normal to experience a bumpy road at first, and it's much safer to let the cats work out their concerns on the sock rather than on each other. Be ready with treats or toys to help the cat associate something pleasant with the unfamiliar cat's scent.

Do the sock exchange a couple of times a day until you feel everyone has become familiar and relatively comfortable with each other's scent.

The towel swap—The next step after the sock exchange is the towel swap. Place a small, clean towel over each cat's bedding to collect some passive scents from the area. Take the towels and put one cat's scent-filled towel in the other cat's room. Don't put the towel on the other cat's bedding. Place the towel in neutral areas of the rooms to give the cats the choice of sniffing them or even resting on them without interfering with their own areas of comfort and security. After a few days, swap the towels back into the original rooms. Hopefully, they will now contain both cats' scents. Like the sock-exchange method, this helps the cats become comfortable with more of each other's scents.

STEP TWO: CLOSED-DOOR MEALTIME

It's time to let the cats start to associate each other with positive experiences. This comes in the form of mealtime. Feed the newcomer in her room and feed the resident cat outside the sanctuary room with the door closed. When you start your mealtime step, you may need to feed each cat far away from the door at first and then work your way closer in subsequent sessions. If one cat finishes first and begins to get nervous or starts to growl or hiss, have an interactive toy handy to use for distraction. Because the cat will have just eaten, keep the game low intensity. If she can't be distracted, lure her away from the door until the next mealtime.

The door serves as the visual safety barrier, but there will still be enough scent (and in some cases, sound) to remind each cat that someone is on the other side. The meals help the cats associate something they want with the presence of each other.

Pay attention to distance. Each cat must be at ease enough to come to their food bowl and eat without darting back and forth, vocalizing, or looking around nervously. If one or both appear nervous, then you have the bowls too close to the door. Once you find the closest, most comfortable distance, mark it with a piece of painter's tape so you'll know exactly where to place the bowls in the next session. I use painter's tape because it doesn't leave a residue on carpet or flooring.

Now that you've identified the feeding safe zone, you can gradually move the bowls closer to the door. We're talking inches here and not feet, though. Go slowly.

STEP THREE: EXPLORATION

After a couple of days of doing the scent exchanges and closed-door meals, if the newcomer seems at ease, it's time for her to do a little exploring. Place your resident cat in another room with some catnip or a few treats or toys to keep her occupied. If you have multiple resident cats, make sure they all get along with one another without any redirected aggression before putting them in one room. If there is any tension, then they need to be divided up so no one gets picked on. Now, open the sanctuary room door for the newest feline family member to begin checking out her new home. Be ready with some treats or an interactive toy to help make this exploration positive. If the new cat seems too scared or stressed, then lead her back to the sanctuary room and try this again later.

When the sanctuary room door is opened, let the new cat walk out on her own. Let her decide whether she wants to take a few steps out or not. Don't pick her up and drop her in the middle of the living room because she'll probably be upset and end up hiding.

As the new cat walks around, she'll sniff just about everything, but she'll also be depositing her own scents into the main part of the environment. She may even facially rub on some furniture or jump up on the sofa. All of this is good because she's leaving a scent trail.

Let the newcomer explore for about thirty minutes if she's comfortable. Do this a couple of times a day if you can. You can gradually increase to sixty minutes if she's okay with being out of the sanctuary room.

STEP FOUR: ROOM SWAP

Once the cats seem comfortable enough with each other's scent through the sock exchange, towel swap, and eating on either side of the door, it's time to try a room swap. Now, your newcomer will already have done some investigating of the resident cat's area at this point, but she probably hasn't spent time in more private locations. Also, the resident cat hasn't checked out her new soon-to-be buddy's quarters yet.

With this step, it's important to evaluate the stress level of both cats. They each must be comfortable enough with the other's scent before you expose them to this higher level of scent intensity. Signs of discomfort may include growling, hissing, slinking low to the ground, tail lashing, hiding, remaining frozen in one place, or trying to dart out of the room. For the room swap, place the new cat in another room and then let the resident cat check out the sanctuary room. Keep the door to the sanctuary room open to allow your cat the option to leave whenever she wants. The room swap shouldn't be attempted if it appears to cause your resident cat any distress. It's better to wait a few more days rather than rush this step.

If the above step goes well, you can give the newcomer a chance to check out more of the resident cat's main turf the next day. Place your resident cat in a room in which she's secure and then let the newcomer do more inspecting.

Pam's CatWise Caution

Never trap the resident cat in the newcomer's room by closing the door. The resident cat always needs the choice to leave.

STEP FIVE: VISUAL CONTACT

Now that the cats have gotten used to each other's scents, eating on either side of the closed door, and the room-swapping sessions, the next step is to add in another sense and let them have a little visual contact. Their exposure to each other should be brief, positive, and at a safe distance. Open the sanctuary room door and let the cats see each other while being offered a treat or a meal. Similar to when you began the closed-door feeding, you may have to start on opposite sides of the room so the cats don't feel threatened. To increase the success of this step, choose treats that you already know the cats love. This isn't the time to experiment with a brand-new treat.

To keep the mood light, keep the cats somewhat happily distracted. If there's another family member available, you should each play with a cat, using interactive toys. If you are by yourself, try puzzle feeders or Mylar crinkle balls to keep the cats engaged. You already know what entices your resident cat, so use that knowledge.

To provide extra security, place something in the doorway so the cats can't charge each other. You can install a temporary screen door there or even a couple of baby gates stacked one on top of the other. The cats could certainly scale the gates if they wanted to, but having them there buys you a little time to put up a visual blockade or close the door if needed. The baby gates or the screen door will also serve as a psychological barrier to the cats. They might feel a little less exposed with the gates or screen in place, rather than with a completely wide-open entrance.

Another option is to install a hook and eye or other clasp that prevents the door from opening more than just a few inches.

When at the visual stage with cats, always keep a thick towel nearby. The towel can be used to drape over the gate if you need to adjust how much visual contact you want the cats to have. If using a screen door, you can control the amount of visual contact by taping a large sheet of paper on the screen so just a small part of the opening to the sanctuary room is visible. Keep a towel with you no matter what you put in the doorway. The towel will come in handy if things go sour and the cats attack each other; you can toss it over them if a fight breaks out. Try not to let it get to that point, though. Pay attention to signs of escalating tension so you can end the session before any confrontation.

When you do the visual sessions, it's always more productive to end on a positive note each time so you can build on the good experience in the next session.

STEP SIX: SUPERVISED VISITATION

When the previous phase has gone well, it's time to let the cats have more time to interact. Keep the sanctuary room set up because you'll want to put the newcomer back in there at night and when you're not around to supervise, but you're now ready to let them begin to build their relationship. As for supervision, keep it nonchalant in appearance so the cats don't feel as if you're hovering over them. You want to see their reactions, and they may not act as naturally if you're too close because they'll pick up on your tension.

Conduct a parallel play session by letting each cat enjoy an interactive toy. This is obviously easier if you have a family member or friend to help so the cats can be kept at a distance. If you're alone, put a toy in each hand so the cats don't compete for one toy. To learn more about this type of group play, refer to chapter 5.

When the cats are together, periodically toss treats to keep up the positive associations. Always keep toys within reach to use if you notice one cat starting to stalk another or if they seem to be too intensely focused on each other. You can also roll a Ping-Pong ball down the hallway or toss a Mylar crinkle ball to shift the focus. Keep everything positive, so use cat-friendly methods of distraction. If, however, an attack happens or is about to happen, make a noise to get them to move away from each other. If one cat starts stalking another, use a towel, large piece of cardboard, or anything else that will serve as a visual barrier to break the stare. Then, carefully guide the cats away from each other and put them in separate rooms. Never pick up an agitated cat and never get in the middle of a cat fight. In fact, when doing a new cat introduction, keep objects handy that can serve as visual blockades. A large, sturdy, flat piece of cardboard works great and can be easily stashed behind a chair or sofa when not needed.

STEP SEVEN: FREEDOM

This happens only when the previous step has gone well consistently over several days. Before the cats can be together in the house, make sure you've created resources in the locations each cat prefers and there's no need for rivalry. Don't make the mistake of thinking you can get rid of an extra litter box or have the cats eat side by side out of one bowl or place bowls close together. Maintain an environment that allows choice and security.

WHAT IF THINGS DON'T GO WELL?

Never punish a cat for hissing, growling, or displaying any sign of negative behavior at another cat. Doing so will only intensify the fear. Use distraction to lure the upset cat away, close the sanctuary door, and give the cats a break from visual contact. Keep the process positive, calm, and nonchalant. Sometimes introductions take two steps forward and one step back. Don't get discouraged, just go a little more slowly. Don't move on to the next step until the cats are comfortable with the current step. Remember, you're not trying to meet a deadline—you're trying to help cats develop the start of a lifelong relationship.

Sometimes a newcomer may have trouble leaving the safety of the sanctuary room, especially if the resident guards the exit. If that's the case, slow down the process. You may be exposing the cats to each other for too long a period or you may have rushed through one phase of the process. If things aren't going well despite slowing the pace, you may need to keep a screen door up in the sanctuary room in place of a regular door while you extend the introduction. You can buy an inexpensive screen door at a home improvement store. Just make sure it's sturdy enough that an upset cat can't push through it. The screen door will allow the cats to see each other and have closer contact yet remain safe. Hopefully, they will start to become desensitized to each other's presence. This method isn't needed in most cases, but you might feel safer using this option if you're worried about their level of arousal. Keep in mind, though, that the screen door isn't there in place of the behavior work you need to continue doing. Keep using mealtime, treats, and playtime to help the cats develop positive associations with each other.

Clicker training is an option to use as a tool to keep cats focused on good things and to help them see there are good consequences to desirable behaviors. To learn about clicker training, refer to chapter 5.

If any cat seems traumatized by the introduction, keep the cats apart and talk to your veterinarian about a referral to a certified behavior expert. A personalized, detailed plan by a professional may be needed or it may be determined that the cats are just not a safe match. For more information on finding a certified behavior professional, refer to chapter 12.

Some cats will never develop the close bond you were hoping for. They may just get to a point of mutual respect for each other's territory and coexist through avoidance. This may appear to be an okay outcome for some cats, but others might still experience ongoing stress. Consult a behavior professional to help you determine the best course of action based on your case particulars.

OTHER INTRODUCTIONS

How to Introduce a New Spouse or Significant Other

In most families, the cats like the new spouse or significant other and you all can become one big happy family. But what about when things don't go smoothly? What if one or more of your cats hates the love of your life?

Even if the cats liked your spouse while you were dating, a full-time living arrangement can be another matter altogether.

If you and your cats plan to move into your spouse's home or a new home, follow the instructions in this chapter under "Introducing Cats to a New Home."

If your new spouse has furniture that will be coming into your home, try to make the transition gradually. Incorporate the unfamiliar furniture into the home a few pieces at a time. If you're planning one big move, bring over smaller pieces, if possible, before the actual moving day. The more gradual you can make the transition for your cats, the less anxiety you'll have to contend with. It's also very beneficial to maintain your cats' schedules. If they're used to specific times for play sessions or meals, don't deviate from that. The less you disrupt normal daily life for your cats, the easier this transition will go.

One thing to know about and plan for in advance is your spouse's reaction to living with multiple cats. Does your spouse have an allergy to cats? Does he or she have strong feelings about where the litter box should go? About cats chilling on his or her furniture? If one or more of your cats sleep with you at night, how does your spouse feel about that? These are things to talk about in advance of the move so they don't escalate to crisis level later. Your spouse may have enjoyed your cats while you were dating, but having cats sleep in the bed or sprawl on a treasured piece of furniture may not be something open for negotiation.

If you decide it would be best to start locking the cats out of the bedroom, it'll be much better to begin that transition before the spouse moves in. This way they don't have two major adjustments to make at the same time—new person and suddenly getting kicked out of the bedroom. Start keeping your bedroom door closed all the time so your cats get out of the habit of wandering in there during the day. You'll be decreasing territory by closing off that room, so increase it with cat trees, perches, hideaways, or cat shelves in other rooms. If your bedroom was a popular place for some of your cats to spend the night with you in the bed, then you must create other appealing sleeping arrangements before you just shut them out of a room they're used to enjoying. It's something to carefully think about and discuss with your new spouse because of the stress it can cause cats to suddenly lose a location they've come to know as secure and familiar. Work on compromises with your spouse, but it's also important for him or her to understand how upheaval and loss of territory can affect your multiple-cat harmony.

What if some of your cats hate your new spouse? The first rule is for him or her not to try too hard to be the cats' new best friend. While it's important that they develop positive associations with the new spouse, it's also essential that the cats, not your spouse, determine the pace.

Pam's CatWise Etiquette Tips
for the New Spouse or Significant Other

- Be aware of how your presence may be perceived by the cats. Don't use a loud voice or big gestures.
- Be aware of the way the cats react to how quickly you move, the sound of your footsteps, and your energy level. Sometimes cats who have lived only with women may be startled by the footsteps of a male. Cats who are used to only men may be confused by the movements and higher voices of women. Cats used to living with a quiet, low-key person may be unsettled by the arrival of someone with a dynamic personality. Keep in mind that you're dealing with animals who find great comfort in routine and predictability.
- Don't try to pick up a cat until you have established a friendly relationship and it appears that the cat is inviting more contact. If a cat doesn't want to be petted yet, she certainly isn't ready to be picked up and held.
- Don't go into the personal space of a cat who hasn't accepted you. Let the cat approach you.
- Let a cat conduct a scent investigation without interruption. Stand or sit still and let her sniff. This is a chief part of her making sure you aren't a threat in her territory.
- Offer a cat one extended finger to sniff before you reach to pet her so she can do a scent investigation. Just hold it still and let her come to you. It's good cat etiquette that's like nose-to-nose sniffing. This will show the cat that you *speak* her language and are following the rules.
- Help in preparation of the cats' meals but don't hang around where they eat if it makes any of them uncomfortable. It's good to have your scent on the bowls and to let the cats start to associate you with this vital part of their daily lives.
- Take over at least half of the interactive play sessions after the cat parent has initiated the first few. Select some

special new toys (with the cat parent's guidance to ensure the cats will like them) that can help the cats associate you with fun experiences. Move the toys the way a cat prefers. The cat parent can instruct you on each cat's individual play-style preferences.

- Never punish or reprimand a cat no matter what has happened. All unwanted behavior is based on fear, and punishment will only increase that fear and delay a cat's acceptance of you. Instead, look at what might have triggered the unwanted behavior to see what you may be able to change regarding your approach.

- Don't remove a cat from a chair that you want to sit in. If you really need that specific chair, entice the cat off with an interactive toy or treat. You are in the early stages of learning about each cat's preferred areas. Try not to displace cats from areas in which they feel most secure.

- Never stare directly at a cat as that is viewed as a challenge. Challenging a cat you're trying to win over is the last thing you want to do. Instead, use a soft gaze when looking at a cat and don't look for too long.

- Use bribery. Carry treats with you. Get a trainer's treat bag from the pet supply store and stash treats in there to use periodically throughout the day as you interact with the cats. The trainer's bag clips onto your waistband or belt and makes it very convenient to have a treat handy when needed.

Blended Feline Families

It's not only about your kids getting along with your spouse's kids. It's also about all the cats getting along—not to mention any dogs in the now blended family. One of the hardest hurdles a blended family must face in terms of the pets concerns how to introduce the cats. The situation can be made easier if you follow a few basic guidelines.

If you're moving to your new spouse's home, then your cats should be put in the sanctuary room. Slowly help the cats get to know the new human family members and then proceed with a new cat introduction. This is a huge transition for your cats, so they need as many allies as possible. Cats hate change, and a new home, a new human family, and new cats rank high on the cat stress-o-meter. If your spouse is moving into your home, then his or her cats go into the sanctuary room.

If you are all moving into a new home, there are some benefits to that from a cat's point of view. The new home is neutral territory that no cat has claimed yet. Set up two sanctuary areas. A move to a new home is stressful in itself, so just as you would do in a typical new cat introduction, let the cats get comfortable in the sanctuary room before proceeding. Let each set of cats out separately to explore the house a little at a time. To determine whose cats should go out first, choose the group that tends to be a little more frightened. These cats should have first exposure so they won't be initially intimidated by the additional scents deposited by the other cats. After the cats seem calm in the sanctuary area and have checked out the rest of the house, you can start the actual introduction. Follow the steps mentioned earlier in this chapter on how to introduce a new cat.

Don't try to introduce all the cats to one another at the same time. Pick the two cats who are calm and confident and start with them so they can then serve as cat ambassadors to the rest of the feline family.

Introducing Cats to a New Home

Cats take great comfort in the familiarity of their surroundings. Introducing a new environment can be relatively easy for some of the cats and very challenging for others. In general, though, a brand-new territory introduces stress into a cat's expectation of daily life.

Your cats have worked out a social structure in your current home and established individual, personal territories within it. It may have taken some of your cats quite a bit of effort to negotiate their little corners of the world. To them, the move to a new home feels as if a giant came along and shook up the world, and their things landed in all the wrong places.

You should have sanctuary rooms set up in the new place before the cats arrive. How well your cats get along and how many you have will determine how many sanctuary rooms you'll need. Be sure to match together cats who get along even under stress. Put familiar furniture in the sanctuary, but if you're separating cats into various rooms, match cats with their favorite pieces of furniture.

Keep surroundings as familiar as possible. For example, don't go out and buy new furniture all at once if you can help it. Your cats will take comfort in finding their favorite chairs, even if they're not all in the location they remember. If you normally keep throws or afghans on your furniture, don't launder them right before moving. Being able to detect their familiar scents will provide more security for the cats.

Even though you'll probably be exhausted and overwhelmed yourself by the move, take care to keep your cats' daily schedule. The more they can hold on to what's familiar, the better. Don't neglect those daily play sessions—your cats need them now more than ever. Help your cats develop positive associations with the new home by conducting games in various rooms. The new home may present opportunities for increased territory through cat shelving. Perhaps your previous location had limited space for that, but the new home has higher ceilings or more unused wall space. Take advantage of that and consider how adding more vertical space could help increase feline harmony.

Despite all the stress of moving, you may find an unexpected bonus. Because a new home starts out as unclaimed territory, some of the cats who didn't get along previously might have a less tense relationship. The preferred area divisions may change enough to make more of the cats feel secure, especially if you've moved to a larger home.

Introducing Cats to Babies and Children

Cats and children can form wonderful and close bonds, but some preparation is needed to help cats adjust to this major life-changing event. Many people mistakenly believe cats retaliate out of jealousy when a baby enters the family. This is false. Any behavioral changes that occur, such as elimination outside the litter box, for instance, are the result of the anxiety and uncertainty surrounding the sudden change. Remember, cats hate change and are territorial creatures of habit. So imagine the stress of finding there's a strange-smelling, very loud little creature in their territory. On top of that, none of the humans in the home are acting normally and the daily schedule usually gets totally turned upside down. Nobody consulted the cats about this change, so they often find themselves overwhelmed.

When you have more than one cat, you may find that with the arrival of the baby, the dynamics among the cats change. One may become more anxious when the baby comes home, and that can trigger some of the others to then get concerned. It can create a chain reaction of anxiety because the nervous cat is no longer acting normally and that confuses her cat companions. The cats who may initially get the most stressed out are typically the *Velcro* kitties—the lap cats who are most bonded with you. Because you're spending so much time with the baby and maybe aren't keeping up with the normal cat rituals, they become confused. You may see behavioral changes—mostly unwanted ones. One cat may eliminate outside the litter box and the scent of the urine may cause concern and confusion in the other cats. When you have more than one cat, it's not just the cat with the behavior issue you must address—you also must be aware of how that cat's behavior affects the rest of the cat family.

The best solution is to plan ahead so the cats aren't faced with the sudden shock of a new baby. Start by doing nursery preparations well in advance so you can go gradually. If you're going to convert a room that some of your cats currently use, begin getting them used to other places in a positive way. If you have a cat tree in that room, move it to a very appealing location, being careful not to place it in another cat's preferred area, especially if the cats don't get along. Take time to play with your cats at the newly located tree to get them comfortable with this change. Since you'll be decreasing horizontal territory, make some vertical increases. This will also come in handy later when the cats want places to get out of the baby's reach. Incorporate more perches, cat shelving, cat stairways, and maybe even cat skyways. An additional cat tree, at the very least, will help add vertical territory.

Do the nursery decorating gradually to give your cats time to adjust to all the different scents. Don't paint, wallpaper, install new carpet, and bring in the new furniture all in one weekend. This is key if one of your cats tends to stress out if you so much as buy a new end table or rearrange the living-room seating.

Even if you don't mind if the cats come and go in the nursery, the one place you want to make sure they don't camp out is the crib. There's no truth to the myth that cats steal the breath from babies, which probably began before sudden infant death syndrome (SIDS) was identified. However, since a newborn baby is unable to turn, you don't want anything in the crib anyway—not even a blanket. Because some of your cats may view the empty crib as a great place to nap, start the training process right away.

Get a bunch of empty soda cans and plastic bottles. Make shake cans by putting a couple of pennies in each can and taping over the opening. Put pennies in the bottles as well and then recap them. Fill the crib with the cans and bottles so the cats can't find a comfortable place anywhere. Keep the cans and bottles in place until the baby arrives. If you do it early enough, the cats will make the connection that the crib isn't such a great place to be. Another option is to line the crib bed with a plastic carpet runner. Use the kind with the pointy feet on one side and place it in the crib with the feet side up. After the baby comes, if you're still concerned about a cat jumping in there, you can purchase a crib tent. Choose one that's strong and won't sink down under the weight of a cat and just become a cat hammock. It was my experience that the best cat deterrent in the crib was the ear-splitting noise emanating from the wailing baby.

To help cats get used to the scents of the baby, the mother-to-be can start wearing baby lotion and powder. When preparing my cats, I also found it helpful to buy and play with some of the larger and noisier baby toys in advance so they had time to get used to the often-startling sounds they make.

If your cats have never been around babies, you can start exposing them gradually by inviting friends with babies over for short visits. Make the visits brief and as low stress as possible. Timing will be important because you don't want the friend to bring the baby over when she's due for a nap and might be cranky. You can also play sound effects of baby noises (include baby crying sounds). Play it at a very low volume while you conduct interactive play sessions or offer treats. Gradually increase volume in subsequent training sessions.

One big mistake cat parents make is they shower their cats with an exceptionally large amount of attention before the baby comes, thinking this will help ease the stress afterward. This backfires because the parents can't maintain that level of attention after the baby arrives, and the sudden decrease in what the cats have come to expect as normal increases stress and loneliness. It's better to establish a realistic routine before the baby comes home so you'll be able to maintain it afterward.

If you don't already have cat furniture for your cats, don't delay any longer. Get those things in advance of baby's arrival so your cats have time to get comfortable with them and learn they can rely on those locations for security. It also gives the cats time to work out any preferred elevated area compromises that need to be made. When the baby starts crawling, the cats need areas of escape, and going vertical is a good choice.

This is also the time to start making litter box adjustments. The boxes may eventually have to be relocated out of the way when the time comes that baby is mobile. Place additional boxes in baby-free areas, and then if the original boxes need to be moved, relocate them a few feet a day until they're in the chosen areas. Once they're next to the new boxes, you can remove any unneeded ones. Keep territorial considerations in mind: Which cats use that box most often, and will it go into an equally secure area?

If the baby has arrived and some of the cats aren't handling it well, you can still make things better. One of the activities you shouldn't skimp on is the interactive playtime. Try to maintain the twice-daily schedule. You'll even get coordinated enough that you will be able to hold the baby while maneuvering a fishing pole toy. I'm not known for my coordination and ability to multi-task, and yet I found that it was easier than I thought to tend to my infant daughter and still keep a cat entertained. If there are other family members available, enlist their help with play sessions when you're busy with the baby.

Even if you can't interact with your cats physically because you're feeding, changing a diaper, or playing with the baby, you can interact with them verbally. Use a soothing tone of voice to talk to them. Mention their names often and describe what you're doing. You may find they'll be reassured to hear their names, rub up against you, and curl up near you while you feed the baby.

Incorporate the use of puzzle feeders to keep cats occupied and content when you're busy with the baby. Learn more about how to use puzzle feeders in chapter 6.

Watch for preliminary warning signs that a cat is getting upset or fearful around the baby. Don't wait for a cat to strike out. Distract her at the first sign of potential trouble. It's best to catch behaviors early and divert them so a cat doesn't begin to associate the presence of the infant with a negative.

As your children grow, it'll be important to teach them how to interact gently with the cats in a positive way. When babies first learn to touch, they tend to grab with the subtlety of a sledgehammer, and that won't go over too well with your cats. Start early and be consistent in teaching your children how to pet gently with an open hand. Hold your child's hand to prevent grabbing and making a fist. You'd be surprised how early that message of gentleness can be conveyed to the child. It also helps your cats become used to a child's touch and learn they can trust it.

Don't ever let your children tease your cats, and teach them as soon as practical to become familiar with basic feline body language. Teach the message about off-limit times and places. For example, cats are to be left alone when eating, sleeping, using the litter box, and hanging out in their perches or cat trees. Help children learn to read the body language of a cat who is saying *I'd rather be left alone.*

If a cat who normally gets along with a child suddenly starts acting aggressively or terrified, one of the things you need to investigate is the possibility of unintentional rough handling or, sadly, even potential abuse. While in most cases a child hurting a pet is accidental, there is a possibility of intentional cruelty. Children who abuse animals are usually very secretive about it, so you must be vigilant when it comes to the relationship between your children and your pets. Never leave a child alone with a pet if you suspect anything.

Introducing Your Cats to a Dog

Just when you think you've gotten the stress in your feline household down to a healthy level, a dog comes bounding into your life. Suddenly, the cats are diving under the bed or leaping onto the highest perches in the house.

A dog can be a delightful addition to the family, but you need to teach them all how to interact with one another in a safe and nonthreatening way. As with all other aspects of introducing cats to anything new, planning makes all the difference.

Cats and dogs can be closely bonded companions, but everyone must get started off on the right foot. Dogs and cats speak different languages, and you need to help them find common ground. Although you won't have the same territorial issues to deal with as when you bring a new cat into the house, you'll have to work on canine/feline social etiquette and communication. Dogs and cats have different ideas on how to play, and that can cause problems. Dogs play by chasing and wrestling. Your cats may run, and the dog will interpret that as an invitation to play. The more the cats run, the more the dog chases. This sets everyone up for continual frustration because the frightened cats will be conditioned to run every time they spot the dog.

As a highly social animal, a dog also doesn't understand the protocol of feline greetings. Take a dog to the dog park and, chances are, within minutes she'll find another canine buddy. Two cats will never be friends in the space of a few minutes. The trick is to help the dog learn how to approach.

Here's how basic training sessions should go:

Step one—Sanctuary room. Incorporate some of the techniques described in the section on introducing a new cat. If the dog is coming into the cats' house, make sure the dog has a safe room and a crate. This will help the cats feel as if most of their territory were still safe. If the cats are coming into the dog's home, then the cats need the sanctuary room, where they can come and go, but the dog can't.

Step two—Scent investigation. Let them get to know one another's scents in their environments without making visual contact. Keep it positive and use treat rewards for calm/positive reactions.

Step three—Closed-door mealtime. Just as with the cat-to-cat introduction, find the zone where both will eat comfortably on either side of the closed door. Gradually work your way closer, being careful not to rush.

Step four—More scent investigation and room swapping. Let the dog investigate the cat areas by placing the cats in a separate room so she can go around the house and not only check out the feline scents but spread some of her own. Let the cats check out the dog's area by leaving the door to her room open and either place her in another room or take her out for a walk.

Step five—Visual contact. The dog should be on a leash and the cats should be loose in a room. Start off with a baby gate blocking the entrance where the cats are so the dog can't get to the cats should the leash slip out of your grasp. You may want to do the first few sessions with just one cat—the most potentially dog-friendly one. Have some dog treats in your pocket and a dog toy in your hand. The goal of this session is to get the dog to focus on you and not the cat. When she relaxes and focuses on you, offer an irresistible treat. If she tries to move toward the cat, walk her farther away from the baby gate to get her to refocus on you. When the dog responds, walk a little closer toward the baby gate. If all goes well, practice walking back and forth in front of the baby gate. Work up to being able to remove the gate in future sessions. This is a slow process, so don't rush anything.

You can use clicker training during these sessions. Click the second the dog does what you want and then deliver a treat. Clicker training can be helpful because it immediately lets the dog know what you want from her. As you proceed through these sessions, you can progressively inch closer in the direction of one of the cats. These sessions will show the dog that cats are neither toys nor prey to be chased. They will also help the cats realize that the very sight of the dog doesn't mean they're in danger. Details on clicker training can be found in chapter 5.

Pam's CatWise Caution

If a dog growls, attempts to bite, or shows any sign of aggression toward a cat, separate them immediately and contact a behavior professional. This is a very dangerous situation.

Even if things seem to be going well, don't be in a hurry to remove the leash. A leashed dog is easier to control. When you get to the point where you don't feel you have to actually hold the leash in your hand, let the dog drag the leash around so you have the option of stepping on the end of the leash in an emergency, for instance, should the dog suddenly lunge toward the cat. Don't allow the dog off the leash in the house until you are completely satisfied that the animals have formed a safe and friendly relationship.

It's important to have a well-trained dog under any circumstances, but with cats in the house, you must make sure everyone feels safe. If you're unsure whether you can trust the dog with the cats, consult a certified dog behavior consultant or qualified dog trainer. Never leave a dog and cat unsupervised until you're positive they have established a safe relationship. It can take weeks for a cat to become comfortable with the dog. Be prepared, as well, for the realization that some cats never adjust to living with a dog.

Environmental adjustments are typically necessary when a dog joins the feline family. Litter box locations need to be secure so the dog can't ambush a cat in the box. You may even discover that the dog visits the litter box for something to munch on. It seems gross to us, but some dogs frequently seek out cat poop due to its high protein and fat content. If you find that to be the case, block the doorway to the litter with a baby gate. Place a sturdy box, table, or chair on the other side of the gate so the cats have something to jump onto if they're reluctant to jump the top of the gate. If you have a large dog, you may be able to raise the gate a few inches off the ground so the cats can scoot underneath. You can also cut a hole in the baby gate, depending on what it's made of, and create a cat door within it. Glue slats of wood to make a frame around the cut opening to keep it sturdy.

Pam's CatWise Caution

Don't be tempted to get a covered litter box for your cats to prevent the dog from gaining access. A covered box only sets cats up for being ambushed and trapped. Cats need as much visual warning time as possible.

Another more long-term option if you have a large dog is to install small pet doors on the interior doors to rooms where litter boxes are located that only the cats can fit through. The downside of this is that the dog may camp out at the door, ready to spring a surprise ambush. Training is the most practical solution. The baby gate is also a better option because it allows the cat to see what's on the other side. You'll have to decide what works best in your household to keep the litter box locations safe for all the cats.

The feeding station is another area that may require some modifications. If you previously had ground-level stations, you may need to elevate them all or relocate the food to rooms where the dog is not allowed. Continue to work on training, though, to teach the dog and the cats they are to eat only from their own bowls. Again, training is the best long-term solution.

Cat trees, elevated perches, or cat walkways will also be helpful. The cats need safe places for retreat. If you have a very large dog who can access the taller perches, training is needed so she learns the trees are off-limits.

Vertical space for the cats, in the form of trees, walkways, and skywalks, allows them to have choice. Stress levels are reduced when cats feel they can control their surroundings and have the choice of whether to engage and of just how much interaction they prefer. The more choice you offer, the more peaceful the long-term multiple pet environment will be.

WHAT IF THINGS DON'T GO WELL?

You never want to put a cat or dog in physical danger or emotional distress. If you feel as if you've hit a brick wall in the introduction process or are concerned about either animal's safety, contact a qualified professional to help guide you. Ask your veterinarian for a referral to a veterinary behaviorist, certified dog or cat behavior consultant, or a qualified dog trainer. If the cat is the one having problems, be sure you contact a veterinary behaviorist or certified cat behavior consultant. A dog trainer is not qualified to guide you on cat behavior problems.

Pam's CatWise Caution

An introduction that should never be attempted is between cats and their natural prey. If you have a pet snake, bird, caged mouse, gerbil, and so forth, do not allow the cats access to where these pets are kept. A cat is a hunter, and even if you have a very secure cage setup, it's extremely stressful for the caged pets to live in such close proximity to a natural predator. A fish tank in the room the cat uses has to be totally cat-proof, not just covered.

Enriching the Environment

An unhealthy, stressful, or boring environment can contribute to feline behavior problems as well as illness. Cats in these environments are at risk of developing boredom-related or stress-relieving behaviors. Those problems can include litter box issues, intercat aggression, depression, compulsive behaviors, changes in appetite (overeating or undereating), vomiting, attention-seeking behavior, and more.

How an environment is set up also plays an enormous role in how cats get along. In chapter 1 you learned about the feline social structure, and in chapter 3 you read about territory. By now, you should have a good idea of how the setup of your environment is either helping your cats coexist peacefully or how it might be preventing household harmony.

A successful cat environment provides the following:

- Safety
- Easy access to key resources
- Multiple resource locations
- Personal space
- Opportunities to play and exercise
- Vertical territory

- Stimulation for the senses
- The choice to interact or avoid
- The ability to hide
- Predictability
- Positive and consistent human interaction

START WITH THE BASICS

Before cats can engage in the fun aspects of environmental enrichment such as playtime or social interaction, they first must know they're safe. This applies to the overall environment and daily life. Do any of your cats stay constantly hidden because they're terrified of being attacked by another cat? Are disputes occurring at the food bowl or is a cat consistently ambushed in the litter box? Are you maintaining veterinary care and addressing indications of illness or pain? As you go through this chapter, you'll find ways to increase the fun factor in your cats' lives, but it's essential to start by creating safety and maintaining the health of your cat family.

Most features of environmental enrichment are fun and creative, but other aspects relate to being diligent, observant, and using common sense to ensure a happy cat family. Don't overlook the basics to get to the fun part, because everything needs to start with a firm foundation.

The basics start with:

Veterinary Care

Keep up with routine veterinary visits regardless of the size of your cat family. Every cat needs to see the veterinarian on a yearly basis (more often for older cats) for vaccinations and wellness exams.

Nutrition

Each cat should eat good-quality food appropriate for their life stage, age, activity level, and health condition. Maintaining a good nutritional regimen is more challenging in a multicat environment, but it can, and must, be done. For help with mealtime issues, refer to chapter 6.

Safe and Clean Environment

Every single cat needs to feel safe and deserves a clean and healthy environment in which to thrive. The larger the cat family, the more waste is deposited in litter boxes, the more cat hair is left on furniture, and the more food bowls need to be washed. Don't skip the less appealing portions of living with multiple cats. Maintain an environment that's healthy for the cats and healthy for you.

Minimize Stress

Stress ruins everything. When you're stressed, it can be all you focus on and it can prevent you from enjoying daily life. Chronic, persistent stress begins to wear you down and can affect your health. The same applies to your cats.

Address ongoing stress. That may be the most important message in this book. For example, if you have a couple of cats who don't get along, it's time to do the necessary behavior work to repair the relationship. If your cats never adjusted to your new spouse or if they're stressed out by any recent family change, deal with it now. Stress just eats away at everyone's joy and, eventually, overall health.

See chapter 10 to learn more about reducing stress triggers in your cats' lives. If you can't figure out the underlying cause of stress, ask your veterinarian for a referral to a veterinary behaviorist or certified cat behavior consultant.

Key Resources

The foundation of environmental enrichment is the ability of a cat to engage in normal activities, free from fear or stress. The key elements here: litter boxes, scratching posts, meals, places to sleep—you know what I'm talking about. An appealing litter box setup, clean and in a location in which a cat feels safe and comfortable, will help contribute to physical and emotional health. Access to scratching posts and pads helps to maintain claw health and allows cats to stretch and mark, and thus contributes to good health, stress relief, and intercat communication. The mealtime setup and a safe and comfortable place to sleep are also crucial. When thinking about environmental enrichment, start by ensuring the most basic needs are being met in a way that helps your cats thrive physically and emotionally.

Now, let's get into the fun stuff!

PLAYTIME

Daily playtime is important for your multicat family. You may think it's unnecessary because some or all of them play with one another now and then. If you just leave it up to the haphazard play schedule a few of your cats may sometimes follow, you won't be able to use playtime as a valuable behavior tool. Take more control to ensure everyone is enjoying play sessions that are satisfying.

Playtime, in a multicat environment, if done correctly, can

- help ease tension between cats,
- refocus a cat who tends to cause issues,

- be tailored to fit each cat's individual physical limitations,
- help an intimidated cat feel more confident,
- help cats make positive associations with previously negative locations,
- assist in the introduction process,
- strengthen bonds,
- help in appetite regulation,
- provide exercise in a fun way, and
- help with weight reduction.

To understand how cats play, you first must understand how they hunt. It's not about throwing a ball and having a cat fetch it. Playtime is a simulated hunt. Cats don't hunt by engaging in long chases; they are ambush predators. They don't have the lung capacity to chase prey to exhaustion. Their skill is in their stealth. For cats, the hunt is as much mental as it is physical. It isn't just luck that's involved in being a successful predator—it takes planning, stealth, speed, good timing, and accuracy. Cats hunt by silently scouting the area, alert to any sound, scent, or movement that might indicate potential prey. When prey is detected, a cat uses his exquisite stealth to stalk his target, inching closer and closer. The cat relies on any available objects in the environment for cover, such as a nearby tree, bush, or tall grass. His body and head are low to the ground. Whiskers and ears are in the forward alert position. The unsuspecting prey goes about its business as the cat effectively closes the gap. When the predator gets to within ambush distance, the cat pounces on the prey with lightning speed. If his aim is good, the prey will instantly be killed by a well-placed bite to the spinal cord. This is referred to as the killing bite.

Pam's CatWise Feline Fact

Adult cats don't engage in social play unless they're familiar social companions.

There are a couple of different types of daily play. One is interactive playtime and the other is solo (object) playtime. Interactive play involves you. You control the movements of the toy. The cats connect your presence with this fun activity.

The other, solo playtime, involves the cats coming across toys or other fun objects in the environment that can be investigated, batted, or manipulated in some way. Even though you won't be directly involved with the actual solo play sessions, you are still an integral part based on your toy selections and how you set them up. They may do this together or alone, depending on their relationship. Cats do not hunt in packs, but it doesn't mean your cats won't cooperate together as they discover solo toys.

Your approach to interactive play should be to simulate a hunt. You want to make this mental and physical experience as realistic as possible for the cat, short of bringing in a live mouse. A good way to become more familiar with beneficial play technique is to observe how a cat hunts. Notice how your cats track a bug in the house or go after a toy mouse. Does the cat prefer prey moving on the ground or flying in the air? Watch videos that show outdoor cats hunting prey. If you can understand what movements stimulate cats the most and how they react, you can make the play session have an advantageous effect.

Interactive play requires a fishing pole–type or wand toy. This design is important because of the following:

- You can move it like real prey.
- It keeps a safe distance between your hands and the cat's teeth.
- It allows a worried cat to maintain personal space.
- It's a powerful trust-building tool.
- The cat doesn't have to work to make the toy come to life.

Since you control the toy's movements, the cat can shift into play mode and enjoy the game. Believe it or not, many cat parents don't play correctly with their cats, and that can lead to a disinterested, overstimulated, or frustrated cat. If done correctly, interactive playtime can not only be a fun experience for the cat and for you, it can also help you correct behavior problems.

You should use interactive play in two ways. First, set up a daily schedule for maintenance sessions. Don't let the word *maintenance* fool you, though. You'll look forward to these sessions, too, as it strengthens the bond with your cat. This is especially important if you've felt a little distance from a cat due to any recent behavior issues. The second way to use this playtime is for on-the-spot sessions in response to specific behavior issues happening in the moment. Hopefully, though, the daily maintenance sessions will help you prevent behavior problems from cropping up in the first place. Play sessions also provide the necessary mental stimulation that predators need as well as the obvious exercise to keep cats healthy. No cat treadmills or exercise wheels will be needed at your home. Playtime is a great way to prevent boredom, combat depression, and alleviate stress.

You'll use the on-the-spot play sessions to diffuse a tense situation between cats, help a frightened cat to change his association with a particular area or cat, and help a cat adjust after a negative experience. During playtime, endorphins that contribute to feelings of well-being are released.

Even if you currently enjoy play sessions with your cats, if you aren't doing it daily, you may not be supplying them with the amount of physical activity and the mental stimulation they need.

In a free-roaming environment, a cat would probably hunt about ten to twelve times a day. That's not to say he would successfully capture a dozen mice or birds, but he would engage in approximately that number of physical attempts. That's a lot of activity. Now imagine your own cats. How much daily activity do they engage in? Don't count being chased by another cat, because I'm referring to positive, confidence-boosting activity, not stress-inducing escapes.

The truth is that even though kittens seem to be able to play endlessly, many adult cats fall into the couch potato category. Since these feline couch potatoes gradually become less and less active, many cat parents don't really notice the change until the annual veterinary exam when the cat is diagnosed as overweight. "Overweight? My kitty? How did that happen?" That's when you come to the realization your cat's only physical activity consists of the walk from the couch to the food bowl.

When you think of the benefits of daily play, compare it to an exercise regimen you might have. If you engage in activity only sporadically, it doesn't benefit you as much as if you exercised on a regular basis. Doctors repeatedly advise us to do a little something every day. The same applies to your cats. Ideally, you should try to do two fifteen-minute interactive play sessions every day with your cats. This chapter shows you how to conduct both individual and group play sessions, so if you have many cats, you won't have to quit your job to stay home and entertain them. If you don't have time to play with them all every day, divide them up so some have morning playtime and the rest take the evening shift. It's not as beneficial as twice-daily play sessions, but do the best you can. In this chapter I'll go through some enrichment activities you can set up to entertain your cats when they're home alone, but nothing takes the place of the interactive play sessions you conduct. They are a bond-strengthening, highly customizable way to bring joy into a cat's daily life.

Mousers, Bird-Watchers, Spider Snatchers, and Cricket Nabbers

One reason to get a variety of toys is because a cat is an opportunistic hunter, and he never knows what prey will become available. The technique the cat uses to catch a bird will be slightly different from the one used to capture a little snake. Although the basic concept of stalking and pouncing are the same, the cat must adjust for each individual hunt. If you provide an assortment of interactive toys, you give cats the opportunity to test their skills. We all like a little variety. One note, though—you'll probably find cats will develop a favorite toy. If that's the case, you'll know which one to use when you need to distract that cat. If you do have a cat who wants to play with only one toy, that's fine, but periodically keep trying other toys as well. You may find that once he gets into a routine of the daily play sessions, he'll be receptive to other prey.

A critical note on interactive toys. They should be stored in a safe place. Never leave these toys out, because the cats could chew and swallow the strings or get tangled in them. Also, you want to keep the toys special, and if you leave them out, they'll lose their appeal. Leave out safe toys for solo play—such as the furry mice (buy a good supply because they always end up under the refrigerator). Store the interactive ones in a cat-proof closet. You may even need to rotate where you store the toys, or you might find your cats sitting and staring at the closet door. Interactive playtime is *that* powerful.

You may have a basket filled with toys for your cat, but they are just *dead* prey. In order to make them move, the cat must do all the work. With an interactive toy, the prey comes to life. There are numerous kinds of interactive toys available, but you'll want to use toys that you'll be able to move like prey. Two favorites I've recommended for years because of their ongoing strong cat appeal are very basic but very effective—Da Bird and the Cat Dancer. Da Bird is an outstanding toy that consists of bird feathers attached to a swivel on the end of a string that hangs from a pole. When you move the toy through the air, the feathers whirl around so it looks and sounds like a bird in flight. The other toy I always bring on house calls with me because I know it will have a positive reaction is the Cat Dancer. It's inexpensive and couldn't be simpler: a long, flexible wire that has small, very tightly rolled-up cardboard rods attached to the end. It may not sound glamorous, but trust me, this toy is a big hit with cats. With just the slightest movement from you (or the cat), the toy bounces and jerks all over the place. It's like the erratic movements of a fly. I'm sure you've seen how crazy your cats get whenever there's a flying insect loose in your house. The Cat Dancer is especially effective for cats who are high energy and athletic.

These two toys are just a couple of the abundant options available. When you go shopping for toys, keep a couple of things in mind: match the toy to a cat's age, ability, and hunting preference. Also, make sure the toy is safe and durable.

Tips for Picking Top Toys

Safety and durability—Inspect the toys to make sure there are no glued-on parts that could be swallowed or sharp pieces sticking out. For solo toys that will be left out, there shouldn't be any strings or yarn attached. When I bring home furry mice for my cat, I pull off any glued-on eyes or nose pieces and inspect to make sure tails are securely fastened. Over the years, none of my cats has ever seemed to care whether the mice they hunt are missing eyes or noses.

For interactive toys, make sure they're securely made with

heavy string or wire that will withstand countless play sessions. Look at how the toy on the end of the string is attached to ensure there are no pieces poking through that could hurt your cat's mouth. And no matter how well an interactive toy is made, you still will have to put it away when the play session is over to avoid the risk of cats chewing on the string and the risk of strangulation.

In order to avoid spending money on toys that are unsafe or poorly designed, check out online reviews such as the ones found on Amazon. I've noticed many very helpful reviews warning of the poor quality of some popular cat toys. Even if there's a celebrity name attached to a line of toys, it doesn't mean they're safe or well made. Depend on other cat parents who can possibly save you from spending money on toys that could potentially put your cats at risk, or, at the very least, be a wasted purchase if the toy breaks after two minutes of play. My hope is that manufacturers will pay more attention to the warnings of reviewers and put more effort into improving the quality of their toys.

Type of cat toy—There are toys meant for solo play and ones meant for interactive sessions. Don't choose just one type and leave out the other. Although cats are naturally curious and playful, don't depend on solo playtime to provide all the enrichment.

When it comes to solo playtime, there are toys to simply bat around, stalk, pounce on, roll, and flip into the air. There are also reward-based toys that provide the cat with a treat for a job well done. Food-dispensing toys (puzzle feeders) are very popular now and easy to find. These toys provide activity for your cat and a food reward at the same time. Some puzzle feeders require a little training to help your cats get the idea, but it shouldn't take long before they figure out that solving the puzzle will result in a tasty reward. In addition to food-dispensing toys, there are also puzzle toys that reward cats with a little toy for their successful work. More on puzzle feeders in chapter 6.

How the cat toy moves—Cats are hunters, so when it comes to toy appeal, its movements need to resemble that of prey. Even though your cats get top-quality nutrition and their daily existence doesn't depend on being able to capture a meal, their play techniques are still based on how they would hunt. Cats stalk, pounce, and ultimately capture their treasure. Does the toy resemble prey in its appearance, size, shape, or movement? Will a cat be able to manipulate it comfortably?

When it comes to resembling prey, less will depend on how it looks than on the way it moves when the cat pounces or swats it. Does the toy easily skitter across the floor, allowing for a fun chase? Or, if using an interactive toy, can you mimic the movement of prey by how you drag it along the ground or flip it in the air? Much of an interactive toy's success depends on how enticing you make your moves.

Offer a variety of movements to keep your cat interested. Even if the toy is meant to be waved in the air to mimic a bird, do some on-the-ground movements. Experiment with your movements to see which toys work best on different surfaces. One toy may be most irresistible on the floor and not as appealing on carpet.

Size—In addition to being predators, cats are also prey because of their size. When shopping for cat toys, keep that in mind so you don't end up getting a toy that's too large. If the toy is too big, your cats may view it as a challenger and the play sessions may turn into more of a battle.

Sound—I've had many clients show me these large, motorized toys purchased for their cats, but when they set them up, some of the cats became frightened. If you choose a motorized toy, make sure it doesn't make a whiney sound that will be disconcerting to your cats. The typical prey sounds are little squeaks, not whirring, buzzy motors. A cat's hearing is extremely sensitive.

The right toy for the right cat—Pay attention to each cat in terms of size and personality. A timid cat may not view a motorized or large, noisy toy as an opportunity for some fun playtime. Use the information you know about your cats. Does one seem intrigued by little squeaking noises in the house but another one is frightened of the sound? Every cat is different, and you must appeal to individual personalities and comfort levels.

Texture—Texture plays a big role in a cat's life. If you've lived with cats for any length of time, you know texture matters when it comes to the litter in the litter box, the places they like to nap, or the mouthfeel of different brands of cat food. Texture also matters to a number of cats when it comes to playtime as well. Some cats prefer soft toys that are easy to bite, and other cats may like smooth toys that are easier to roll or bat around. Toys come in various textures, styles, sizes, and shapes. You can choose a feather-covered toy, a leather toy, a fuzzy one, a crinkly one, a fabric-covered one, hard, soft, plastic, you name it! There is no shortage when it comes to cat toy selections. Your cats will let you know whether your choice is a hit or a miss.

Toy testing—If you're unsure about what type, texture, or shape your cats will like, experiment by purchasing a few different types. When it comes time to play with each cat, offer one at a time. Don't offer the assortment all at once. You can more accurately evaluate a toy's appeal if you offer it on its own. Very often, *how* you offer it will influence whether it's a hit or miss. For example, instead of just tossing a solo toy in the middle of the floor, place an open paper bag on its side and then toss the toy in there.

If offering an interactive toy, remember, it's the movements that go across or away from a cat's visual field that spark the prey drive. You won't increase the toy's appeal by dangling it right in front of a cat. Mimic the movement of prey—that's the key to igniting a rewarding play session.

Toy rotation—You don't need to have a collection of a hundred toys for your cats. Once you have a core collection of the ones they like, rotate them to help maintain their appeal.

Scent issues—In a multicat home where there are a couple of cats who have a hostile relationship, don't use the same toy for each cat. Playtime is supposed to be filled with fun, discovery, and reward. If one cat smells the strong scent of an opponent cat on the toy, it may stop him from enjoying the game. If there are serious relationship issues in the home, keep certain toys exclusively for use with specific cats to prevent adding fuel to the fire.

Homemade cat toys—Toys don't have to be purchased. A quick search online will result in many clever toy ideas and instructions. Just be sure your homemade toys are safe.

Changing with the times—Toys that some cats loved when they were younger may not be as appealing as they become seniors or develop mobility issues. Maintain playtime with your cats, but if certain toys are no longer of interest to one or more of the kitties, this may be the time to reevaluate your play technique to accommodate their needs, but also to experiment with some different types of toys. For example, an older cat may no longer find it comfortable to bite down on hard toys and may now prefer a softer feel. A senior or geriatric cat may need to play only on carpet now in order to maintain adequate traction. Movements of interactive toys may need to be less intense. Again, it comes down to knowing your cats and adjusting their playtime environment as abilities change. For more on the needs of older cats, refer to chapter 11.

INTERACTIVE PLAYTIME

First, set the stage. Since cats hunt by hiding and then stalking, look around the room and make sure there are places for a cat to hide. If you're going to play in a big open room, put a couple of boxes or open paper bags in the middle of the floor for the cat to use as cover.

If you want to play with just one cat, do it in a separate room so you don't drive the other cats crazy and so you don't create intimidation. Do the session when others are napping. You can also set up some puzzle feeders for them in another room or play a cat-interest video.

> **Pam's CatWise Caution**
>
> Don't send mixed messages to a cat. If you don't want him to scratch the couch, be careful not to toss the interactive toy up there or dangle it near the side. He may accidentally dig his claws in as he pounces on his prey. Play near cat trees and scratching posts instead, to keep training consistent.

Now for your interactive playtime technique. I've mentioned already that the secret is to move the toy like prey. No dangling the toy in your cat's face. Although the cat may paw at the toy, it's not the way he would naturally hunt, so you won't be triggering that important mental part of the game. If you're doing playtime to increase a cat's confidence or relieve stress, the mental aspect is as important as the physical. The target at the end of the string should go across or away from his visual field. Prey doesn't offer itself up as lunch by running toward the cat. Dangling a toy in a cat's face changes the cat's impression of the toy from prey to potential threat.

The other big mistake is to wave the toy frantically and make the cat go on an epic run. This is just physically exhausting for the cat and very frustrating. Even if you have an overweight cat who needs to shed pounds, exhausting him to the point of heart failure isn't the way to do it. Stick to what is natural for a cat. A cat is an ambush predator—he doesn't endlessly chase. He must make quick decisions and plan his movements efficiently. He depends on stealth, speed, timing, and accuracy. If you keep the toy in constant motion, then your cat doesn't have time to sneak up and plan the attack.

To move the toy effectively, keep a couple of things in mind. First, you want this to be a positive, confidence-boosting experience, so make sure the cat has several successful captures throughout the game. Also, vary your movements. In order to move like prey, *think like prey*. What would a mouse do if it found itself in your house? It would scurry around and dart from one hiding place to another. It might hide behind the leg of a table and peer out to see if the coast is clear. The mouse might dash under the sofa and quiver. For a cat, it's just as exciting when the prey stops moving for a moment, hides, or just quivers. It's at those times that the cat can plan his next move or prepare to pounce. Just try it and you'll see for yourself: have the toy peek out from around a corner or out from under a piece of furniture. Alternate between fast moves, slow movements, and just staying still.

Matching a Cat's Play Preference Style

A cat's hunting preference (even if the cat doesn't go out to hunt) can influence the success or failure of a toy. Many cats will go after anything and everything that moves if it's not so large as to be viewed as threatening. That prey could be a bird or butterfly in flight, a cricket hopping along, a lizard darting around, a mouse skittering from hiding place to hiding place, or a little snake slithering its way out of sight. Each creature requires modifications in how the cat would seize his intended prize. Some cats, though, have preferences when it comes to the type of prey/toy. A cat may be excellent at going after birds and even getting one as it begins

Pam's CatWise Tip

If you have a shy cat who might initially be intimidated by an interactive toy, start by doing low-intensity sessions using something as simple as a peacock feather or string attached to a pole. Use a very sturdy string, though, and be watchful that your cat doesn't chew it. As the cat gets more comfortable, you can then start to introduce an actual interactive toy. Keep your movements gentle and let your cat set the pace of how much interaction he wants.

It's also helpful for a timid or frightened cat to be able to sniff and investigate the toy before the session. Place the toy on the floor and let him check it out. Then begin the game slowly.

to fly or land. Another cat may do best sticking to prey that can only move horizontally.

In addition to knowing what toys are safest for your cat and addressing texture, size, shape, and sound preferences, it's also helpful to move those toys in the most enticing way. For example:

Ground hunters—You may have a cat who prefers going after prey/toys that only stay close to the ground. It could be he feels he can stay hidden more effectively that way as he inches toward his target, or it may be due to limited physical mobility.

An overweight cat may know it takes less effort to go after toys limited to horizontal movement. If you're trying to build trust with a frightened cat, he might feel too vulnerable to leap in the air and come too far out of hiding. Pay attention to how each cat reacts when movements of a toy go vertical. If a cat loses interest, it may not be that he dislikes the toy itself, it may just mean he dislikes the way you're moving it.

Air hunters—When you play with a cat, does he really enjoy the toy movements that include going up in the air? Interactive toys based on a fishing pole design are great for making both ground and air movements. In addition to stalking along the ground and pouncing, a cat who enjoys air hunting will include leaps and mid-air captures.

Air hunting may be something a cat has always enjoyed doing, regardless of age. It could also be something that was enjoyable when he was younger, had less joint pain, or was thinner, but has now become too much of an effort. Play-style preferences can change as a cat ages or experiences less mobility, sensory decline, age-related cognitive decline, or increased pain. If your cat was always an athletic in-the-air hunter and has recently shown less interest, make sure he gets seen by the veterinarian to identify any medical problem. Also, adjust your technique to accommodate him. It may be time for more horizontal movements so he can still enjoy the fun of playtime.

Even enthusiastic air hunters will appreciate some ground movements so they can stalk and pounce. Don't make all the toy's movements over a cat's head. Additionally, when waving the toy in the air, don't continually keep it out of reach. If the toy becomes impossible to catch, a cat may lose interest or possibly hurt himself as he wildly leaps into the air. Playtime should be challenging but also fun. If a cat never gets to enjoy successful captures, then all you'll have accomplished is to frustrate him and leave him physically worn out.

Peek-a-boo hunters—Some cats like to be out in the open and right in the middle of the action during playtime while others may prefer to remain hidden throughout most of the game. A cat may pounce and then dart back behind furniture or under the bed, waiting for the next chance to pounce. If you have a peek-a-boo hunter, set up boxes, bags, tunnels, or other objects to provide extra cover for him.

Pam's CatWise Tip

If you think a cat doesn't have an interest in play, it may actually be because:

1. It's the wrong kind of toy or perhaps one he has grown tired of.
2. You're not using the right technique.
3. The cat doesn't feel safe enough to focus on the game.

Don't Forget the Sound Effects

Very often, the sound of a mouse scurrying through the grass or a chipmunk hiding in the leaves will be what first alerts the cat. I'm not suggesting you squeak like mice or chirp like birds. I'm referring to the enticing sounds a toy can make on different surfaces. The toy can create an enticing scratching sound if you slide it against the side of a box or bag. Have the toy dart inside a paper bag that's on its side and tap or slide the toy against the sides. It probably won't take long before your cat dives headfirst into the bag. Even the sound of a toy skittering across a floor can spark a cat's interest.

The Importance of the Gotcha

Because you want this to be a positive, fun experience for a cat, let him successfully capture his prey several times during the game. In a real hunt, the cat might catch the prey between his front paws, where it might stay, wriggling to get away. Do that type of movement with the toy as well. If the cat grasps the toy and holds it down with his front paws, let it sit there for a few seconds. This is the time he's using his carpal whiskers to detect movement. After a few seconds, gently start to wriggle it free.

And the Winner Is . . .

Don't leave a cat revved up at the end of the game. If you suddenly just stop playing and put the toy away, you'll leave the cat in an excited state. From his point of view the hunt may not have been over. When you know you want to end the game, wind the action down gradually, almost as if the prey is injured. If using a flying toy, keep the movements on the ground, as if the bird has a broken wing. This will enable your cat to have one final grand capture. At the end of the game, give your cat a treat or time the play session to be right before mealtime. Wind down the intensity to help your cat settle back to normal. Having satisfied both the mental and the physical aspects of the hunt, the cat will enter back in the general cat family as a more relaxed kitty.

Pam's CatWise Playtime Reminders

- Set the stage.
- Vary the types of toys.
- Respect each cat's play-style preference.
- Alternate the speed of movements.
- Let the toy hide and quiver so a cat can plan his attack.
- Let your cat capture the toy several times during the game.
- Wind the action down as the game comes to an end.
- Allow for one final grand capture.
- *Optional:* Offer a treat or meal after a play session.
- Store interactive toys in a safe place.

WHY I DON'T RECOMMEND LASER LIGHT TOYS

These toys are popular because most cats have an immediate reaction to them. Laser toys are a very tempting way to guarantee a cat gets lots of physical activity.

There are problems with laser light toys, though. People using this toy often move it too frantically. This results in a cat not playing in the natural way. His movements become frenzied, fast, and he must abandon his normal instinct to stalk, plan, and pounce. Although it's very amusing to watch a cat chasing a laser light and leads people to think they're giving their cats exercise, this isn't mentally beneficial.

Cats are tactile animals and the laser light never lets them capture anything. A cat may think he has the prey under his paw, but his carpal whiskers are telling him there's no movement, and when he lifts his paw there is nothing there. How unrewarding and frustrating is that!

In some cases, chasing laser lights can cause cats to develop a fixation with any flickering light, and they may end up displaying OCD-type behavior. This warning has been issued by several behavior and veterinary professionals.

Then there's the subject of safety. Manufacturers claim laser lights are safe, but there's concern about the light accidentally getting pointed at a cat's eyes. Not all laser lights are made to the same standard, so if you do purchase one, extreme caution must be used to ensure you don't shine the light in the cat's eyes. That's something rather difficult to avoid when you're dealing with an excited cat who is moving unpredictably. Use interactive toys instead. They are safer and the cat gets the tactile satisfaction of capturing something.

GROUP PLAY SESSIONS

Group play sessions, if done correctly, can help cats become more comfortable around one another. They can be a wonderful way for a timid cat who normally would sit on the sidelines to take a more active role in playtime. This only works, however, if you have a technique to prevent a more assertive cat from bulldozing his way through the game. Group play is also a time-saver if you have many cats and you want to make sure they all get their playtime.

Group play can be done with two or three cats at a time. Try to combine cats who are of the same energy level and who already get along well. If you're using a group session to help cats learn to like one another a little better, then stick to two cats only so it'll be easier for you to control the dynamic. If one of your cats hasn't been active in a long time, is scared, shy, or stressed, he'll need quite a few individual sessions to build up confidence before he's ready to play in a group.

To start, you'll need two interactive toys. Hold a toy in each hand. It'll be easier if you choose two of the same type of toys so your movements will be more coordinated. It may seem very awkward at first, but you'll get better with practice. I can hardly walk and chew gum at the same time, and I can handle two toys very easily. If there are other family members willing to help, it will obviously be much easier to do a group session if you each only have to handle one toy instead of two.

Use the two toys so the cats aren't competing. If both cats are focused on a single toy, they'll become more concerned with watching to see who'll pounce first, and the game will no longer be fun. Competing for one toy can also intensify a timid cat's fear; he won't take the chance of pouncing and risk attack by the other cat.

Basically, the concept is that the cats will be playing *near* each other but not *with* each other. Cats who have a good relationship may learn to play cooperatively with one toy, but why create potential conflict when with just a little more effort you can create a positive environment? As you're playing, if one cat loses interest in his toy and eyes the other cat's toy, slow the movements of the popular toy and increase the action on the other toy to refocus the cat's attention. With a little practice you'll have this technique down to a fine art and will look like a maestro conducting the orchestra.

USING PLAY FOR DIVERSION

Here's a scenario: one of your cats is sitting on the cat tree or window perch, looking out the window peacefully. Another cat enters the room, spots the other cat, and assumes that low-to-ground, slinking posture associated with stalking. The cat near the window remains unaware that he is about to be ambushed. What do you do?

Previously, you may have yelled at the stalking cat or chased him out of the room. Although your motives were good, these methods scare the innocent cat as well and keep both cats in a negative state of mind. A more positive option would be to divert the aggressor's focus with a fun little attention-getter.

For the diversion technique, any toy will do. You can keep toys like the Cat Dancer stashed in several rooms or you can carry little toys in your pocket or keep a few conveniently located for easy access. The next time you see a cat about to cause trouble, quickly grab a toy and divert his attention away from the intended victim. The sight of the toy will likely put him in play mode. If you use something like a Ping-Pong ball, fuzzy mouse, or Mylar crinkle ball, just toss it in the opposite direction of the unsuspecting cat to put a greater distance between him and the cat you're trying to distract. The instant play opportunity will likely change the cat's mind-set from negative to positive, or at least it may lower the intensity of his desire to go after the cat on the window perch. The prey drive in a cat can usually be instantly triggered by the sight of a toy moving, and this is an effective way to shift focus.

The great thing about the diversion technique is that even if you misread the cat and he wasn't about to cause trouble, he got a bonus opportunity to pounce on a toy, so there's no harm done. If you had chased him or yelled, it would've left things on an unnecessarily negative note.

Now, of course you can't always be in the room when two cats are about to go at it. There will also be times when you won't see the behavior until the aggressor is too close to the targeted cat or they've already locked eyes on each other. The key to the diversion technique is timing. You need to get the cat's attention before he gets too focused on his target. If you notice the problem too late and the cats are already in a struggle, then make a noise to startle them so they'll separate. Once the two cats have gone their separate ways, get a toy and causally offer the attacked cat some low-intensity playtime to help get him out of that frightened, negative state. If he's really upset after a serious fight, then leave him alone to calm down. Lower the lights and let him have time to himself. Never physically get in the middle of a cat fight.

The diversion technique can be applied to other situations as well. For example, if one of your cats is still adjusting to indoor life and cries at the door to go outside, divert his attention to an on-the-spot play session before he gets to the door or starts crying. Fortunately, because cats are such creatures of habit, you should be able to pick out his pattern rather quickly. This can also help a timid cat who dives under the bed whenever company comes over. Another use is when one of your cats is spray-marking. In addition to following the instructions in chapter 7, divert his attention when you notice he's backing up to an object or walking toward a favorite spraying target. There are so many uses for the diversion technique. Think of it the next time you want to change a cat's negative state of mind to a more positive one.

THE GRAVEYARD SHIFT

If you live with several cats, there's a pretty good chance you've received the four a.m. wake-up call. Whether they want food, a place on your pillow, or just a bit of playtime, cats can be very persistent.

If you're guilty of getting up to fill a food bowl because a cat was sitting on your chest in the wee hours of the morning, then you've reinforced the behavior. Even if you try to hold out as long as possible before you simply can't stand it anymore, every time you get up lets a cat know his persistence paid off.

When a cat relentlessly meows at you while you're trying to sleep, you must ignore it. And I'll warn you right now, he's going to rev up his approach and meow even more. A cat can get very dramatic. This increase in the unwanted behavior occurs because you have previously rewarded him for it. Eventually, if you ignore his vocal pleas, the cat will see his behavior offers zero reward and he'll give up. This is known as an *extinction burst*.

When it comes to evening activity, cats tend to be most active at dusk. This is the time when you're typically winding down from the day. After engaging in several catnaps during the day, a cat is ready for play when the sun goes down. You also must keep in mind that if you've been gone all day, when you come home at night your cats are stimulated by your presence.

Fortunately, there's an effective and fun method for curbing nighttime activity based on natural cat behavior.

Normally, you may come home, feed your cats, play with them, and then settle in for the night. Perhaps the cats curl up next to you after dinner as you check email or watch TV. Then it's off to bed. While this routine is great from a bonding/affection standpoint, it doesn't address a cat's energy needs.

To shift a cat's internal clock, I think of the cat's most basic behavior cycle: *hunt, feast, groom, sleep.* Cats engage in the basic activity cycle multiple times in a day. First, a cat goes through the stimulating activity of the hunt. Once the prey is captured, the cat enjoys his feast. After the meal, a cat fastidiously grooms himself to remove any traces of the prey's scent. This important survival skill is done so the scent won't alert other prey or make the cat the target of a bigger predator. With a full stomach and his grooming duties completed, the cat is ready for sleep. Keep this cycle in mind to change the unwanted behavior. Do an interactive play session right before bed, in addition to any other play sessions earlier in the evening. Okay, that takes care of the hunt, and now it's on to the feast. If you feed your cats on a schedule, divide up their portions so you can include the pre-bedtime feeding without increasing their overall amount of food. After the meal, the cats will groom themselves and settle in for the night. If you leave dry food out for your cats, take it up in the earlier part of the evening and put it back down at bedtime. If you don't want to take up the food because of complaints from some of the cats, then just make a big ritual out of topping off the dry food right before bed, or at least offer a bedtime treat.

Even if one or two of your cats aren't so food motivated, you'll improve the chances of a restful night's sleep if you get on a schedule of doing pre-bedtime play sessions. These sessions may have to be a bit longer than the usual fifteen-minute sessions, but it's worth a little extra time to ensure a good night's rest.

For those cats who seem to defy the need ever to sleep, set up some activities to keep them occupied at night. Put out some special toys that only make their appearance right before bedtime.

Use food-dispensing toys, set up some tunnels and place toys inside, or hide some treats around for treasure hunts. Note: If you have a dog in the family, make sure none of the cat's toys and puzzle feeders are left out in areas he can access.

FOOD ENRICHMENT

Puzzle feeders are a great way to increase the fun factor surrounding meals. The principle of the puzzle feeder is that the cat must either move the toy or manipulate it in some way to release the food reward. To learn how to incorporate puzzle feeders into your enrichment plan, refer to chapter 6.

WATER ENRICHMENT

Cats love movement, and water provides a natural fascination for them as well. For cats who like to play with the water in their bowls or who like to drink from faucets, a pet water fountain may be the answer.

Water fountains come in many different styles, from waterfall types to faucet types to bubblers. You may have to do some homework to figure out which type your cats would like, or maybe get a couple to offer variety. In addition to the enrichment and fun, water fountains may encourage a cat to drink more because the movement keeps the water oxygenated so it tends to taste fresher.

Water fountains need to be taken apart and cleaned regularly, regardless of whether they contain filters. Filters also need to be changed as often as recommended by the manufacturer.

Look online and you'll find several brands. Read reviews and choose a sturdy one that's easy to take apart and clean.

TUNNELS AND HIDEAWAYS

Tunnels serve double duty as great places to play but also to provide concealment for a cat who is trying to remain invisible in the environment (see chapter 3).

There are numerous soft-sided tunnels available in pet supply stores and online. You can also create homemade ones out of boxes or paper bags.

Hiding places (also discussed in chapter 3) are important for environmental enrichment, to allow a cat the choice of whether to interact. Hiding is a valuable coping mechanism because it provides a place for a scared or unsure cat to calm down and assess the situation. I've talked quite a bit about the need for safety, and something as simple as a hiding place provides much safety for a cat, and that's a big stress reliever.

MAKING CAT CARRIERS FRIENDLY PLACES

The cat carrier doesn't have to be this feared object that comes out only to take that dreaded trip to the veterinary clinic.

If you have trouble getting a cat into a cat carrier when it's time for travel, leave the carrier out to help desensitize a cat and change his association. Periodically toss a treat in the carrier for positive association. You can also feed a cat near and then eventually inside the carrier.

If you have room, you can leave carriers out all the time for cats to use as cozy napping hideaways. Line the inside with soft towels or bedding to make them extra comfortable.

REACH FOR THE SKY

Vertical space. Cats love to climb and take comfort in the ability to access elevated locations, as discussed in chapter 3. Adequate vertical territory can make a difference in how your multicat family gets along and whether squabbles are settled peacefully or not.

Look online and you'll find so much inspiration regarding how to create vertical options and increase the territory in a multicat (or single cat) home. You can keep the arrangement basic or, if time and budget allow, create a vertical feline wonderland. Just remember, every piece must be sturdy and secure. There must also be multiple escape options so no elevated spot becomes a dead end, making a cat susceptible to ambush.

CAT FURNITURE

Trees and other climbing equipment also increase vertical territory (see chapter 3). Cat trees come in a variety of styles, colors, heights, and prices. Various perches at different heights allow more than one cat to share that elevated location. Multiple perches also make it easier for a cat to climb to the top without having to make a giant leap. Cat trees are portable, so if you don't want to do an installation of cat wall shelves, the tree is the perfect alternative. Cat trees can also be moved to other rooms if situations change within the cat household.

While a good-quality tree is initially a larger expense than you might have expected, its value will soon become apparent as you watch your cats climb, nap, scratch, play, and enjoy this piece of furniture that is exclusively theirs.

Scent is important to cats, and a cat tree becomes a piece of furniture identified as belonging to the felines alone. Your other furniture will contain changing scents due to visitors to the home, but a cat tree's scent remains consistent. Cats can claim 100 percent own-ership. If you move to another home, the cat tree remains a reas-suring and familiar scent object in the strange new place.

If you don't have room for a tall tree, or you simply don't want to have a large tree in your home, a couple of small ones will work just as well. It's all about elevation, but that height doesn't have to reach to the ceiling.

Don't underestimate the physical and emotional benefits of cat trees. When you provide a cat tree, it decreases the chances that your cats will seek out unapproved elevated areas, such as table-tops, bookshelves, or counters.

SCENT ENRICHMENT

Your cats need to have places to deposit and find their own com-forting scents throughout their environment, including the spaces they share with you. For example, you may notice some discolor-ation on doors or doorframes at about the same height as your cats. While you might be tempted to clean those spots, don't do it. Those discolorations are physical indications of where your cats have been lip and cheek rubbing. This is how they deposit the facial pheromones that help them identify the area as familiar to them.

Scent enrichment is also about *not* having artificial scents added to the environment. Remember how sensitive a cat's nose is, and be careful about the cleansers and room fresheners you use. Don't place plug-in room fresheners in areas where cats spend time. It's especially tempting to place a plug-in near litter boxes, but that's one of the worst locations. The best litter box odor control is to keep the box clean rather than cover up the smell with a strong ar-tificial scent. Be respectful of your cats' noses and don't overwhelm them with scents associated with household products and sprays. This even applies to personal beauty products. If you use hair spray, make sure your cats aren't in the room.

Potpourri and essential oils aren't a good fit with cats. Potpourri is used quite a bit during the holidays, and essential oils have become extremely popular in the past few years. Many people put essential oils into air diffusers. Keep in mind that almost all essential oils, whether in potpourri or for human health use, are toxic to cats. Even in diffuser form, tiny droplets of the oils are being dispersed through the room. These can be toxic to cats if they get them on their fur or their skin, since they can ingest them when grooming.

If you want to use an essential oil diffuser in your home, use it in a room where the cats don't spend time. Position diffusers where cats can't get anywhere near them.

If you use essential oils directly on your body, apply them in areas that will be covered by your clothes, to prevent your cats from rubbing against the oil or licking it. Wash your hands after applying essential oils so they don't get transferred to a cat's fur during petting. If you have questions about any essential oils you use and the safety of your cats, talk to your veterinarian.

Now, let's talk about good scent enrichment.

The Joy of Catnip

This is the ultimate in olfactory enrichment. Catnip is a gift Mother Nature has reserved exclusively for cats. It is certainly an asset when it comes to environmental enrichment, but many cat parents either don't incorporate it into their cats' lives or overuse it, which can leave cats immune to its effects. Start with understanding how catnip works.

Catnip contains a volatile oil, nepetalactone, that creates the famous catnip effect. Catnip reduces a cat's inhibition and creates a euphoric feeling that lasts about fifteen minutes. Cats may roll in, lick, or eat the herb, but the actual effect is achieved through inhalation. Catnip shouldn't be left out all the time, because if cats are constantly exposed to it they can become immune. Interestingly, the response to catnip is an inherited gene that about one third of the cat population lacks. Catnip should be given only to adult cats. Kittens don't respond to the herb nor do they even need it, considering all their seemingly endless energy.

Catnip benefits—Catnip can help spark a couch potato to get off the couch and engage in a play session. If you're working with a cat who hasn't played in a while, catnip can be a great start. It's a wonderful tension reliever, so use it after your cats have had a stressful experience—for example, after you've had company or after you return from a trip.

Catnip is also a great way to help a shy cat come out of his shell. It's a wonderful start to an interactive play session for a cat who is too timid to focus on a toy otherwise.

Catnip cautions—The first time you introduce catnip, offer it to each cat separately in individual sessions. Some cats may cross the line from play to aggression while under the influence of catnip. You'd want to know that before offering it to the whole group at one time.

How to use catnip—You can grow your own, or you can buy packaged dried catnip, catnip spray, or catnip-infused toys. If you grow your own, don't grow it outdoors if other cats can get into your yard or you'll be the most popular house on the block. If you do grow your own, dry the catnip by hanging it in bunches upside down in a dry, dark place. After the herb has dried, strip off the leaves and blossoms and store in a tightly sealed container. Don't crush the leaves until you're ready to use the catnip, because you don't want to waste it by releasing the oils prematurely.

If you buy packaged catnip, look for brands that use only leaves and blossoms. Catnip that contains a lot of stems is of lesser quality. If the catnip is in a bag, repackage it in a tightly sealed container. When you're ready to offer the catnip to your cats, rub some between your hands to release the oils. You can offer catnip loose, put it in refillable catnip toys or in a sock (knot the top), or just sprinkle it on a paper plate or directly on the floor. I keep a few furry toy mice marinating in catnip so they'll always be ready for action when it's time for a catnip party. Rub some catnip on scratching posts periodically as well, if you're in the middle of training a cat to use the post or if a post hasn't been getting much scratching action lately.

Don't buy catnip-filled toys unless you know the quality of the manufacturer. You're better off using refillable toys and buying your preferred brand of catnip. Some catnip toys are filled with low-quality catnip, and some may not be filled with true catnip at all.

In addition to offering catnip during times of stress or after an anxiety-producing event, use it on a maintenance basis but not more than once or twice a week. Keep it special.

Keep catnip in a place the cats can't access. You'd be surprised at how determined a cat can be. I've seen many plastic containers get demolished by cats when cat parents have inadvertently left them out on kitchen counters. And if you use a catnip spray, never spray it directly on or at a cat.

Catnip Alternatives

Catnip isn't the only game in town. If one or more of your cats don't respond to it, there are other options. No one has to be left out. Many cats also respond to silver vine. In fact, some cats have a stronger reaction to silver vine than they do to catnip.

Other Fun Scents

In addition to the scents associated with fun things such as catnip and silver vine, provide your cats with other opportunities to enjoy interesting scents. Bring in dried leaves from outside for your cat to sniff. The added crinkly texture will also create tactile enrichment if your cats decide to bat them around in play. Supervise during play to make sure no one starts to eat any of the dried leaves.

A bird feather provides another scent opportunity.

Be creative, but always be aware of the sensitivity of a cat's nose. Never introduce a scent that could be viewed as threatening, such as an object that contains an unfamiliar cat's or dog's scent.

Pam's CatWise Caution

The scents of flowers and plants can be very enticing, but almost all are toxic to cats. Keep all indoor plants out of reach. If you have large floor plants that can't be moved, spray the tops and bottoms of the leaves with a bitter antichew product made specifically for plants.

VISUAL ENRICHMENT

Window Views

Let's start with the easiest way to create visual enrichment—windows. Set up window perches, place cat trees there, or create some comfortable access near windows to give your cats the opportunity to view the outdoor activity. Depending on whether there are outdoor cats who come around, you can also set up a bird feeder or birdbath outside to increase your indoor cats' viewing pleasure. For many cats, just having the curtains or blinds open to allow the sun to stream in is welcomed. For a cat, what could be more relaxing than having a long nap, stretched out in a patch of sun?

If you open windows, crack them open only enough to let the breeze in, because cats can easily push through screens, especially if the appearance of a bird or animal gets them excited.

Visual enrichment can also be provided by leaving a TV on for your cats. YouTube has many videos showcasing birds, insects, and other creatures of interest to cats. Don't play videos of cats, though, because as cute as all those videos are, they will cause stress and maybe even incite aggression between your cats.

Fish Tanks

Another option is to set up a fish tank. The tank must be fitted with a totally cat-proof cover. Fish tanks are often entertaining for cats and very relaxing for the human family members. If you are considering this, make certain you're ready to do the ongoing maintenance and care required to keep the fish healthy and the tank clean. Fish tank stands must be extremely sturdy so they can't be knocked over by a determined cat. By the way, there are several things you can do to create environmental enrichment for the fish as well. I trained my son's goldfish to do all sorts of behaviors. Just something to think about if you want to explore behavior and enrichment more deeply.

SOUND ENRICHMENT

Many shelters use classical music to help soothe the animals and relieve some of the stress. Periodically leave soothing music on when you aren't at home to help create calm. The sound may also buffer some unwanted noises.

Don't play music all the time, as cats need a break from sound as well.

In addition to soothing, quiet classical music, there is bioacoustically designed music available, created specifically for cats. Yes, your cats can have their own music. The title of one program is *Through a Cat's Ear*, and it is available as a download or via Bluetooth streaming.

Toys can also provide sound enrichment. Some interactive toys and solo toys squeak when touched. A little fuzzy mouse toy that gives off a realistic little squeak when batted by a cat may entice a little impromptu play session.

TOUCH ENRICHMENT

Grooming

Brushing increases circulation, distributes natural oils, and removes dead hair. Brushing your cats is beneficial for them physically, but it can also help strengthen the bond you share. If any of your cats enjoy being brushed, it can provide relaxation and calm. Grooming also gives you the opportunity to do quick once-overs to check for external parasites, lumps or bumps, wounds, or anything else that might need further investigation. While grooming, you may discover that a cat's unexplained aggression might be due to pain from a wound or other physical problem.

If you have a kitten, get him comfortable with being groomed and touched as soon as you bring him home. This will help ensure his comfort with grooming as he matures.

If any of your cats have hair that mats easily, it's important to brush them daily to prevent matting. That's also how you keep the experience a positive one so you don't end up having to tug and pull at a cat's sensitive skin to release tight knots and thick mats.

Petting

Nothing replaces the time cats get to spend with you. For some cats, the time you spend petting, or having a kitty in your lap, represents such a degree of trust, love, and relaxation. Not all cats want the same amount or type of petting or touch, though. Pay attention to each cat's preference when it comes to where on the body stroking is preferred and the spots to stay away from. For some cats, location on the body matters, and for others, it's the length of time you spend petting. I have a cat who has a couple of spots I know to stay away from, and if I adhere to those rules, she enjoys being petted for as long as I am willing. Because I pay attention to her preferences, she never hesitates to come to me to be petted.

If one or more of your cats don't like being petted but they like being on your lap or just near you, respect that and don't push the issue. Cats will let you know if they want more interaction. When you give them the choice, you gain their trust.

Texture

Pay attention to individual preferences when it comes to texture. This applies to texture of toys, as previously mentioned, but also things like bedding, food, and litter. It's common, especially when it comes to food and litter, for cats to have texture preferences. Pet food companies spend lots of time and money evaluating mouthfeel preferences regarding size, shape, and texture of food. See chapter 7 for more on litter and changing textures in the box.

OUTDOOR ENRICHMENT

I believe cats are safest indoors. Indoors versus outdoors is often a hotly debated topic. Some people feel cats should have full, unrestricted access to the outdoors. Others feel the only safe environment is indoors. There are so many dangers outdoors and many risks that are completely out of your control.

Outdoor Enclosures

In chapter 3, I discussed how to increase territory by creating an outdoor enclosure, commonly referred to as a catio, a safe (and fun) compromise that reduces the outdoor risks and still lets your cats experience the good parts of the outdoors. It should be a sturdy, well-constructed, totally escape-proof outdoor enclosure. Don't even think of using a pop-up enclosure or large dog crate. If you decide a catio is a good option for your cats, you need a permanently installed enclosure that creates total safety and allows the cats free and immediate access back into the house.

Outdoor enclosures can ease stress, alleviate boredom, and maybe turn the volume down on intercat tension. It's also a great way to increase territory and scent enrichment and provide fresh air. For some cats, though, an enclosure can introduce more stress and fear because of the ever-changing outdoor scents and the risk of encountering an unfamiliar animal on the other side.

If you decide an enclosure would be a good addition to your environmental enrichment plan, spend time researching online to see all the different designs. You'll get some great ideas and you'll also learn from others' mistakes.

Leash Training

Many people include outdoor enrichment for their cats by walking them on leashes. Not every cat is a good candidate for leash walking, though. You also must gauge whether you live in an area that's safe enough to pursue this activity. When you take a cat outdoors, even on a leash, he can become frightened by the sights, sounds, and smells. He can be startled by the dog across the street who may come running over to investigate. He might feel threatened by the sight of an unfamiliar cat roaming around or the sudden sound of a horn honking.

Cats do not need to go outside to be healthy and well adjusted, but leashes aren't just for taking a cat for a walk. Even if you never plan on taking any of your cats outdoors for a walk, I think leash and harness training is a good idea. During some cat-to-cat introductions, or if I'm concerned about aggression, having a cat who is already acclimated to a harness and leash has helped me keep the cat calm and focused. If you ever travel with a cat, you have an extra level of control if you can harness and leash him as a precaution, even though he remains, of course, inside his carrier at all times.

It's important to remember that for a territorial animal who finds comfort in predictability, the experience of being outdoors can produce uncertainty and fear. Trying to control and wrangle a panicked cat as you hurry back to the house is dangerous for you and for the cat. Another thing to consider is how the cats in your family who didn't go out for the leash walk might react to the returning cat if he smells unfamiliar. Think very carefully about whether this will enrich a cat's life or create an added problem. You know your cats best, so use that knowledge to make the best decision.

Before you attempt to put a leash on a cat, he must be desensitized to the process gradually or else you'll have one very panicky, traumatized, and ticked-off cat on your hands. Here are the general guidelines to get started the right way. Get a lightweight leash and a harness made for cats or a walking jacket. I recommend a walking jacket. Follow the manufacturer's instructions for how to measure your cat in order to pick the correct size.

Leave the harness or walking jacket and the leash on the floor for the cat to sniff and investigate.

Put the harness or walking jacket loosely on the cat while he gets offered some treats or a meal. He may roll onto his side, so don't be surprised. Cats commonly flop over on their sides and refuse to walk when you first put something on them.

Gradually increase the time spent wearing the harness or walking jacket until you know the cat is comfortable with it. Work up to where you can also adjust the harness or walking jacket so it fits properly.

Attach the leash and hold it loosely while the cat walks around indoors. Be armed with treats to keep the cat distracted.

Keep training sessions short and positive.

If your cat doesn't react well to being attached to the leash, hold a treat a few inches in front of him as enticement to walk forward.

Don't attempt to take your cat outdoors until he is completely comfortable on a leash indoors, even when he feels the leash tug a bit. Also, use the indoor training time to ensure the harness or walking jacket fits perfectly and the cat can't escape out of it. If there are any safety issues, you certainly want to discover them indoors rather than outdoors.

Before going outdoors, your cat needs to have ID in the form of a visible tag and an implanted microchip. Escapes can happen, so increase the chances of getting your cat safely returned to you by having both forms of identification.

If you also have a regular collar on your cat, include "indoor cat" on the tag so should he manage to escape out of the harness, anyone who might find him will know he isn't supposed to be roaming around alone.

I recommend that you carry a thick towel over your shoulder when leash walking a cat so you have something to wrap him up in should he begin to panic. You may also decide to carry a soft cat carrier with you that you can sling over your shoulder to be out of the way during the walk.

While outside, your cat is at risk for parasites. Keep your cat on flea and tick preventative. A cat who goes outdoors must be up-to-date on vaccinations. Cats can also get heartworms. Talk to your veterinarian about your cat's risk factors and whether he needs to be on heartworm preventative.

Confine your leashed walks to your own yard or your own street, if it's a quiet one. Don't go far from home in case your cat starts to panic. By sticking close to your own area, you're also more familiar with any dogs or cats who live on the street, so it decreases the risk of unwelcome surprises.

CLICKER TRAINING

If you've heard of clicker training, you may only associate it with puppy-training classes. This method of training works very well with cats, too. Cats quickly learn certain sounds indicate a reward is about to follow. Think about how a cat comes running when he hears the cat food can pop open or you shake the bag of cat treats. You can use clickers in a variety of situations.

Clicker training can help a cat feel more in control in his environment. It can focus a cat away from an unwanted behavior and toward a desirable one. It offers him a choice—and choice is a powerful tool when it comes to feeling secure and not stressed.

Clicker training is an effective communication technique that creates a common language between you and your cat. It is a reward-based technique that provides a type of road map to success. It communicates to your cat what you'd like him to do rather than merely telling him what not to do. With clicker training, you can click and reward for the most subtle behaviors or baby steps you normally wouldn't be able to acknowledge.

You'll need a few tools for this type of training. First, you need a clicker. This is a small device that makes a cricket-type noise, similar to the sound of opening or closing a ballpoint pen, or clicking the button on your smartphone when taking a picture. The clicker is known as a *secondary reinforcer*. It's used as a consistent method to mark a displayed behavior. When the clicker button is pressed, the sound lets the cat know that a very specific behavior exhibited is desirable and will result in an immediate reward. Clickers are available at your local pet stores as well as online. Buy more than one, because they're small and easy to misplace.

You will also need rewards. Treats are the most common reward. The reward is the *primary reinforcer*. Choose treats that are of high value, meaning they are hard for a cat to resist. If you're working with a cat who isn't so food motivated, though, find something else that can serve as a primary reinforcer. Some cats may prefer to be gently petted or scratched under the chin. Other cats may view a fuzzy mouse or Mylar crinkle ball as a reward. If a cat loves to be brushed, then a few short and gentle strokes with a soft brush may be the perfect reward. Find what motivates the cat in order to use that as the reward.

Now that you have the clicker and the reward, they need to be paired together. You must teach the cat to associate the sound of the clicker with the reward. This is what gives the clicker its communication value. The first training sessions will consist of clicking the clicker and then offering the cat a reward. Once you've clicked and offered the treat, wait for the cat to look at you before you repeat the process. This is how you train the cat to associate you as the supplier of the reward. Repeat the sequence about ten to fifteen times. Click, reward, wait for the cat to look at you, then repeat. Once the sound of the click has been paired with the treat, you're ready to train.

Using clicker training, you can train a cat to do fun behaviors such as sit, high-five, turn in a circle, look at you, jump through a hoop, and so on, but the real value is to use it to correct unwanted behavior. This reward-based training increases the likelihood of a behavior you want to see again get repeated, because the cat learns there's something good in it for him.

For fun and simple behaviors, start with ones that a cat naturally does on his own, such as sitting or looking at you. Have your clicker and your treats ready. The second you see the cat sit, click and reward. Do this every time the cat sits. Start with basic, easy behaviors and be consistent in your click and reward. Timing is everything.

Once a cat is reliably offering a wanted behavior such as *sit*, you can then put it on a verbal cue. As the cat starts to sit, say, "Sit." Soon you'll be able to verbally cue a behavior before the cat begins to exhibit it. With verbal cues, you will be able to direct a cat to exhibit a particular behavior. This is what you've commonly seen with dog training when trainers use verbal cues for *sit*, *stay*, *down*, etc. The behaviors aren't put on verbal cues until the dog is reliably performing them, and then they are paired with the audible part of the training. In addition to verbal cues, you can also use visual hand cues.

Now that your cat understands clicker training and you both have this common language, you have the tools to click for a behavior you want to see again. Ignore unwanted behavior that you don't want repeated. Focus on the positive. This is how the cat learns he has a choice. For example, click and reward when

- a cat scratches on the scratching post instead of the furniture;

- a cat walks by a companion cat whom he has typically swatted at or shown aggressive behavior toward;
- a cat doesn't spray when walking by or pausing at a spot he has previously targeted; or
- a fearful cat comes out of hiding or takes a baby step toward interaction.

If the clicker training session isn't going well, it could mean the food reward isn't tasty enough. The cat may also be too tired; training sessions should be short. The cat may not be hungry enough or he could be too hungry and getting frustrated. Another thing to be careful of is that the behavior you're requesting might be too challenging. This is supposed to be fun!

Pam's CatWise Tip

No matter how excited you get over a behavior the cat has displayed, click the clicker only once. Remember, it's all about timing and being precise with the click and immediate reward. Repeated clicking just confuses the cat.

There are so many ways to use this positive, confidence-inspiring way of training. Clicker training can be a fun part of environmental enrichment in terms of mental stimulation to

- help change unwanted behaviors,
- increase the bond between you and your cat,
- decrease stress, and
- boost confidence.

Managing Mealtime in a Multicat Home

You started out with one cat, and just when you got the whole feeding ritual down, you introduced a second cat. Maybe you always had two cats and it wasn't until you introduced the third cat that mealtime changed from peaceful to chaotic. Living in a multicat household is filled with joy and fun, but sometimes you hit bumps in the road. One of those bumps may appear at mealtime.

When you live with multiple cats, you need an effective mealtime strategy. Those single-cat days of placing a bowl of food on the floor and not having to worry about who did or didn't eat are over. These days you may be faced with one or more cats on special diets, cats who like to graze, cats who push other cats out of the way, and cats who gobble food like vacuum cleaners. There are, however, methods you can use to help make life a bit easier when those hungry little faces are all looking up at you in the kitchen.

START WITH THE RIGHT SUPPLIES

Bowl Preferences

Cats can have preferences when it comes to the type of dishes used for food and water. What you put the food into may not seem that important to you, but it could make a big difference to one or more of your cats. There are many choices out there when it comes to pet bowls. You'll find bowls in all styles and price ranges.

Plastic—This is a common choice, but plastic tends to retain odor and your cats may object to the old smells of previous meals. Plastic also scratches easily, and bacteria can get trapped in the tiny lacerations. Many cats can develop skin problems around the chin area (such as feline acne) from eating out of plastic bowls. Plastic is also very lightweight and can end up being pushed around the floor when a cat is trying to eat the last bit of food in the dish.

Stainless steel—A good choice for food or water. It's virtually indestructible and easy to clean. To keep stainless steel bowls in place, choose the type with a rubber base.

Ceramic—Before buying a ceramic bowl, run your fingers over it carefully to make sure the surface is completely smooth. Any imperfections or rough spots can irritate a cat's tongue. Don't use a ceramic bowl once it has become chipped or you'll risk injury to a cat's mouth or tongue.

Glass—Another option for food or water. If you choose this, just be careful when washing to prevent chips. Throw out any glass bowl that gets even the tiniest chip or crack.

No matter how many cats you have, don't skimp on using the right type of dishes. Don't use old food containers or paper plates. Stainless steel, glass, or ceramic bowls are worth the investment because they'll last a long time and won't create a struggle for the cat to access the food.

Whisker Comfort

In addition to the preferences individual cats may have concerning what the bowls are made of, you also must address bowl size and shape. Cats don't like having their whiskers squished or bent while eating or drinking. Whiskers are exceptionally sensitive. If the food or water bowl is too deep, a cat may resort to dipping her paw in the bowl to avoid whisker discomfort.

Choose food bowls that are shallow to allow a cat's whiskers to remain spread out, so they don't come in contact with the sides. The shallow, flat food bowl will also allow a cat to keep watch over the environment as she eats. When a cat must bury her head into a bowl to retrieve food or water, it puts her at a disadvantage in case an opponent walks into the room.

For water bowls, choose ones that also allow for the cat's whiskers to remain straight and comfortable. Another option is to use a pet water fountain so the cat can drink from the running or dripping spout. One of the reasons many cats drink from kitchen or bathroom faucets is to avoid stress and discomfort to their whiskers. Keep this in mind when choosing the type of water bowl for your cats. If you choose a traditional water bowl instead of a water fountain, be consistent in keeping the water at a level that doesn't cause a cat to have to stick her head far down into the bowl.

Separate Food and Water

Don't use divided dishes for food and water. Food particles can easily land in the water and contaminate it, making it less desirable to drink. Many cats prefer not to have their food too close to their water. If a cat is thirsty and not hungry, she won't want the smell of food so close by. Since cats may look for a drink of water several times throughout the day and between mealtimes, have water bowls stationed all around the house, most specifically, at least one water bowl in each cat's preferred area.

SEATING IN THE CAT CAFETERIA

Free-Choice Feeding (Not Recommended)

Since food is a powerful training tool, if you decide to feed free-choice style, meaning leaving food available all the time, you lose that beneficial tool. Free-choice feeding works best with dry food only, because wet food quickly spoils when left out. If you want to limit the amount of dry food you feed, or you want to feed only wet food, then free-choice meals aren't a good option.

If your schedule demands it, or you decide for another reason to do free-choice feeding, with a multicat household it's not a good idea to have one community bowl. Tension between cats, anxiety, and aggression often extend to the feeding station. Even if all your cats get along, there may come a time as they mature when territorial issues come up, and one or two cats may start crowding others out. You want to create an environment in which each cat feels safe enough to eat in peace. Set up more than one feeding station so one cat doesn't have to cross into another cat's area. If there isn't any aggression between your cats, you can create different feeding stations in one location, such as the kitchen. In a tense multicat household, though, create stations in multiple locations. You may also have to create stations on different levels. If there's a cat who isn't at ease eating on ground level, she may need the security of an elevated feeding station. Another cat who is extremely timid may prefer a more hidden eating area, and if you have a dog, you need to place bowls in locations where the pup can't access them.

With free-choice feeding, you must keep a careful eye on weight. Some cats will eat all day if food is left available. Don't contribute to the growing obesity problem in cats, please.

> ### Pam's CatWise Caution
>
> Cats don't eat where they eliminate, so never set up a feeding station near a litter box.

Scheduled Feeding (Recommended)

If you feed on a schedule, everyone should have their own food bowl and be fed in the same position each time. With a large cat family this can be a challenge, but since they're creatures of habit, consistent routine can help create more security.

How far to separate the bowls will depend on the dynamics in the household. Some cats may be comfortable eating three feet apart, while others may need to eat in completely different rooms. Cats aren't social eaters. Even cats who enjoy each other's company at other times may still prefer their own bowl in a secure location where they don't have to worry about competition or intimidation.

How to Transition from Free-Choice to Scheduled Feeding

If you've been feeding out of a community bowl, you have some shopping to do. You need a separate bowl for each cat.

The easiest way to stop is to simply pick up the food bowl. Clean the area where the bowl was to remove trace bits of food.

The next step is to determine the schedule. Several meals per day will be easiest for the cats to adjust to and it's also more natural, since they have small stomachs. The number of meals will also depend on your own daily schedule and the age of the cats (kittens need more meals than adults). If you work away from home, the most practical schedule will be three meals a day:

- Breakfast in the morning
- Dinner when you come home
- Late-evening dinner right before you go to bed

If your schedule is such that you're home during the day, you can include lunch in the daily schedule. It's important that whether you choose the three-meal or four-meal schedule, you remain consistent. Don't feed lunch just because you're home two days a week, because it confuses the cats the other days. Cats do best with consistent, predictable schedules. Pick the times for scheduled feeding and adhere to them seven days a week.

If you notice a cat hanging out where the food bowl used to sit 24/7, that's the time to engage in some extra playtime. Get her mind on something other than food.

Scheduled meals are much healthier for your cats, so it's worth going through the adjustment period. You'll be better able to control food portions, be aware of changes in appetite, and feed specific diets to the cats who need them.

Involve Your Veterinarian

If you have questions or concerns about your cats' feeding routines or whether a change from free-feeding to scheduled feeding is appropriate for a cat's health, discuss the situation with your veterinarian. The doctor can best advise you on specific health and nutrition issues based on a cat's current health status and individual needs.

NEVER UP AGAINST A WALL OR IN A CORNER

Don't place bowls up against a wall or wedged in a corner, because cats can feel vulnerable with their backs to the entrance of the room. Slide bowls out enough so a cat has the choice of how to position herself at the bowl when eating. This gives her the option of keeping an eye on her surroundings.

ELEVATED LOCATIONS

Scheduled feeding may also be made more peaceful by using levels. Some cats prefer eating on an elevated surface like a perch or side table. For example, to keep an overweight adult cat from nudging a younger cat away from the food bowl, place the younger cat's bowl on an elevated surface that's too difficult for the overweight cat to access. If that doesn't work, the cats should be fed in completely different locations. When choosing an elevated location for feeding, avoid kitchen counters or other areas where food preparation for humans is done.

CATS AREN'T SOCIAL EATERS

When doing a new cat introduction, mealtime is a good time to help them form positive associations, but the distance between them is essential. When feeding cats, adequate distance is very important so that each cat can remain well within her comfort zone. If a cat stops eating and starts looking at another cat, then it means the bowls are too close together. If you notice there's a problem with one cat becoming too possessive around the food bowl, or if some cats are afraid even to enter the feeding area, then separate stations are needed.

I know setting up and maintaining multiple feeding stations creates more work, but it's important to create security. In many cases, if you don't have many cats, ensuring security and making sure everyone eats out of his or her own bowl may just require your presence in the room, separating the bowls a few feet apart and keeping a close eye on the diners (and praising their good manners). If you're consistent and are doing other behavior work to help maintain multicat harmony in your home, then the routine should sink in and the cats will likely head to their individual bowls without incident. If not, then separation is the key to peace and to avoiding any feline food fights.

Pam's CatWise Tip

To help you keep track of each cat's preferred bowl in a large multicat household, use a permanent marker to write a cat's name on each one. This will also help when other family members or pet sitters oversee mealtime.

HOW TO HANDLE SPEED BARFING

No, it's not the latest Olympic sport. It's the cat who eats so fast she ends up barfing it back onto the kitchen floor a few seconds later. This happens with a cat who is worried other cats will nose her out of her bowl, and it can also happen with a cat who's been placed on a diet, or a rescue cat who had difficulty getting enough food in the past. For this cat, make sure the mealtime environment is protected so that no one can push her out of her own bowl. She may need to have a separate feeding station in another room. Also, use a slow-feeding bowl to help her take a little longer to finish her food. This type of bowl has built-in obstacles in the bottom that the cat has to eat around to get to the food.

Slow-feeding bowls are very popular for dogs. You may also want to consider puzzle feeders for the cat who eats too fast.

HOW TO FEED DIFFERENT DIETS IN A MULTICAT HOUSEHOLD

This situation may arise if you bring a kitten into a household of adult cats. It can also be an issue if a cat must go on a prescription formula due to a medical condition or if you are mixing medication into a cat's food. Your veterinarian may also want one or more of your cats on a reduced-calorie formula due to a weight problem.

Scheduled feeding is the obvious choice when you have cats on special diets so you can be sure everyone is eating what they're supposed to, unless you plan on keeping certain cats separated 24/7.

Elevated options—In some cases, just elevating the regular food may prevent a cat (for example, an overweight cat) from reaching it if her excess pounds can't win the battle against gravity. And while we're on the topic of overweight cats, it may help to feed an overweight cat smaller meals more often. Her stomach won't be empty for such a long time, so she'll feel more satisfied. You may need to put her in a separate room for her special mealtimes. You can also try using puzzle feeders to help her get a little playtime and exercise and to encourage slower eating. More on puzzle feeders in the next section. Just be sure not to increase her daily amount of food. Portion out the amount recommended by the veterinarian and then divide up the food in order to feed smaller meals more often or to put into puzzle feeders.

With a kitten, if she's getting close to her first birthday, is healthy, and is a good weight, your veterinarian may allow her to transition to adult food a bit early. This may help if you're struggling to keep your adult cats out of the growth-formula food.

Don't make the early transition without the veterinarian's approval, though. Kittens need the extra fat and protein in growth formula.

Separate locations—Feed the cats in completely different rooms and close the door during mealtime.

Baby gates—This works best with cats who aren't as athletic, such as overweight or senior cats. Feed in the same area but put a baby gate up for separation.

Feed in shifts—Feed a cat on a special diet at a different time by placing her in a separate room, or lock the other cats in another room during her mealtime. Be mindful when doing this method that you don't end up with cats hanging around right outside a door meowing and crying because they know there's a cat eating in there.

Be the food monitor—Depending on the number of cats in your household and their relationship to one another (no fighting), you may be able to feed different food just by staying in the room and acting as the cafeteria monitor.

Automatic smart feeders—These feeders are programmed to open when paired with a cat's microchip or special RFID (radio-frequency identification) collar. If you have a cat who likes to graze throughout the day, this type of feeder may be a good option. My only concern, though, is that although the feeder prevents other cats from opening it, there isn't a way to prevent them from hanging around and trying to push the "approved" cat away. Any feeding arrangement you set up shouldn't cause anxiety or opportunities for intimidation. The automatic smart feeders may be a good choice, but that depends on the personalities in your multicat household.

THE BENEFITS AND FUN OF PUZZLE FEEDERS (FOOD-DISPENSING TOYS)

Depending on the design, these toys are either rolled, knocked over, reached into with a paw, or a cover must be slid open by the cat's paw in order to retrieve the food reward.

You may initially think puzzle feeders make cats have to work for food and that may not seem fair, but it's a natural concept for a hunter. In fact, it's not as much work as it is discovery and playtime.

Puzzle feeders can be used

- for extra playtime,
- to distract a cat from less desirable behavior,
- to encourage a fast eater to slow down,
- to entertain cats during the wee hours of the morning,
- to provide all-important mental stimulation,
- to spark the instinct to hunt and forage,
- to help a dieting cat feel satisfied between meals, or
- for stress relief.

There are multiple types of puzzle feeders available for purchase. Do an online search for puzzle feeders and you'll see the various options for wet or dry food. But it's also just as easy to make homemade ones. You can also find instructions for all sorts of homemade puzzle feeders online. Making homemade feeders can be a fun family project.

Make It Easy at First

Your cat is used to walking over to her food bowl and seeing a meal all ready for her. Now you're expecting her to use a little skill in order to procure her dinner? Make the introduction easy and avoid frustrating your cat and she'll quickly find out it's fun. Cats love to seek, discover, and paw at things. They're attracted to objects that move, especially when the movement is enticing. If your cats have ever knocked objects off tables or batted toys on the floor, they can very likely work a puzzle feeder. They just may need a little puzzle-feeder basic training.

Try Different Puzzle Feeders

Every cat is an individual with certain preferences, so try a couple of different types of puzzle feeders. Just as with toy selection, you may find some of your cats have specific likes or dislikes. If you purchase puzzle feeders, some are designed for beginners and others are intended as level 2 or level 3. Cats are very smart, but since this is supposed to be fun, start at the easiest level (whether homemade or purchased) and work your way up. Don't be discouraged if a cat doesn't show interest in the first one you try. It may be too difficult, not the right size, or maybe your cat wasn't hungry enough.

Pam's CatWise Tip

A PVC elbow fitting purchased from your local home improvement store can be turned into a simple and easy puzzle feeder. An ice-cube tray makes another quick and easy level 1 puzzle feeder for wet or dry food.

Starting Out with Puzzle Feeders

First, your cat needs to be hungry, but don't wait until she's starving because that might lead to frustration when she's in puzzle-feeder training.

Here's an easy dry-food puzzle feeder: Use a small water bottle placed on its side and partially filled with dry food. Before filling the bottle, cut holes all around that are much bigger than the size of the food pieces. This way, all your cat must do is basically touch the bottle and food will be released. You can even place a few bits of food right next to the bottle, so when your cat gets close to the food her nose may touch the bottle and another piece will magically drop out. As she becomes more proficient, make fewer holes in the next water bottle so she must put more effort into accessing the food. Always make the holes larger than the size of the piece of food or else this will turn into an exercise in cat frustration.

For wet food, start out with something like an ice-cube tray or muffin tin. It will get your cat comfortable with the idea of foraging in each compartment.

The LickiMat, for example, is good for a cat who eats wet food. Spread the food over the raised design surface and it will take more time for the cat to get all the food.

With the popularity of food-dispensing toys, there are many varieties available. Just search online and you'll see how many styles and types there are. Remember, you can also make home-made ones. In addition to the water bottle or ice-cube tray, you can use the cardboard tubes from paper towel or toilet paper rolls to make disposable puzzle feeders. Cut holes in the cardboard tubes, put some dry food or treats in there, and fold the ends in.

Anything that encourages your cat's foraging instinct will work. Just make sure it's safe and fun. Even the most basic idea of portioning the food into each compartment of a muffin tin creates some degree of discovery. It may not seem like an exciting challenge but it does entice your cat to search for the food and to eat more slowly.

Remember, if your cat isn't showing an interest in the puzzle feeder, try a different type. You may have to experiment with a few.

Many of my clients' cats enjoy the Catit Senses 2.0 Digger. It has narrow and wide tubes that stand upright in a base. The cat has to reach her paw in to retrieve the treat. It also has a sloped surface in the front with enough space for you to place a little food there to get your cat started. This puzzle feeder is also very easy to clean.

Puzzle Feeder Toys Should Never Be Frustrating

Don't push cats beyond their ability. Even though a puzzle feeder is meant to work the brain, it's still supposed to be a game that brings enjoyment. Some cats will never graduate beyond the most basic puzzle feeder, and some may not take to the idea at all. Don't insist on it. If it's not fun for a cat, then don't force the issue, and don't let the cat go hungry if she resists this method of eating or hunting.

Keep Puzzle Feeders Clean

Even though your cats may get every morsel out of the puzzle feeders, it's important to wash them after each use. Puzzle feeders can have little bits of food stuck in corners, which can lead to contamination. There will also be saliva on the toy that needs to be washed off. Residue or odor of old food may make the toy unappealing. Wash puzzle feeders in mild dish soap and rinse thoroughly.

Create a Safe Environment When You Introduce the Puzzle Feeder

Mealtime, whether it's by way of a puzzle feeder or a traditional food bowl, should always be a safe and peaceful time for cats. When you offer the puzzle feeder, make sure it's in an area where a cat won't be at risk of an ambush by other companion animals. In a household with a dog, offer the puzzle feeder in a location where the dog won't have access. In addition to the stress this could cause the cat, you don't want a dog eating cat food, and even worse, chewing or swallowing pieces of a puzzle feeder.

Pam's CatWise Caution

If one of your cats has the habit of chewing on plastic, don't use plastic water bottles or easily chewable materials to make puzzle feeders. Choose a store-bought puzzle feeder made of a sturdy material, maybe even one intended for small dogs. Safety is always the most important concern.

Not Everything Is a Good Idea for a Puzzle Feeder

Although you can turn many items around your house into puzzle feeders, don't use pill bottles. Plastic pill bottles seem like a natural, but your cat may mistake a bottle filled with pills for a puzzle feeder. Stick to safe items. Never use medicine containers or cleaning containers.

TREASURE HUNTS

If you decide not to use puzzle feeders, or if one or more of your cats just don't seem to take to them, do simple treasure hunts instead. Hide treats around the areas where your cats spend time. As a cat walks near where a treat is hidden, her nose will guide her to the reward.

FOOD THIEVES

Counter Cruisers

With multiple cats, it often takes more of a concentrated effort when it comes to training everyone to stay off the counters where food (yours or theirs) is being prepared. Even if you feed one or two of the cats on elevated surfaces, there are areas where you probably don't want your cats to have access—for example, the dining-room table and the kitchen counter. This becomes particularly important if you hope to make sure nobody runs off with the uncooked piece of chicken or gets into the Thanksgiving turkey seconds before you're about to serve it to your company.

To keep cats off the counter or other surfaces, first determine where the cats will and won't be allowed. Make sure everyone in the family knows the rules as well, because consistency is important. A cat who receives mixed messages won't get trained successfully.

Get a plastic carpet protector that comes in a roll. Choose the kind that has pointy feet on the underside. These carpet protectors are the type you typically see in model homes. The pointy feet help the protector grip the carpet; for feline counter cruisers, though, you'll use the protector with the feet side up. Cut out squares of the carpet protector to fit the different sections of the counter or table you want to cover. Place the protector all along the counter and your cats won't be able to find a comfortable place to hang out. Keep the protectors in place whenever you don't need the counter or table space. You can also keep part of the counter covered whenever you're working on another side of it, to prevent a cat from quietly sneaking up onto the counter when you're distracted.

If the upside-down carpet runner isn't effective enough, go to the next level, which is to place strips of double-sided tape on plastic place mats and lay those along the counter surface.

The above methods work well because they change a cat's association with the area without directly connecting it to you. After a couple of weeks of consistently keeping the protectors or place mats in place, you can start to remove them one at a time, leaving the ones closest to the edge until last.

One basic rule when it comes to training cats who like to counter-cruise for food—don't leave food out. Remove temptation by keeping food covered or put away. In addition to not wanting any cats to get extra calories or the fact that paw prints in the pumpkin pie won't go over well with your guests, you also don't want to risk their ingestion of something poisonous.

If any of the cats like being on the counter for reasons other than trying to grab a quick snack, establish what the motive is so you can supply an acceptable alternative. For example, if the cat wants the elevated location because she feels safer there, then provide another elevated location nearby, such as a cat tree, cat shelf, or window perch so she uses that instead. If the desire to be on the counter is an attention-getting behavior, then make sure she's getting enough playtime with you before you go into the kitchen to prepare meals. Leave a puzzle feeder out to occupy her

Pam's CatWise Caution

Decide which elevated surfaces are off-limits to your cats and remain consistent. Don't send mixed messages by allowing cats on the dining-room table when there isn't food there, but then shooing them off during meals. It's also important to be consistent when it comes to what foods are allowed. If you don't want your cats licking ice cream from the open container on the counter, don't let them lick the remaining ice cream from the dish you've just finished.

so she can be nearby without having to be on the counter. By the way, if it is an attention-getting behavior, it's important that when you remove her from the counter you don't talk to her, kiss her, make eye contact, or pet her. All those things provide some form of attention. Instead, just gently pick her up and place her back down on the floor.

HOW TO USE TREATS EFFECTIVELY

Treats can be very effective when training cats. Use them specifically for training purposes and trust building. Don't just give them out for no reason. I know you love your cats and want to reward them, but providing top-quality nutrition, affection, playtime, and a loving environment will more than make up for that handful of treats. If you overdo the treats you can interfere with nutrition and you may find a cat loses interest in her regular food.

When you use treats for training, break them into pieces. Most cat treats are generous in size, and if you break them into halves, you'll get more mileage out of them while not overloading the cat with calories. During training, a cat needs only a small taste of this special treat and not a stomachful. Remember, it's a *treat*, not a *meal*.

Some cats will love any treat you offer, and others will be a bit picky about flavors or textures. I have found that dehydrated chicken treats are extremely popular with most of the cats I work with. There are so many brands of treats available, and your cats will surely let you know when you pick the perfect one.

Pam's CatWise Mealtime Reminders

- Don't place food and water near litter boxes.
- Don't feed cats out of one community bowl.
- Separate food and water.
- Set up feeding stations in areas where each cat feels most comfortable.
- Wash water bowls daily and replenish with fresh water.
- Use shallow, flat bowls for food to prevent whisker stress.
- Don't allow moist food to sit out for more than a half hour.
- Make mealtime peaceful.
- Make sure everyone gets the appropriate amount of food.
- If any cat displays a change in appetite, see your veterinarian.

How to Maintain a Happy Multicat Litter Box Environment

When I'm on TV or radio, I'm always asked about litter box problems. Everyone is looking for that two-minute miracle answer. The best I can give you in a nutshell is my three-step approach to dealing with cats who aren't in sync with their litter boxes. This approach isn't a magic wand to avoid doing the work you need to do, but it does give you a place to begin. Here's the order in which to proceed when tackling litter box unhappiness:

1. Rule out medical issues.
2. Evaluate the litter box setup.
3. Address intercat or household stress.

Litter box problems can occur in any household, regardless of the number of cats, but the chances certainly increase as you add more cats into the mix. Many cat parents assume the litter box is just the place cats use for elimination—the feline version of a toilet—and if they keep it filled with litter, everyone will be happy. Oh, if only it could be that simple. In reality, a cat's relationship with the litter box is more complex.

No miracles. Just common sense and good detective work. So, let's get started.

IS IT MEDICAL?

Any change in litter box habits can be an indication of an underlying medical problem. There are quite a few conditions that can cause a cat to eliminate away from the box. It's also common for a cat to associate the box itself with any pain he is experiencing during urination or defecation, and that can be another reason why he chooses an alternate location. Don't assume a litter box problem is behavioral until you've had the cat checked out by the veterinarian. Urinary problems can be fatal if the urethra becomes totally blocked, especially in male cats, who have long, narrow urethras.

Medical conditions that create discomfort when walking can also lead to litter box issues if the cat is too stiff to get to the box or has difficulty climbing inside.

In geriatric cats, age-related cognitive issues could be causing the change in litter box habits.

Cats experiencing medical conditions such as kidney disease, diabetes, or urinary tract infection may not be able to make it to the box in time due to an urgency to urinate.

Changes in a cat's litter box habits should be brought to the veterinarian's attention immediately.

Even if a cat is diagnosed with a medical condition, there are steps you can take to create a more comfortable litter box experience, such as increasing box sites and making sure sides are low enough for a cat to enter.

THE LITTER BOX SETUP

Cleanliness

No matter how many cats you have (or how many litter boxes), all the boxes must be kept clean. Nothing will drive a cat away from a box faster than smelly mounds of soiled litter. You should sift and scoop the litter a minimum of twice a day. This is a shock to you if you've been getting by with peeking at the box only every other day, but trust me, you're headed for trouble. The easiest method is to scoop first thing in the morning and then again before bed. If you really want to avoid potential problems, take a few seconds for an extra litter check when you come home from work. And of course, if you happen to pass by a litter box in the middle of the day and you notice it has been used, stop and scoop.

Your scooping technique can vary based on the litter you use. For scoopable (clumping) litter, have a sturdy slotted litter shovel. For nonscoopable litter, use a slotted shovel to sift through litter for solid waste and a nonslotted litter shovel to scoop out wet mounds of litter. The sooner you remove soiled litter, the happier your cats will be.

If you're on a twice-a-day scooping schedule, you can get a small trash bag and make the litter box rounds and then toss the bag in the outside trash can. If you want to scoop more often, keep a small container with a tight-fitting lid (or use a commercial litter receptacle) near each box. Line the container with a small trash bag to make it easier to throw the contents away. You can lay your shovel on top or get a litter rake container as well. After you scoop, put the soiled clumps in the container and snap the lid back on. At the end of the day, make the rounds to clean them out. If you make it convenient, no matter what type of setup you create, you'll be more likely to scoop as often as needed. Scooping more regularly is not only hygienic for your cats and your house, but it may also cut down on tension between cats; some won't use the box after another cat has gone there.

The schedule for completely cleaning out the litter and washing the boxes will depend on the type of litter and the habits of your cats. Don't underestimate the importance of washing the boxes even if you're using scoopable litter. Not all the urine and feces lands exclusively on the litter itself. The sides and bottoms of the boxes will get dirty and need to be washed. Clean the boxes, soiled litter containers, and litter shovels in mild dish soap and then rinse thoroughly. Don't use household cleaners because they're too heavily scented, and don't use ammonia because that'll smell like urine to the cats.

Boxes with nonclumping litter should be emptied and washed every three to four days. Boxes filled with scoopable clumping litter need to be emptied and washed about every three to four weeks.

Number of Boxes

When you have more than one cat, you need more than one litter box. You should have as many boxes as you have cats, plus one extra. I know you may be groaning right now at the thought of all the extra maintenance, especially if you have a larger cat family, but if you want to decrease the chances of having a litter box issue, this is one of those cat rules you can't break. Although the thought of scooping and scrubbing several boxes may not sound like fun, it's much better than having to replace carpet or refinish floors due to ongoing elimination issues.

Box Size

Ideally, a litter box should be one and a half times the length of a cat from tip of the nose to base of the tail. Choose boxes that fit the cat and not your location choice. On the other hand, don't get a box so enormous that you'll be reluctant to wash it and refill it with fresh litter. I have seen some people use extremely large plastic concrete mixing tubs, thinking that one gigantic box will work for a houseful of cats. The problem is that the tub becomes too difficult to empty and clean. The other issue is that one gigantic box still limits all cats to one elimination site. Not a good plan.

Box Type

Uncovered—The best choice. It provides the cat enough room to move around and makes it easy for you to notice soiled litter. It also gives a cat more visual warning time to see who might be entering the room, and provides multiple escape options. More about escape in a bit.

Covered—In a multicat environment, the use of covered litter boxes is almost always a mistake. I actually believe they're bad choices in general. A covered box traps the odor inside. Cat parents may love that, but cats aren't so crazy about that aspect. Think of how close a cat's nose is to the litter when in the box, and how sensitive that nose is. Having the litter smell trapped in the box can created an unpleasant concentration of odor. The cover also prevents proper air circulation, so it takes longer for the litter to dry. When it comes to scooping, many cat parents may be less likely to stick to an adequate schedule because of the inconvenience of having to remove the lid. Imagine how unpleasant it must be for a cat to step into a dark box filled with damp, smelly litter. Covered boxes also mean twice as much work when it comes time to wash the box because you must clean the lid and the base.

In a multicat home, covered boxes pose a potential danger: *lack of escape potential*. Humans prefer privacy when it comes to taking care of personal business, and we tend to assume that really matters to our cats as well. To a cat, privacy takes a back seat to safety.

A covered box limits the cat to one entrance/exit. While in the process of elimination, a cat is very vulnerable, and he certainly doesn't want to get ambushed in there by another cat. In some households, one cat may sit on the lid while another unsuspecting cat is in the box. The cat stalker waits for his moment and then pounces just as the victim is exiting the box. In other cases, the unsuspecting cat may try to exit the box and come face-to-face with his adversary at the box entrance. It may take only a couple of these startling encounters for a cat to decide to eliminate in a safer location. If all the litter boxes are covered, that new location may end up being your living-room or bedroom carpet. Even if your cats aren't feuding, a surprise appearance by a second cat can cause the same reaction. A cat may do all he can to avoid the risk of being trapped there again in the future.

Next on my list of negatives about covered boxes has to do with size. The boxes may look large to you, but the actual elimination area may not be any bigger than a regular litter box. If you're worried about litter scatter or you have cats who spray inside the box or over the sides, get plastic storage containers and use those as litter boxes. I've found regular litter boxes all to be too small anyway. The storage containers come in all heights, lengths, and widths. This is helpful when you must have boxes in several locations and need various sizes to accommodate different-size cats. They're also great if you need a couple of extra-large ones in the most frequently used areas.

Many manufacturers make storage containers. I like the Sterilite containers because they have flat bottoms, which make it easier to scoop. They also come in a good variety of sizes and heights. You can find storage containers in most discount stores as well as online.

To address litter scatter and poorly aimed urination attempts, choose a high-sided storage container. Cut a low entrance on one end, using a Dremel tool or a multipurpose tool. You can also drill three-quarter-inch holes and use a pair of tin snips. Use sand-paper (80 or 100 grit) to smooth any sharp or rough edges. The three high sides will contain the litter and urine spray, but the openness at the end of the box will make it convenient for you to scoop. The cats will also have adequate escape potential. If you're concerned that your cats may not adjust to the change in the litter box, place the original litter box in the storage container at first and then you can eventually get rid of the original box and simply put the litter substrate directly into the plastic storage container.

Pam's CatWise Caution

Be very careful when cutting the entrance in the litter box. Plastic containers can be slippery and you can lose your grip on them, and the cut edge is sharp.

Self-cleaning boxes—Some cat parents with large numbers of cats may think these boxes are a time-saver, but the downsides, in my opinion, outweigh the positives. The electronic boxes may deter cats from entering if they approach while the motor and rake are still cleaning up from a previous cat's visit. I also find the actual litter surface areas of these boxes to be too small. The box itself seems large, but that's just because it must house the motor and the soiled litter receptacle. The rake can jam if the litter clump is exceptionally large. The rake may also get stuck on large clumps of diarrhea as well.

Some electronic boxes are also covered, which adds another cat-negative aspect.

As for manual self-cleaning boxes, you'll spend just as much time flipping them over and emptying receptacles as you would if you'd just scoop with a shovel. These boxes also must be washed at some point, so you'll end up cleaning the top, the grate, the base, and the receptacle.

Don't be tempted by manufacturers trying to sell you on ways to avoid cleaning the litter box. It may not be the most pleasant part of living with cats, but the value it provides by potentially being an early warning system of possible medical issues far outweighs any negatives. Keep the setup simple, cat friendly, easy for you to clean, and easy to see what is or isn't happening in the box.

Top-entry box—Ugh! This is awful for so many reasons. This is the type of box designed strictly for the cat parent's convenience by avoiding litter scatter or pee overshoot. For a cat, though, the box is a nightmare. Any cat with even the slightest physical impairment or weakness will struggle entering and exiting this box. While in the box, the cat is totally vulnerable to a feline aerial attack. To have any warning time, the cat in the box would have to be willing to pee and poo while looking straight overhead the entire time, and even at that, he would have no place to escape.

Even if there aren't adversarial relationships between your cats, I wouldn't blame a cat for rejecting this box just on principle.

The Litter

You may be lucky enough to have a household where all the cats happily use the same brand of litter. It may even stay that way forever, but in some cases, a cat or two may have a preference when it comes to texture or scent (or lack of scent).

A litter box rule is not to change brands or types of litter abruptly, because cats are creatures of habit. You'll be asking for trouble if you suddenly decide to buy a different brand because it's on sale that week. When a cat steps into the box, he expects to find the same texture and scent as the last time he visited there.

Perhaps you do want to try a different litter, or maybe you sense one of the cats might be displaying an aversion to the litter. How do you make a change? There are two methods:

Litter box buffet—If you suspect one or more cats might prefer a different type, do a test run by setting out an extra box or two filled with the new litter. Place the new box near the ones you think are used the most by the discontented cats. You can even set out a few types of litter to give the cats more of a choice.

When a cat has a litter aversion, he may eliminate without digging first or covering afterward. His mission is to get in and out of the box as quickly as possible. Now, some cats never dig or cover, but it's important to notice if there's a change in typical behavior. If a cat who normally scratches at the litter suddenly stops or scratches at the side of the box, the wall behind it, or the floor around it, he may be experiencing a litter aversion (it can also be that the box is too dirty and he's trying desperately to cover the odor). He's attempting to cover but doesn't want to have any more physical contact with the litter than is necessary. He may also perch on the edge of the box, so his hind legs are propped up on the edge. This results in poor aim, but from the cat's point of view, at least he's in the box. A cat might also perch by resting his front paws on the edge. At least the latter position keeps his aim well within the target zone. A litter aversion can also be the cause if the cat is getting as close to the box as he can but never actually steps inside. He may eliminate right next to the box or on a nearby mat. It's important to remember that cats may display this behavior due to an underlying medical condition or because the box is too dirty.

In big feline families there may be a couple of cats who prefer a specific type of litter. You may need to keep a few boxes filled with that preferred litter type. You won't be able to stop other cats from using it, but at least you can accommodate preferences.

Pam's CatWise Reminder

Cats are very tactile, and the texture of a litter is important. With multiple cats you must be prepared that not all will share the same likes or dislikes.

Gradual changeover—This is another method of changing litter brands or types. You add a small amount of the new litter into the current brand. Every few days you gradually increase the proportion of new to old. If you notice the cats seem reluctant or uncertain when approaching the box or standing in it, or if you see less covering of the waste than normal, it means you're moving too quickly. Slow down. If you still notice a problem, it may indicate the type of litter you chose will not be acceptable to the cats.

Keep in mind that when switching to a different type of litter, such as going from clay to scoopable (clumping) or from scoopable to another alternative litter, the performance of the litter will not be optimal because of the noncompatible formulations. Scoopable litter will not clump effectively while there is still a large amount of regular clay litter in the box. Hang in there during the transition, because the litter performance will improve as the proportions change.

When adding a new cat into the current household, if he has been accustomed to a particular type of litter, use that in his sanctuary room while he gets adjusted to his new environment. You can then do a gradual changeover. If you aren't sure which type of litter the cat would prefer, or if you're rescuing a stray cat, it's usually best to start with unscented scoopable litter, since an outdoor cat would have been used to eliminating in sand and soil. If you normally use a very specialized litter in your home, set out two boxes in the sanctuary room (one containing unscented scoopable) so the new cat has a choice.

Litter Levels

When you go from one cat to two or more, your days of buying small, easy-to-carry boxes of litter are over. You have probably entered the world of the warehouse-club shopper, or you order your pet supplies online so they can arrive at your doorstep. You may also have switched to lightweight formula litter. There are two things you know you can't run out of: food or litter.

Along with your good scooping and sifting schedule, you'll also need to maintain a consistent litter level. Depending on how much a box gets used, you'll have to top off the remaining litter with a fresh supply. In general, you'll probably have to do this every few days. One thing I often see on house calls is an insufficient amount of litter in the box. Although you have five or six boxes to maintain, this isn't the place to economize. Even if some of your cats don't mind the low litter level, it'll mean a smelly box as the urine just sits unabsorbed in the bottom. On the other hand, don't fill the box to the brim with litter because that's a waste. It makes it harder to scoop, there's more of a chance of litter scatter, and some cats may object to having to perch on mountains of litter. In general, a consistent three-inch depth is about right.

Litter Additives

A new or sudden litter aversion can occur for reasons you might never think of, even if you use the same brand of litter you always have. If you recently started adding scented commercial litter additives, the scent changes may be unpleasant and overpowering to cats. If you maintain a good scooping schedule, there isn't need for an additive. Most additives are merely introducing a strong fragrance to cover up the urine odor.

A human's perception of an attractive scent and a cat's perception can be quite different. Cats prefer to smell their own scent. Cover-up fragrances are never cat friendly. For example, we associate citrus scents with being fresh and clean. Cats find citrus scents to be aversive. Refrain from using any additives, as well as air fresheners or plug-ins. Keeping the box clean is the best odor control.

Litter Liners

If you use plastic liners, your cats may dislike the sound or feel of them. Many cats dislike the way their claws can get hung up in the plastic as they try to scratch the litter. Liners are a bad idea anyway because they often don't fit right and create pockets where urine can puddle. Just don't use them.

Litter Box Locations

Never locate the box near the food and water. Cats don't eat where they eliminate. On the most basic level that makes common sense. Humans don't tend to eat in the bathroom either, but for a cat this behavior is rooted in survival. The cat eliminates away from the nest so he won't attract predators with the scent of his waste. Even the most pampered indoor cat shares this instinct. If a litter box must be kept in the same room as the feeding station (such as in a sanctuary room), it should be placed on the opposite side of the room.

Litter Box Life Expectancy

Litter boxes don't last forever. Boxes become scratched from cat claws and they get worn out. In a multicat household, litter boxes get quite a workout. The lacerations harbor bacteria and that leads to a smelly box. Eventually, it gets to the point of no return. Litter boxes should be changed out every two or three years (or sooner if needed).

Territorial Considerations and Preferred Areas

With multiple cats you not only need multiple litter boxes, you need multiple litter box locations. You may think you're being efficient by creating a *litter box room*, but you run the very real risk of creating an aversion problem. As you remember from the earlier chapters in this book, everything in your home is part of overlapping home ranges and territories. You don't want a cat to have to take a pathway that forces him to pass right by an adversary in order to gain access to the box.

Some or all your cats may have established preferred areas where they tend to spend the most time or where they feel the safest. Make sure each cat has at least one litter box in their personal preferred area, or at the very least, has multiple options for accessing one safely.

As I suggested earlier in the book, draw a basic floor plan to get a better idea of preferred areas, neutral locations, and where confrontations, if any, occur. This can help you plan the most practical litter box locations.

Escape Potential

Privacy is important when it comes to human bathroom behavior, and we mistakenly believe we need to provide an abundance of that for our cats as well. Yes, a certain degree of privacy is needed; after all, very few cats would feel comfortable with the litter box right in the middle of the family room where the children are noisily playing video games, but some cat parents go to extremes to create privacy. Although many people don't want litter boxes in the main living areas, too much privacy can be to a cat's detriment.

A cat is extremely vulnerable when in the litter box. It's a time when adversaries may choose to ambush. A cat caught eliminating in a box that is claimed by another cat may find himself backed into a corner before he can finish urinating. The need for escape potential isn't only limited to feline confrontations: dogs and young children can also appear to be a threat from a cat's perspective. When a cat is taking care of his litter box business, that's not the time he should have to worry about defending himself.

There are two steps to creating optimal escape potential. First, provide an open box so the cat has several ways to leap out in a hurry if needed. This way, if a perceived threat approaches from any direction, the cat in the box can go the opposite way. Even if you have uncovered boxes, if they're hidden in closets or wedged in corners, you've reduced the cat's escape potential by half. Keep the box in the open and slide it out several inches from the wall. Often, that can be enough for the cats to feel they can dart out the back or side if necessary.

Second, provide adequate *warning time*. When a cat is in the box, the more visual advantage he has to see if someone is approaching, the better. If there's a litter box location aversion issue, there's a good chance the soiled areas are in *escapable* areas. The frightened cat doesn't want to be caught off guard in the litter box, so he may choose a room where there are two entrances, such as a dining room or open-plan living room. He may pick a room where there aren't many pieces of furniture blocking his view of the entrance. The cat may eliminate on the carpet near the wall opposite a door. This way, he has the most visual warning to see who might be coming. Cats lower in status may also choose rooms that aren't claimed or ones that aren't used often by the family. That's another reason why dining rooms are often a popular choice. Not only do most dining rooms have two entrances, but in many families they are used only when entertaining company. Guest rooms are another popular choice. The cat may view those places as a perimeter. Some cats may also choose the cat parent's master bedroom because they think of that as a safe haven. Those cats need escape potential but also are comforted by the safety the cat parent's scent represents.

Pam's CatWise Tip

Be sensitive to what each cat needs. Litter box placement in a multicat home may have to be creative to address the needs of the privacy-seeking cats and the escape-seeking ones.

Place litter boxes in areas of rooms that allow a cat to see the doorway. If he can see down the hallway as well, even better. Create as much of a visual advantage as possible while still maintaining enough privacy to satisfy you and your cats. Pay attention to each cat's preference based on how they act while approaching a litter box, how they behave while in the box, and how they exit.

Consider escape potential before deciding to put a litter box in a basement with a cat flap in the basement door. I've even seen cat parents insert pet doors on laundry-room doors. The pet door means one cat still faces the risk of suddenly encountering another cat without warning at very close range.

LITTER BOX PROBLEMS

Identifying the Cat(s) in Question

Surveillance—This is the most accurate way to determine which cat is eliminating outside the box if you don't witness the behavior firsthand. Set up a surveillance camera in the area being targeted. With the popularity of home surveillance systems, it's easy to set up cameras, even for those who are electronic novices. There are many single wireless camera options that connect through an app to your smartphone. These cameras are not expensive and work well. Just be sure to insert an SD card in the camera so you can view previously recorded footage.

Camera surveillance is the best way to identify the cats as well as provide clues to what may have triggered the behavior.

Fluorescein method—This is an okay method although not always reliable. Fluorescein ophthalmic dye is used to detect injuries to the eye. In a multicat home, it can also be given orally to help identify which cat is urinating outside the litter box. Fluorescein causes urine to fluoresce under a black light. Your veterinarian can put fluorescein in a capsule for you to administer to the cat you suspect is most likely the one urinating or spraying outside the litter box. Fluorescein isn't 100 percent reliable, though. Cameras are better.

Confinement method—I really don't recommend this at all. The problem with separating a cat from the others to identify the unwanted behavior is that the behavior may temporarily stop if two feuding cats are apart. You still won't know which cat is the correct one.

Crayon shavings—For use in identification of a cat leaving fecal deposits outside the litter box, brightly colored, nontoxic crayon shavings can be added to the food. The shavings will show up in the feces. Again, camera surveillance is better.

Pam's CatWise Feline Fact

Sadly, elimination outside the litter box is often the most common reason cats are relinquished to shelters or abandoned to the outdoors.

Urination Outside the Litter Box

Before you can address the litter box issue, you must identify the behavior. There's a difference between *spraying* and what many refer to as *indiscriminate* or *inappropriate urination*. The word *inappropriate* was, for many years, the common term used when describing urination outside the litter box. Fortunately, many experts and veterinarians are moving away from that word because it doesn't accurately identify the behavior. There's nothing *inappropriate* about a cat who pees outside the litter box. If a cat feels he has no other option due to environmental or medical reasons, it's a very normal and practical behavior. Calling it *inappropriate* seems to label the behavior as something that should be punished, or something deliberately done as a misbehavior. Even though the behavior is certainly unwanted by the human family members, it's important to remember that behaviors are displayed and repeated because they serve a function. There's a payoff for the animal. It may not be a payoff we like, but in the animal's mind, the behavior served a valuable purpose. So, while experts continue to search for the ideal word to best describe this behavior, I'm going to refer to it in this book as *undesirable* urination. I acknowledge that having your cat pee on the carpet or your bed is undesirable, but when thinking like a cat, it's certainly not inappropriate.

Pam's CatWise Caution

Never rub a cat's nose in his urine or feces. This is inhumane, frightening for the cat, and will backfire on your training. The cat will think you're punishing him for the very act of elimination and not just his choice of location. Punishment erodes trust and will damage the bond you share.

Identify Spraying vs. Undesirable Urination

These are two different behaviors that can have very different causes. Undesirable urination is typically displayed on horizontal surfaces. The cat takes the normal position of squatting, just as he would in a litter box. In many cases, the cat will completely empty his bladder. In the cases of undesirable urination due to a medical cause, though, such as a urinary tract infection, the cat may only urinate in small amounts because of pain. With urination outside the litter box, the cat will also typically attempt to cover as he would normally do in the litter box.

With spraying, the cat's posture will be different. A cat about to spray will back up to a vertical object, he'll start twitching his tail, he'll usually tread with his front paws, then he'll send out a stream of urine. You may even notice that while spraying, he partially closes his eyes.

Spraying

Spray-marking is a behavior displayed by both confident and less-confident cats. It's not just turf marking, but rather a complex form of communication used by males and females. It's a language all its own. It can be an announcement of reproductive availability, a territorial marker, a display of aggression, a response to another cat's threat, a victory display after an aggressive confrontation, or a display of uncertainty. It's important to realize that where cats roam freely, spraying is a normal aspect of feline life. It's an aspect of their social structure that serves a function. Even though it's not a behavior you want displayed in your home, it's important you not view it as willful misbehavior. It's not about a cat being *bad*. When a cat sprays, he's reacting to a specific situation in a typically feline way. That said, it doesn't make it a good thing when it's happening in your living room. Note: If you have an intact male, he's eventually going to spray. You will never solve a spraying problem if the cat isn't neutered.

Pam's CatWise Reminder

SOME COMMON REASONS FOR SPRAY-MARKING
- To look for females in heat (with intact males)
- To mark territory
- To establish pecking order
- To self-soothe
- As a challenge to other cats
- When a new cat has been introduced into the environment
- A change in household routine
- A move to an unfamiliar environment (such as a new home)
- A victory display after an altercation with another cat
- A new person in the home
- On a person's belongings if he's unsure whether the person is a threat
- On unfamiliar objects (such as furniture) brought into the environment

Spraying is typically displayed against vertical objects but can also be performed on horizontal objects such as a bed or sofa. Your clue that's it's spray-marking will be that the urine appears as a thin stream as opposed to a puddle. Sometimes spraying is mistaken for undesirable urination because the cat parent notices only the urine puddle on the carpet by the wall and isn't aware that it dripped from the vertical target.

A higher-ranking cat may spray in more than one area to make sure other cats in the home understand his wide reach. A confident cat entering a new turf may spray as an announcement of his arrival. An outdoor cat will often routinely spray as he goes around the perimeter of his territory.

A cat lower in status may tend to limit his spraying to one area, often to carve out a little territory for himself, gather information (as a response to a direct threat from another cat), or as a passive display of aggression. If a less-confident cat is confronted with a direct threat, he may feel more comfortable spraying after the opponent has left because he knows the other cat is too strong or high-ranking to provoke. In this case, spraying becomes his response to a threat without risking an actual confrontation and potential injury. With ongoing disputes in the environment, lower-ranking cats may engage in a spraying war instead of face-to-face confrontation.

Some cats spray any new objects brought into the home, such as furniture, suitcases, delivered packages, and even grocery bags—anything that introduces an unfamiliar scent into the territory.

Although most people associate spraying behavior with male cats, females may also spray when threatened. In free-roaming environments, it's normal for females to spray when entering a hunting ground.

Sometimes a cat will exhibit a spraying posture without actually spraying any urine. A less-confident cat may display this because he might be too nervous to risk the response. It's almost as if he knows he won't be able to back up this threat.

Spraying by a less-confident cat is often used to gather very valuable information. The less-confident cat will spray to see what kind of "spray reaction" he gets in response. This is commonly the case when a new cat enters the "sprayer's" environment. The new cat's response to the spray-marking cat gives the one who did the initial spraying the information he doesn't have the nerve to gather through a direct encounter.

Managing Cats Who Spray

In a multicat household, you first must identify the sprayer. Unless you've witnessed the spray-marking, the best form of ID is camera surveillance, as with litter box issues. The other benefit of having camera surveillance is that you will not only see which cat did the spray-marking, but also what may have triggered it. Cats don't just spray without a reason, so you must examine the social environment within your cat household. It's time to play cat detective.

Discover the cause—Where is the cat spraying? Under what circumstances? Is it in one area? Perhaps a lower-ranking cat is trying to establish a little piece of territory. Did you bring a new cat into the home? Every time you add or subtract a cat it shakes up the social groups. If that's the case, it's time to do a proper cat introduction to help everyone feel more secure. Did something traumatic happen in the home? Increased stress? If there has been a traumatic event in your life, remember that cats are little emotional sponges who easily absorb the stress human family members are exhibiting.

If the target areas are under windows or near an entry door, the problem could be that one of your cats has noticed an unfamiliar cat on the property. If you have surveillance outdoors, check your camera to see if there was a feline interloper in your yard. If the spraying is due to the appearance of an outdoor cat, you'll need to block viewing access.

Don't restrict yourself to thinking the spraying is either the top-ranking cat asserting himself or the lowest-ranking cat trying to establish some piece of territory. It could easily be one of the middle cats. Sometimes it's the cat you didn't expect. That's why I stress the use of video surveillance. It can save you a lot of guessing so you can get right down to doing the necessary behavior work.

Pam's CatWise Caution

Don't confine a cat who is displaying litter box avoidance in a small room, such as a bathroom, with the litter box. He hasn't forgotten how to use it and doesn't need this in-your-face reminder. This method will only increase his stress level. It also does nothing to help you find the underlying cause of the behavior.

Seek and Destroy (the Urine Stain and Odor, That Is)

While some sprayed areas may be obvious to the eye and to the nose, others may not. Some cats pick the most unlikely places, and you must find all the soiled spots. Use a black light to identify all areas that need to be cleaned. You can buy a black light at your local pet product store or online. In a darkened room, the light will cause urine to fluoresce. You can either clean each area as you go, if there aren't too many soiled spots, or you can mark all the areas for easy identification and then do one big cleaning. What matters is that you get every spot identified and cleaned.

When I'm dealing with multiple areas in a client's home, I outline the soiled areas with painter's tape so I won't miss any spots. The tape is easy to remove and doesn't leave a residue. When doing your identification process, be sure to mark soiled walls, floor, carpets, and furniture. A cat may have gotten onto a piece of furniture and marked the wall behind it. Check closets, under beds, and behind doors. Some cats spray shoes and clothing, so run the black light over everything in the bottom of your closets as well as the lower portions of hanging clothes. It's also important to use the black light at the litter box areas in case one (or more) of the cats is spraying around the box itself, the room entrance, or the walls nearby.

Be prepared when you first turn the black light on. Things may look much worse than you imagined. The black light illuminates urine, but it will also illuminate spots where cats have vomited or had diarrhea accidents, so don't panic when you shine the light across the carpet and everything looks polka-dotted. In a multicat home where hairballs are a way of life, you're bound to see many illuminated spots that aren't urine stains. Some black lights have pictures on the packaging or on the manufacturer's websites to help you determine what urine stains typically look like when illuminated, compared to other stains. This isn't one of the more glamorous jobs when it comes to living with cats, but if you're going to solve the spraying problem, you must be a relentless detective and urine destroyer.

Clean and Neutralize

Even as you're trying to figure out the cause of the behavior, you must clean the soiled areas to prevent repeat visits as well as to prevent triggering other cats to start spraying.

If the soiled area is on the floor, cleanup is much easier because you simply wipe up the urine and then treat the spot with an odor neutralizer. If cleaning carpet, use paper towels to first absorb as much liquid as you can, being careful not to drive the urine down deeper into the carpet. When cleaning, use a product labeled specifically for cat urine stain and odor removal. Regular carpet or household cleaners will only mask the odor, and the residual odor molecules can still be detected by a cat's sensitive nose. To use the odor neutralizer, spray or pour it over the soiled area and treat according to the manufacturer's directions. In some cases, where urine might have gone through the carpet and into the padding, you might need a second application after it has dried. Manufacturers have toll-free numbers on their products or information on their websites, so be sure to get your questions answered if you're concerned about the safe use of a product on a specific fabric or surface.

Pam's CatWise Caution

Never carry a cat to the litter box and place him in there. Trust me, he knows where the box is and doesn't need to be reminded. Forcing a cat into a litter box isn't going to accomplish anything other than making him fearful of you. Training methods should never damage the bond you share with your cat.

Change the Cat's Association with the Area

Even if you've discovered and destroyed the spray marks, the cat can return to those areas repeatedly if you aren't also doing behavior work. Fortunately, you can break the behavior pattern.

Interactive play—To change a spraying cat's association with the area, conduct play sessions with him near those targeted spots. One of the best ways to improve a cat's mind-set is to trigger his prey drive. Conduct individual sessions a couple of times a day in the area. If there are several urine-sprayed areas, rotate your sessions to cover each one regularly. These sessions will help the cat think of these previously insecure areas as safer and more positive. Interactive play will also work on improving the cat's sense of confidence. Keep interactive toys stashed in the rooms where the cat is targeting so you can quickly access one if needed.

Redirect the cat's attention—When using this technique, it's important to get to the cat before he engages in the spraying behavior. You won't be able to distract him once he begins spraying. While your immediate reaction might be to want to yell or chase him away, this is counterproductive. If you yell, chase, or throw something at him, you'll only prevent the spraying behavior in that area at that specific time. He'll likely become a more secretive sprayer. Yelling at him doesn't alleviate his need to urine-mark and it also damages the trust bond between the two of you. Instead, use a positive form of distraction to change his current focus. Toss a toy or treat gently to get his attention. You can use any type of toy you know he likes. If you're in the midst of a spraying crisis, keep a couple of toys and treats in your pocket. I recommend to my clients that they wear a trainer's pouch (available at pet supply stores and online) so they can always have a supply of treats and small toys immediately handy.

Remember, this distraction method, playtime, and other techniques are to assist you while you work on uncovering the cause of the behavior. They must be used in combination with addressing the underlying motivation.

Clicker training—Another technique to include in your toolbox is clicker training. Use this training method to reward the cat for *not* spraying a target area. If he approaches a previously sprayed area and walks away or just sniffs without spraying, click and reward. I like to include clicker training because it gives control to the cat. He is making a choice on his own. If he sprays, he won't get a treat, but if he doesn't, he gets a reward. He quickly learns the desirable behavior will provide a benefit of greater value than the unwanted behavior.

I recommend cats be clicker trained in general. This way, you can use this training method to address whatever individual problems pop up, such as spraying, in this case. For more specifics on clicker training, refer to chapter 5.

Pam's CatWise Feline Fact

Cats who spray will often still use the litter box for normal urination and defecation.

Strategically placed food bowls—This is an old standby technique often used when trying to correct litter box problems in general. Cats don't eliminate where they eat, so if you place a few little food bowls or puzzle feeders at the targeted area, it may help change the cat's connection with the location. When it comes to spraying, sometimes the desire to spray-mark in that area can be stronger than the instinct not to urinate near a feeding station, so use this method in combination with the other training.

Visual blocking—If a cat sprays perimeter areas such as near the entry door, under windows, or near garage doors, it could mean there's a cat hanging around outdoors. Your cat is putting out a not-welcome sign. When outdoor feline intruders come around, it's typical of an indoor cat to choose an entry area for marking.

Use your black light to identify and clean the areas. Place opaque window paper over the bottom part of the windows to block your cats from seeing the outdoor cat. It also may cut down on the outdoor cats coming around if they can't see the cats inside.

In the evening, go outside and use the black light to check for spray marks from the intruder cat. Check around doors and windows. Clean any targeted spots. This may discourage other outdoor cats from spraying. It may also help any of your indoor cats from smelling the urine-spray near doors or windows.

Discourage outdoor cats from visiting by not feeding any strays where your indoor cats can see. If you have bird feeders, you may have to move them out of your indoor cats' view or take the feeders down altogether.

As a last resort, try installing a motion-activated water sprinkler to keep unwanted animals away.

Add a litter box—If an area is repeatedly targeted, try placing a high-sided litter box, like a tall plastic storage container, in that spot. Don't use a covered box. Cut a low entrance on one end as described earlier in this chapter. You may find the cat becomes satisfied with spraying inside the new box.

Pheromone therapy—As an added tool, use pheromone therapy in the areas being targeted. Pheromone diffusers contain synthetic feline facial pheromones that may help a cat feel more comfortable in the area. Pheromone products are available in pet supply stores and online. If you decide to use a pheromone product, you still must do the necessary behavior work, though.

Maintain consistent scent profile—If you know a cat gets upset and tends to spray unfamiliar objects, minimize scent intrusions. When bringing in new furniture, cover the piece with sheets, towels, or clothing that contains your scent to facilitate familiarity and help the object take on the household scent. Put a clean sock on your hand, gently wipe the cat's cheeks to collect some facial pheromones, and then rub the sock along the furniture legs or corners to help speed up scent recognition.

Leave objects such as bicycles, suitcases, or strollers in the garage or in areas where the cats don't go.

Address intercat stress issues—Changing a cat's impression of soiled areas is only part of the job. You also must help spraying cats and their adversaries come to a peaceful understanding. If you make only environmental changes, the cats' relationships with one another may remain negative.

It's time to work on relationships with a more intense form of diversion. When cats are interacting, watch for specific body postures and use a toy to redirect the aggressive cat's behavior. This is important to break any ongoing agonistic behavior patterns cats may have established. Try to divert the aggressor's attention *before* any actual confrontation occurs. You're trying to change the mind-set of both the intimidator and the intimidated. That's why timing is important. If you're late in the redirection and the intimidated cat is already scared, then it's not effective.

If the relationship between the spraying cat and one or more of the others is continually tense or even overtly hostile, they need a reintroduction. Sometimes the best way to correct the situation is to start from scratch and gradually expose them to one another under positive and controlled circumstances. If spraying behavior is caused by the addition of a new cat, keep the newcomer in the sanctuary room and slow down the introduction. You may have hurried through some of the steps.

Pam's CatWise Reminder

DEALING WITH SPRAY-MARKING CATS
- Thoroughly clean and neutralize all targeted areas.
- Identify the sprayer.
- Identify the trigger(s).
- Change a cat's association with an area through playtime or meals in that location.
- Address household stress.
- Increase vertical territory.
- Increase the number of safe areas such as hiding places.
- Increase the number of litter boxes and scatter them throughout the house so no one must pass an opponent's area.
- Increase the number and locations of feeding stations so no one can intimidate.
- Incorporate the use of synthetic pheromone therapy.
- Use distraction to change a cat's mind-set from negative to positive.
- Do twice-daily maintenance interactive play sessions.
- Reevaluate whether more overall or customized environmental enrichment is needed.
- Talk to your veterinarian about a referral to a behavior professional if you aren't seeing an improvement.

UNDESIRABLE URINATION

After your cat gets a clean bill of health, it's time to go through your checklist to see if it's a litter aversion, location aversion, too-dirty box, unappealing box setup, overcrowding, discomfort getting into the box, lack of escape potential, and so forth. Use the black light to find those soiled areas and clean them completely. Very often, the location a cat chooses will give insight into the reason for the behavior. For example, if you have a covered litter box, he may be urinating in an open location in order to have more visual warning time. If most or all the boxes are in the preferred areas of others, then this cat may be forced to eliminate on the carpet in an area where he feels safe.

If a cat repeatedly soils in a particular area, place a litter box there for now. He's letting you know his location preference and it'll ease his tension while you work on what could be triggering the behavior.

Sometimes a cat forms a negative association with the box during an illness, urinary infection, constipation, or any other cause for discomfort during elimination. In that case, it can often be resolved by setting out another litter box with a different type of litter.

Pam's CatWise Reminder

SOME SIGNS OF URINARY TRACT PROBLEMS
- Frequent litter box visits
- Voiding little or no urine each time
- Crying during urination attempts
- Blood in urine
- Straining during urination
- Frequent licking of genital area
- Urination outside the litter box
- Decreased appetite
- Depression
- Irritability
- Restlessness

The treatment for correcting undesirable urination starts as it does for the previous section on spraying. You must uncover the cause. In some cases, it could be obvious, such as a dirty box or a move to a new home, but in other cases it could be very subtle, such as a change in the relationship between certain cats.

Pam's CatWise Reminder

POTENTIAL REASONS FOR UNDESIRABLE URINATION
- Underlying medical problem
- Dirty litter box
- Loss or arrival of a cat
- Overcrowding
- Location aversion
- Litter aversion
- Wrong type of box
- Too small a litter box
- Abrupt change in litter brand or type
- Inadequate level of litter in box
- Move to a new house
- Renovation or construction
- New baby or family member
- Loss of family member (divorce, college, death)
- Change in schedule
- Negative association due to a medical problem
- Punishment
- Tension between cats or change in relationships
- Abuse
- Separation anxiety
- Social tension with a human family member

PANDORA SYNDROME

Feline urinary tract problems are difficult to diagnose and treat. Urinary tract problems used to be labeled under the umbrella term FLUTD (feline lower urinary tract disease) or FIC (feline idiopathic cystitis).

In 2011, a study was done at Ohio State University, led by Dr. Tony Buffington. The research revealed that when it comes to urinary issues, they are about more than just the bladder. There is a connection between the urinary recurrences and stress. Dr. Buffington coined the term for these urinary issues—*Pandora syndrome*—after the Greek myth of Pandora's box. The research connects the cat's big enemy, stress, to frequent recurrences of FIC.

FIC is so labeled when no identifiable cause can be found for the chronic bladder inflammation. The condition waxes and wanes. The research out of Ohio State University shows FIC to be one result of many problems triggered by stress.

Stress can affect all systems of the body (immune, gastrointestinal, cardiovascular, and so on), so it's not unusual for cats with Pandora syndrome to also exhibit other sickness behaviors such as loss of appetite, diarrhea, vomiting, etc.

The cats who are most susceptible are the ones who are more nervous, fearful, and sensitive in general. It is believed these cats have an abnormal stress response system. They startle more easily than other cats and stay hyperalert.

Diagnosis of Pandora syndrome is difficult since the problem has many causes. A thorough exam, along with urinalysis and blood-work, is performed. A thorough behavioral history is needed as well. Your cat's veterinarian needs to know about the home environment, stressful events, or any trauma. Did something happen in the cat's life that was traumatic and as a result the cat remains in a state of stress, even in the absence of any threat? It's also important for the veterinarian to know whether the cat was orphaned, if the cat was socialized as a kitten, and anything else that will help put the pieces of the puzzle together.

Addressing Pandora syndrome—Your cat's veterinarian will prescribe as needed, including pain relief and anti-inflammatory medication. The rest of the treatment involves reducing stress in your cat's environment. For a cat with Pandora syndrome, don't overlook any potential stress trigger. The cure will come from what you can do to lower stress and provide an ongoing sense of security.

Cats in a multicat household experience a higher degree of stress due to conflicts within the various social groups, about availability of resources, and simply over whether there's enough personal space to go around. If you have one or more cats who experience recurring urinary problems, it may mean more has to be done when it comes to stress management.

Think beyond what your average cat needs when it comes to helping a cat suffering with Pandora syndrome. Regarding mealtime, for example, it may not only be that the cat needs a separate, quiet feeding station. He may need you there when he eats. He may get stressed if the food temperature is inconsistent, or if the meal schedule isn't consistent. If you feed him in the kitchen, the dishwasher shouldn't be running. This isn't the time for a family member to be loading or unloading the dishwasher or handwashing dishes that could cause clanking, banging sounds.

Cats with Pandora syndrome need the following:

- Safe, personal space
- Safe placement of key resources
- Safe playtime
- Social contact in the way the cat prefers
- Consistent schedule
- Very gradual transitions
- No conflicts with other cats or pets in the home

- Reduced noise in the home
- Choice
- Avenues of escape
- Hiding places
- Time with you

At this point, you should have a good understanding of why personal space, safety, stress management, and enrichment matter in a cat's life. You've learned about the social structure of cats, the need for territory, and ways to create secure resource availability. If any of your cats has a litter box issue that is not medically caused, it's time to reexamine whether some aspects of your cats' social structure or environment might have fallen through the cracks.

The problem relationship may not even be between cats, so keep that in mind as you do your detective work. The tension may be between a cat and a human family member. This could be due to a person who is new to the family, punishment from someone in the family, inconsistent interaction, or even abuse. As you examine the relationships between the cats, also carefully review the social relationship between cats and the rest of the family.

Soiled Areas Can Provide Clues

Very often, *where* a cat chooses to eliminate can provide clues as to *why* he's not using the box. Here are some common examples:

Elimination near the litter box—This often means the cat is trying to go in the box but either something about the box conditions are bad (too dirty, too small, too difficult to step into, covered, unsafe) or it could be that due to a medical reason he just couldn't get there in time. If the cat gets a clean bill of health, go through a litter box checklist to see what it is about the box setup that is unappealing or unsafe. Remember to look at it from your cat's point of view and not yours.

Eliminating on a person's belongings—If the person is the cat parent, it could be a distress call due to a change in schedule or separation anxiety. The cat may be trying to self-soothe by mixing his scent with the person's scent. If the belongings are those of a guest, it could be stress due to not knowing if this person is a threat or not. It could also be a cat's attempt to mix scents with the unfamiliar person to share information. Although not pleasant, it's not necessarily hostile; it's just the cat's way of doing information gathering in the most efficient method—through scent. Either way, the cat is in distress and the situation needs to be addressed by uncovering the cause of the cat's concern, then creating more security, improving confidence, and incorporating enrichment activities.

Elimination on the bed—The cat parent's bed contains the most concentrated scents and it can be comforting for a scared or intimidated cat to choose that location for security reasons. A cat may also pee on a cat parent's bed if experiencing separation anxiety.

The bed, being an elevated location, also provides more visual warning time for a cat to see who might be coming. Beds, as well as upholstered furniture, when you think about it from a cat's perspective, meet the requirements of litter substrate for the most part. The surface is soft and absorbent. Even though the cat is unable to cover his urine, the need for safety that elevation provides becomes more important.

To address this, look at potential stress triggers such as intercat relationships or changes in the home. If it's due to separation anxiety, make improvements to your environmental enrichment plan and reevaluate whether recent inconsistencies in your schedule or your increased absence could be causing this anxiety. Address any intercat stress and make sure litter box setups and locations are appealing. If you think separation anxiety is the cause, refer to chapter 10.

Elimination on kitchen counters—Being elevated, the cat can have extra warning time to watch for adversaries. With the wall right behind him, he also has the added security of knowing no one can sneak up behind him.

To address this, get to the root of whatever intercat conflict is occurring so you can work on creating harmony. This cat is clearly afraid. Do the necessary behavior work to ease the tension between the cats, and that might mean a total reintroduction. If this is a repeated pattern, set up a security camera so you can identify the trigger.

Elimination in the open part of a room—Often this is due to a medical problem. The cat is on the way to the litter box and simply can't make it. It's common when there's a urinary tract issue for the cat to retain his urine as long as possible due to the pain he feels upon urination. You may even notice the cat attempts to cover afterward.

Once medical reasons are ruled out, it could be that the cat simply feels more comfortable eliminating in an open area where he can see all around him. Look at the litter box setups and make sure he has boxes that aren't covered or hidden in corners. If there isn't a box in the room in which he is urinating, then he might be telling you this is his location choice.

Elimination in hidden locations—This is a very frightened cat. He will eliminate behind furniture or in closets, often making no attempt to cover, and then when he has finished urinating, he immediately leaves the location.

The underlying cause of his fear must be uncovered. Address intercat issues and make sure he has safe access to all resources.

Cats who have been punished for elimination outside the litter box may also choose more secretive locations. If there are pariah cats (very low ranking in the hierarchy) in a multicat environment, they will often resort to eliminating in hidden areas.

For more specifics on stress reduction, refer to chapter 10.

Guarding, Patrolling, and Being First

In a multicat home, you may discover a litter box being guarded by a cat. Guarding behavior can be obvious, in the form of physically blocking the box, or it can be so subtle you may miss it. What may appear to be a cat casually lounging in the hallway outside the room where the litter box is located may actually be a cat on guard. The hallway can be a neutral pathway, so the other cats may not suspect the blocking or ambushing about to take place. The cat on guard may not even need to engage in an actual confrontation—mere intimidation may work well enough. That's another reason to ensure your litter box locations allow easy access, escape, and visual warning, and to be sure there are ample litter box sites.

A common and very normal behavior often occurs when it comes time for you to wash the litter box. Have you noticed when you've just washed the box and replenished it with fresh litter, there's one cat who always insists on being first to use it? He may impatiently pace back and forth as he waits for you to finish. In some cases, he might not even wait until you've finished refilling the box, or he might sit and watch with intense focus as you handle "his" box. It's not unusual for a cat with higher status to make sure he's the one to christen the fresh litter or spend time in the box. This is normal behavior.

POOPING OUTSIDE THE LITTER BOX

As with the previous sections on urination issues, rule out medical issues first. There are several medical conditions that could cause a cat to feel discomfort in the box during defecation, such as constipation, diarrhea, inflammatory bowel disease, and more. If you have a covered litter box, a cat may feel too cramped in there while trying to position himself to defecate, especially if he's already experiencing physical discomfort.

Separate Boxes for Separate Functions

There are some cats who don't defecate in the same location designated for urination. It may be that urination has more territorial connection. Only the cats know the reason and none of them has disclosed their secret yet. A simple solution is to make another box available for defecation. Don't place the box next to the original box or it'll be viewed as one big box and the cat may still reject it. Put the second box in the same room, but at a distance—perhaps on the opposite side. In some cases, though, you may have to place the second box in a separate room. Your cat will let you know when you have the correct distance between the boxes.

It Could Be a Safety Issue

Cats often take a bit longer to defecate than urinate. In a multicat household where there is intercat aggression, it may be too stressful for a cat to stay in the litter box too long. If the box is covered, wedged in a corner, or hidden in a closet, this also reduces escape potential. He may feel it's safer to defecate in another location that provides more visual warning.

Provide uncovered boxes and make sure there are enough boxes located throughout the home. Don't place them in areas where a cat would feel trapped or confined. Reduce the chances of a cat getting ambushed.

Litter Preference

A cat may have a substrate preference when it comes to litter texture for defecation versus urination. If you think that might be

Pam's CatWise Reminder

PREVENTING LITTER BOX ISSUES

- Always rule out medical issues first and address any ongoing medical concerns.
- Feeding stations should create peace and security for each cat.
- Have litter boxes in each cat's preferred area so no one must cross another cat's turf.
- Keep litter boxes clean.
- Don't use covered litter boxes.
- Provide adequate personal space.
- Provide opportunities for climbing and access to elevated locations without dead ends.
- Incorporate interactive playtime and solo play.
- Set up cozy hiding places.
- Address conflicts between cats and do reintroductions if needed.
- Ease cats through changes in the household.
- Do a positive, gradual introduction of any new cat or dog in the home.
- Provide activities for the cats to prevent separation anxiety.
- Provide appealing places for scratching and stretching.
- Don't wait until a problem has been ongoing before addressing it.
- Never punish a cat for an unwanted behavior. (Remember, every behavior serves a purpose.)

the case, offer another litter box with a litter that has a different texture. In general, cats prefer a soft, sandy texture. If your cat is defecating on the floor or other hard surface and won't go in the box even after you've tried different litters, set out an empty box with no litter inside. If the cat poops in the box when there's no litter, keep the box available to him and then eventually add a very small amount of litter. If he continues to accept that, you can gradually increase the amount.

The Cleanliness Factor

If there is any waste already in the box, a cat may decide it can't be used. He may urinate in the box but then feel it's now not clean enough for defecation. Make sure you scoop at least twice a day. Reevaluate whether you need to increase the number of boxes as well. And although I am not a fan of electronic self-cleaning boxes, if you have a cat who simply will not use a box that has been soiled at all, you may need to add a self-cleaning box in his area in addition to traditional boxes.

NEED MORE HELP WITH LITTER BOX PROBLEMS?

Since litter box issues can often be a deal breaker when it comes to whether a cat stays in the family or ends up taking that one-way trip to the shelter, talk to your veterinarian if you're unable to resolve the problem. Ask for a referral to a veterinary behaviorist or certified cat behavior consultant. Don't give up on your cat. Refer to chapter 12 for more information on contacting a behavior professional.

Scratching the Surface: Training Cats to Scratch Where You Want Them To

It's imperative that as cat parents we understand scratching behavior and how to supply what cats need. Failure to do both will likely result not only in damage to furniture but damage to the relationship with our cats. And remember, with multiple cats you have just that many more claws to think about.

SCRATCHING 101

Many people believe cats scratch just to sharpen their claws. Scratching is an innate behavior and provides the opportunity to remove the outer dead sheath from the nail, but that's only a minor part of the story.

Marking

As you've read, a cat is a master at communication and makes use of every form of communication available to keep things running smoothly in and around her turf. When a cat scratches an object, the claw marks serve as a visual marker. Since cats keep the peace through avoidance and respecting distance, this sign is very helpful. An approaching cat can see the mark from a distance and perhaps avoid trouble by realizing she's in someone else's territory. There are also scent glands in the cat's paw pads, so when she presses her paws against whatever she's scratching, she leaves a scent.

Marking through scratching is not just about keeping other cats away. It's how a cat finds comfort when she returns to an area, sees her scratch marks, and detects her familiar scent.

Emotions and Displacement

Scratching is one way a cat may display emotion, such as excitement when you walk in the door at the end of the day. She may run over to the scratching post when she hears your key in the lock. In anticipation of dinner, she may also scratch when she sees you heading toward the kitchen.

She may also take out her social frustrations or other stresses on the post. Displacement may be exhibited by scratching. If a cat is denied access to something she wants, she may relieve her frustration by engaging in a healthy scratching session at the nearest post.

Stretching and Toning

Finally, it's about the incredible stretch a good scratch provides. A cat has a very flexible spine, and she can curl up in the tightest ball during naps. Imagine how incredibly good it must feel to sink her claws into the top of the scratching post and stretch her back and shoulder muscles. It's not at all unusual to see a cat head for the scratching post immediately after napping or after a long session of windowsill bird-watching.

Scratching Is an Important Part of Being a Cat

Scratching is a behavior you want to encourage, as it contributes to a cat's physical and emotional health. When it comes to marking behavior, a cat's choice to scratch and not spray is certainly much more desirable. The decision to scratch instead of having a physical confrontation with another cat is a better one as well. Scratching behavior is an important aspect of helping maintain a peaceful multicat environment. People have a problem, understandably, with *where* a cat may choose to scratch, but that's where the right training and the right equipment come in.

CHOOSE THE RIGHT SCRATCHING POST

Cats can scratch on vertical surfaces and some also like to scratch on horizontal ones. Many cats like to engage in both types. Most cats tend to scratch on vertical objects because it leaves a more easily seen visual mark and it better enables them to get a good stretch. As in other aspects of cat life, it helps to pay attention to individual preferences.

Choose scratching posts that are tall, sturdy, and covered in a rough material such as sisal. Carpet-covered posts commonly found in pet supply and discount stores are a waste of money. When a cat sinks her nails into the post, she wants the right kind of resistance to pull off those dead nail sheaths. With a carpet-covered post, a cat just tends to get her nails caught in the fiber loops. Your cats don't care about brightly covered carpets or toys dangling from a spring on the top. If your cats are scratching the furniture, then you probably bought the wrong posts.

Don't settle for just any sisal-covered post. The post should be tall and sturdy with a good, heavy base. If the post wobbles, it's unacceptable (and may be dangerous) and will quickly be rejected by a cat. It also needs to be tall enough for a cat to get a full stretch. The taller the post, the wider the base needs to be to prevent it from toppling over.

If you're into DIY projects, you may want to construct homemade posts for your cats. This way, you can customize the height and ensure the base is sturdy enough. Depending on a cat's preference, wrap the post with sisal or rope. You may have a cat or two with a preference for scratching on bare wood. Pay attention to texture preferences by looking at where your cats tend to scratch now.

For the cats who like horizontal or incline scratching, purchase sisal-covered scratching pads or the very popular corrugated cardboard scratchers. The cardboard scratchers come in a variety of inclines and shapes to accommodate specific scratching needs.

Pam's CatWise Caution

Don't try to teach a cat to use a scratching post by placing her paws on it. It may frighten the cat and create a negative association with the post. Forcing a cat to do something always backfires.

Cats generally take to the right kind of scratching post immediately, but if you think your cats aren't, use an interactive toy and play around the post to get them interested. Place the post on its side initially for your cats to climb on and then eventually stand it up when they get the idea. Once they sink their claws in, they'll become convinced of the post's appeal. If you've ever punished your cats for scratching on inappropriate objects, you may have to entice them a little because they might be afraid to scratch in your presence. Use toys and treats to tempt them, but don't force the issue. Add some interest by rubbing some loose catnip on the post. If your cats respond to catnip, that may just be the secret ingredient for getting them to at least investigate. They may also wait to check out the post when you aren't around.

TOO MANY CATS, TOO FEW POSTS

Since scratching is a marking behavior, provide multiple posts and pads throughout the home to ensure each cat has access. Pay attention to individual scratching preferences so you can meet each cat's needs.

PLACE POSTS IN THE RIGHT LOCATIONS

The first places to put scratching posts are where your cats may already be scratching. When locating posts, keep a few things in mind: (1) territories and preferred areas; (2) where your cats like to scratch; and (3) socially significant areas. Scatter the scratching posts so you cover those three factors. If it isn't in your budget to buy multiple vertical posts, or if you aren't sure about certain locations, scatter a few of the corrugated cardboard scratchers around.

Some cats scratch doorways or furniture near room entrances to mark their turf. If that's the case with your cats, place posts in those areas so cats can comfortably mark their perimeters. Don't put a post in the back corner of a room if a cat's preference is to mark upon first entering. Scratching posts may not be the most beautiful pieces of décor, but proper placement can mean the difference between a nice-looking sofa and a scratched one.

If a cat is spraying in a certain area, in addition to doing the necessary behavior work, place a scratching post in the room to help dissolve the stress she associates with that area. She may be satisfied with scratching instead of spraying.

For cats who get concerned about company coming through the front door, place a post right inside the entrance, or near where cats tend to supervise new arrivals.

If there's an area where the cats tend to spend much of their time, place a couple of posts and/or scratching pads there. Some cats may like being out of the main flow of traffic, but others may feel more comfortable right in the center of the room. Place some posts in open areas and some in more protected locations. This may also help maintain peace within the multicat family.

FURNITURE SCRATCHING

Cats will choose a piece of furniture if there isn't a better alternative for them. When looking for a scratching surface, cats choose sturdy objects with appealing textures and convenient locations. Sofas or chairs are common targets because they're tall, so cats can get a good stretch, and the material allows them to dig their nails in and rake them down the surface.

Since scratching is an innate behavior, you can't prevent it by scolding, hitting, squirting water, or chasing. The desire to scratch will remain, but you will have introduced fear into the mix. You need to redirect them to an appropriate target. If you just try to prevent scratching, the cats will find other locations and will become increasingly anxious. You may think reprimanding works because a cat will run whenever she sees you. You may be convinced the cat who is scratching knows she's being "bad," but what's happening is she's now associating your presence with fear. She's running because her bond with you is deteriorating—not because you have her well trained. Since the cat needs to scratch, every time she has the desire she'll now feel anxious. That only leads her to want to scratch more for displacement, or she may start overgrooming to relieve her frustration and confusion. Either way, the cat isn't happy, and she has been prevented from engaging in a normal, healthy behavior.

To correct furniture scratching, you need a twofold approach. Make the currently used spot unappealing and then create a better alternative. That way, you turn a negative into a positive and allow your cats to engage in this natural aspect of feline life.

Pam's CatWise Caution

If you come home and find a newly scratched area on the furniture, don't bring your cat over to it for punishment. She'll have no idea why you're acting this way and will become afraid of you. This punishment is inhumane and totally counterproductive.

You've probably tried methods such as covering scratched areas with aluminum foil and deterrent sprays and have come to the realization they don't work. There's an easier solution for creating an unappealing scratching surface. Cover the scratched areas of the furniture with Sticky Paws. This is a double-sided tape made for this purpose. The tape's adhesive won't leave a residue. The product is readily available in pet supply stores and online and comes in strips or rolls. It's very easy to use. Just make sure the humans in the family know the tape is in place so nobody leans against it.

If the scratched area of the sofa or chair is too massive to cover with the tape, then cover the entire piece with a sheet or other smooth fabric. Tuck the sheet in all around and secure it at the bottom so cats can't get up underneath.

Now that you've made that spot unappealing, give the cat a better option. This alternative must be not only better but also convenient. Place the scratching post right next to the piece of furniture that was being scratched. In order to shift the cat's focus to the post, the alternative must be obvious. The cat will walk over to the sofa and discover that her usual scratching surface is no longer effective. Instead of having to search for an alternative, she'll find this interesting scratching post right there. Rub a little catnip on the post for added incentive. Leave the Sticky Paws tape in place until you're sure the cat has been retrained to the post.

If a cat is horizontally scratching an area of carpet, place the scratching pad right over that spot. If the cat moves the pad to get to the carpet, put a heavy-duty carpet runner down and then place scratching pads on top and around the area. Even though a cat may be scratching the carpet horizontally, you may want to offer a vertical post as well as a horizontal pad. She may have been scratching the carpet because it was the only effective texture. However, it may be the location the cat preferred.

If the cat is scratching the mat or area rug near an entry door or entrance to a room, it may not be the rug she likes, but the fact that it's the only available scratchable object nearby. It may be that she's trying to mark the entrance. This is where it's very helpful to pay attention to the *why* and the *where* when it comes to scratching preferences.

It's fine for cats to share the posts, too, so long as they don't squabble over them but take their turns. Also, something people often overlook is how each cat uses her scratching areas; some cats prefer horizontal (pads) to vertical (posts). That's why it's really important to pay attention to where cats exhibit behaviors. The clues are always there.

WHEN SHOULD SCRATCHING POSTS BE REPLACED?

A good-quality scratching post should hold up for a long time. Rope-wrapped posts may eventually loosen over time, and you'll just need to tighten up the ropes. You shouldn't have to worry about replacing vertical posts very often.

When you do get to the point of feeling a post needs to be replaced, buy the new one and place it next to the old one. Don't make the mistake of looking at a worn-out, tattered scratching post and thinking you should just trash it for a brand-new one. Your cats have gotten that post just the way they want it. That worn-out post has lots of scents and good visual marks. It's obviously a well-loved, well-used tool in a perfect location. Instead of having it simply disappear, just put the new post nearby. Rub some catnip on the new one for extra appeal.

After your cats have been routinely using the new post instead of the old one, you can then retire the worn one. If it's still getting used, though, my recommendation is to leave it there. It may not look pretty, but by giving your cats that choice you may be keeping everyone happy and content.

NAIL CAPS

Cats are much happier and more confident when they can engage in natural behaviors. If you provide the right kind of scratching surfaces in the right locations, you don't need to resort to unnatural solutions and compromises, like gluing plastic caps on their paws.

I don't like the nail caps for a few reasons. The cat can't dig her nails in to get a good stretch. She also can't leave a visual mark. The application of the nail caps can be stressful. If you can't trim your cat's nails and apply the caps at home, then that means you must take her to the veterinary clinic to have it done on an ongoing basis.

With the nail cap application, you first must trim the nails, put glue in the cap, then properly fit it on the cat's nail. The caps must be reapplied frequently as the nails grow, and it's not unusual for a couple to accidentally pop off in between scheduled reapplications.

I'm not convinced nail caps are totally comfortable for a cat to wear, because the capped nails don't fit back into their sheaths.

Let your cat be a cat. Provide the right posts and pads in the right places.

DECLAWING

Don't do it to any cat. Ever. I had hoped that by the time this book was published, declawing would be illegal all over the world, but sadly, that's not the case. While it is illegal in many countries, it's still not illegal in all states in the U.S. as of this writing.

If you've read the previous sections of this chapter, you understand how important it is for cats to be able to scratch. Having claws is a vital part of being a cat. If you get the right scratching posts, locate them properly, set up effective and humane deterrents, and reward your cats for using the posts, you shouldn't have a furniture-scratching problem. If you still do, then one or more of the elements hasn't been done correctly yet. People also consider declawing because they're afraid of being scratched themselves or having the cat scratch another family member. Cats prefer not to have physical confrontations. They posture so much as a warning to back off. Cats would prefer to escape and only use their claws when all other options are exhausted or unavailable. If you pay attention to your cat's body language and respect a cat's need for *choice* concerning whether to engage or not, then the claws will stay sheathed.

Declawing is a very controversial topic and it's slowly becoming illegal in more places, but not quickly enough as far as I'm concerned. Declawing is inhumane. The bottom line: Don't love your furniture more than you love your cats.

Sadly, for many misinformed cat parents, it has become as routine as vaccinations. The declawing procedure is an amputation of the top joints of the toes. Recovery is extremely painful, and many cats can remain sensitive about their paws long after the healing period. Phantom pain is possible throughout the life of a cat.

Pam's CatWise Caution

THE REALITIES OF DECLAWING

- Cats experience pain during recovery and many endure pain for the rest of their lives.
- Declawing is amputation with the added cruelty that the cat must bear weight on those paws afterward.
- Declawed cats can be reluctant to have their paws touched long after surgical recovery, and in some cases, for the rest of their lives.
- A study published in the *Journal of Feline Medicine and Surgery* reported that declawed cats are more likely to experience long-term pain, bite, have litter box problems, and display increased aggression.
- Cats are digitigrade, which means they walk on their toes, so declawing changes the way they must walk, and they can end up with arthritis.
- Spinal pain can be the result of declawing.
- Case closed.

Declawing takes away the cat's first line of defense should she ever escape outside. It also hinders her ability to escape from an attacker by climbing. Scratching is such a vital part of a cat's physical and psychological well-being that it's tragic when it's taken away needlessly.

If you have one or more declawed cats and you're adding a new cat into the environment, you may be thinking she'll have to be declawed as well to even the playing field. That's not true. Keep the new cat's nails trimmed and she'll be fine. Do a proper introduction and provide the necessary environmental enrichment elements detailed in this book.

Keeping the Lid on Aggression

WHY DO CATS FIGHT?

Aggression is a normal response to a threatening situation in the animal world. While you certainly don't want it displayed in your home, keep in mind it's a natural part of survival. It's how an animal may need to protect himself in response to a perceived threat. To solve the problem, you must uncover what the cat is saying through his behavior. In other words, why does he feel threatened?

Aggression is either offensive or defensive and overt or covert. But in almost all cases, cats would rather avoid actual physical conflict, and that's why they have such an elaborate repertoire of postures. It's to the cat's advantage not to engage in a battle that might leave him injured or worse. In a cat-dense environment such as a large, multicat home, territories are small and overlapping, and some cats feel they are left with no other choice. Fighting is the last resort after all other forms of communication have failed and there's no escape option.

Why Can't My Cats Just Get Along?

- Underlying medical causes that could contribute to aggression, especially ongoing aggressive behavior, must be ruled out before assuming this a behavior problem. Cats with conditions such as hyperthyroidism, hyperesthesia, epilepsy, and others can display aggressive behavior.

- A cat in physical pain can display aggression when handled or touched. A cat buddy may rub up against him, solicit play, or try to share a napping spot and be greeted with an aggressive response.

- The onset of social maturity at about two to four years of age can trigger episodes of aggression.

- Changes in the social structure due to the addition or absence of a cat can also trigger aggression. When a new cat is introduced into the household, displays of aggression may be overt or covert. A cat may go for an all-out physical confrontation, or the aggression may be under the radar, employing more passive methods, such as spray-marking.

- Intact male cats are infamous for fighting, especially when competing for a female.

- Changes to a cat's physical environment, such as a move to a new home, renovation, or furniture rearrangement (especially when rearrangement disrupts territory or if it involves cat furniture), can cause fighting.

- Abrupt changes in daily routine can cause cats to take out frustrations on one another.

- Fighting can occur when cats are defending territory.

- Boredom and lack of environmental enrichment can result in fighting.

- Stress. This is a big one and can be included in all other reasons. Stressed cats can quickly become reactive, especially when stress is ongoing.

- Lack of resource availability can result in fighting and resource guarding.

- Redirected aggression can trigger a cat fight if one cat is already reactive due to something that has caused him to be frustrated, overstimulated, or frightened.
- Fighting can occur when there is a lack of territory—a cat-dense environment with simply not enough space for everyone.

When dealing with behavior problems in general, especially ones as serious as aggression, many people tend to label cats. I get so many calls to my office where the first words out of the cat parent's mouth are "My cat is mean," or "My cat is crazy."

Don't label your cat, because it doesn't help you solve the problem. When a cat displays an unwanted behavior, it doesn't mean the cat will always act that way under other circumstances. Look at behavior as something an animal is doing at that specific time rather than using a blanket label for a cat's temperament. You'll be in a much better position to uncover the cause and correct the problem.

Think of how many cats have probably been relinquished to shelters, abandoned, or euthanized because people labeled them rather than looking at the following:

- Circumstances surrounding the behavior
- Possible behavior trigger
- What the cat was communicating by the behavior
- What could have been done to change the cat's response

Since aggression can lead to injury to animals and people in the home, if you can't find the cause after ruling out medical issues, talk to your veterinarian about a referral to a behavior professional. There *is a reason* for the behavior, and a certified professional can help identify it and provide a customized treatment plan.

In many cases, though, if you look at the specific situation instead of labeling the cat, you can identify the trigger.

Pam's CatWise Caution

- Punishment for aggressive behavior (or any unwanted behavior) is counterproductive and will ruin your bond with your cat.
- Physical punishment increases the cat's fear and can lead to more serious injury to family members.
- Don't yell at the cat, as it only increases fear and defensiveness.
- Don't leave cats alone to "fight it out" because serious injury can occur, and it may permanently damage the relationship.
- Don't try to pick up or restrain a cat showing aggression, because you risk serious injury.

HOW TO TELL IF YOUR CATS ARE PLAYING OR FIGHTING

This is something I'm frequently asked because cat parents don't want to stop a fun play session, but they certainly don't want to allow a fight to continue. Here are some general guidelines to help you figure out whether your cats are fighting or merely enthusiastically playing:

1. Play can often look more aggressive than we'd expect. Even when kittens play with one another, it can look a little rough. During an enthusiastic play session cats can wrestle and tackle one another. It can be easy to misinterpret playtime exuberance for aggression.

2. Cats who normally have an antagonistic relationship or cats who are unfamiliar with one another don't usually engage in play

together. If you notice that two cats who tend to be more opponents than friends are now wrestling, it probably isn't a friendly
encounter. Unfamiliar or hostile cats can develop a friendly relationship and start playing together, but that's something that happens
after some behavior work and after learning to coexist peacefully in
the same environment. They won't suddenly go from being ene-
mies to playmates without interim steps.

3. Body language and type of vocalization are clues to determine whether cats are enjoying a play session or having some
sort of turf war. Here are some typical signs of playtime:

- Claws remain sheathed
- Ears remain in normal position and not pinned back
- No piloerection of hair
- No growling
- No hissing
- No pain shrieks
- Any biting is minimal and done without causing pain or
  injury

4. When wrestling and chasing between cats is done in play,
you should notice the cats take turns. With wrestling, observe
whether they each spend equal time being on the top and bottom. If you constantly notice the same cat pinned on the bottom,
the encounter may not be playtime. Chasing should also be recip-
rocal. Pay attention to whether you see the same cat always in the
position of being pursued.

What to Do If Your Cats Are Fighting

Never put yourself in the middle of the fight or reach your hand
in between them to try to physically separate them because you
will almost certainly get injured, perhaps very seriously. The safe

way to separate fighting cats is to make a sudden noise to startle them. Clap your hands, bang a pot on the counter, or drop a book on the floor. Create some noise that startles them but keeps you at a safe distance.

If the cats separate and then immediately come back together to continue fighting, use something safe to block their view of each other so that you can usher one cat into another room. A large piece of cardboard, a sofa cushion, or anything that will create a visual barrier will do.

Once the cats are in separate rooms, lower the lighting in each room to help them feel calm and hidden. Keep the cats separated for as long as it takes for their behavior to return to normal and for them to be comfortable interacting with you. How long they will need to be separated will depend on the severity of the fight. Depending on how the cats react when they're together again, you may need to separate them for a longer time and do a reintroduction. More on this later in the chapter.

Just Say NO to the Spray Bottle

It may seem like a convenient way to train, but the unintended secondary message the cat receives is to be afraid of you. Spraying a cat for hissing at another cat or swatting at him will stop the behavior in the short term, but it will also teach the cat that you are to be feared. It also does nothing toward helping the relationship between the cats. Aggression will still exist between them, but they'll have the added fear of knowing you are also a threat.

As with all aspects of training cats to do what *you* want them to do, figure out the reason for the behavior so you can supply a better option or help them change their association.

Prevent Cat Fights

If your cats have an antagonistic or unpredictable relationship with one another, do the necessary behavior work to encourage a more peaceful coexistence. Begin by making changes in the environment so they don't have to compete for resources. You may need more litter boxes and feeding stations spread throughout the house. Increase the number of elevated locations, cat trees and/or perches, and hiding places.

In some cases, the cats may be picking on one another because they don't have adequate constructive outlets for their energy. Cats are predators who rely on stimulation throughout the day, in combination with times of rest. Follow a regular schedule of doing at least twice-daily interactive play sessions. In addition to interactive playtime, set up puzzle feeders and other puzzle toys to keep your cats occupied when you aren't home. If the cats have enjoyable outlets to satisfy their need for stimulation, along with the security of having enough personal space, they may be less likely to use one another for target practice.

Pam's CatWise Tip

If your cats have a good relationship but playtime tends to get a little too raucous, monitor the situation in case you need to insert some positive diversion should playtime teeter on the edge of aggression. Roll a Ping-Pong ball, toss some treats, or drop a couple of toys on the floor. It's always a good idea to have toys and treats stashed conveniently nearby, because you never know when a little distraction will be needed.

GET FAMILIAR WITH THE
DIFFERENT TYPES OF AGGRESSION

To solve the problem, you need to identify which type of aggression is being displayed and the circumstances surrounding the behavior. Aggression can be very frightening for cat parents, whether directed at another cat or at humans. Cat bites can be very serious, and aggression is a problem that must be dealt with correctly so no one gets hurt. Here are some common types of aggressive behavior.

Intercat Aggression

Testosterone is a big factor in aggressive behavior between male cats. Toms commonly fight for territory and available females. The solution is to neuter your cats and keep them indoors. If allowed outdoors, do so in a controlled way, such as an outdoor enclosure or leash walking.

The onset of social maturity (between two and four years old) can spark intercat aggression in a home where the cats have previously coexisted peacefully. If you have a couple of cats who are reaching social maturity at about the same time, watch for signs of increasing agitation. Just because the behaviors may not include hissing, growling, or outright physical battles doesn't mean there isn't mounting tension. Watch body postures and pay attention to litter box habits and challenges to territory.

A cat who isn't a member of your household can also spark this type of aggression. If you allow any of your cats outdoors, they could be getting into battles with roaming cats. If your cats are indoor only, the sight of an unfamiliar outdoor cat could trigger spray-marking or redirected aggression toward companion animals.

The addition of a new cat into the household can easily spark aggression that can be overt or covert.

Addressing intercat aggression—Neuter and spay! Without taking care of that first, you'll just be fighting a losing battle.

Reduce territorial aggression and stress by doing a gradual, careful introduction of a new cat, as described in chapter 4.

Work on environmental enrichment if necessary to be sure everyone has ample space. Increase vertical territory, add extra litter boxes and locations, and be perceptive of cat communication.

Separate cats displaying aggressive behavior, even if they've been together for a long time, while you figure out the underlying cause. Depending upon the severity of the problem, you may have to do a total reintroduction, as described later in this chapter.

Cats allowed outdoors can return home in an agitated state and behave aggressively toward companion cats. Keep your cats indoors to prevent conflicts with other outdoor cats and any redirected aggression once they return home. If the intercat aggression between cat companions is caused by the appearance of an unfamiliar cat outside, follow the instructions in the section of this chapter titled "Redirected Aggression."

Fear Aggression

A frightened cat's first choice will be to avoid potential conflict altogether and escape. If he can't escape or if his visual and vocal warnings have had no effect and he feels backed into a corner, a cat may resort to aggression. First, he will display a defensive body posture, such as an arched back with piloerection of fur. He may then crouch with ears rotated back and flattened against the head. His pupils will be dilated, and he'll probably growl and hiss. He may even be caught between two positions at once. His upper body and front feet may face forward, ready to do battle if necessary, but his hindquarters may face sideways, ready to help him bolt at the first opportunity for escape. He will stay in the defensive posture until escape becomes possible or the opponent retreats.

A cat who wasn't exposed to a variety of stimuli as a kitten (such as unfamiliar places, noises, being handled, visitors in the home) may exhibit this behavior more frequently. This is also a common display when the cat is taken to the veterinary clinic, especially if behavior work wasn't done to help decrease his fear of the experience. Animal hospital staff are all too familiar with the tightly wound, unhappy furball crouched at the far end of the examination table.

If the person or animal opponent continues to advance and no immediate means of escape becomes available, the frightened cat may roll from his initial posture into the belly-up position for full defense, or he may strike out with his front claws. The cat may consider the approaching person or animal as a threat in the future as well.

Addressing fear aggression—You can help your cat with some of this fear by making sure children and visitors to your home are respectful of the cat's personal space and don't continue to advance when a cat assumes a fearful position. Teach family members how to interpret basic cat body language so they'll know how to recognize a fearful posture. Work on trust building with your cat as well. Clicker training is a great way to help build confidence and reward a fearful cat for even the smallest of steps forward.

Create a home environment where a cat who tends to show fear aggression has escape routes and options for hiding. Refer to chapter 5 to learn more ways to create security.

With the launch of veterinary professional education programs geared toward eliminating or alleviating animal anxiety in the veterinary clinic, such as Fear Free and Cat Friendly Practice, things are changing for cats. This is a huge help for cat parents who are reluctant to bring their cats in for veterinary exams due to past experience with fear aggression. More veterinary clinics are creating environments that put cats at ease, and veterinary professionals and staff are being trained in low-stress handling techniques. This is a big win for our beloved cats and reduces stress, fear, and aggressive behavior. For more information on Fear Free and Cat Friendly Practice, refer to the appendix.

If the behavior is limited to the veterinary visit, use a carrier that comes apart so the cat can stay in the bottom of it while he is examined. Sometimes being able to stay in the familiar carrier will lessen a cat's anxiety.

A large part of the fear of veterinary visits isn't just about being in the clinic. It also has to do with fear of travel. Often, just getting the cat in the carrier creates a situation in which a cat displays fear aggression. It's important that cats be slowly and gently desensitized to being in carriers and riding in cars. Refer to chapter 10 for information on carrier desensitization and alleviating travel fear.

If the source isn't obviously one of these, it's your job to be the detective. You must figure out what triggers the fear. Is the cat frequently getting ambushed by another cat? Is the cat improperly handled? Has there been a recent trauma or change in the cat's life? There's something causing the behavior. It doesn't just happen in a vacuum. Work on determining the trigger so you can create a game plan to help change how the cat reacts. For example, if the behavior is due to ambushes by another cat, then work must be done to mend the relationship and create an environment that reduces the opportunity for surprise attacks. Increase environmental enrichment and make sure the cats have safe resource access in their preferred areas. You may even need to do a reintroduction of the cats in some cases. If you have home security camera surveillance in your home, look back at the footage to see if you can discover what may have sparked the behavior.

If the cat displays fear aggression when picked up and held, make sure he's not actually experiencing pain. Also, evaluate your approach to the cat and your handling technique. Is the cat being picked up suddenly when he's sleeping? Is he being startled? Is he held like a baby with his feet in the air and belly exposed? Cats don't like that.

Find the cause of the fear and change the circumstances leading up to it so your cat has a *choice*. It's when a fearful cat has no options that he has to resort to aggression.

When a cat is displaying fear aggression, give him time and space to calm down. If you can usher him into a room where he can feel safe, do that, but don't pick him up. Lower the lighting in the room and let him calm down in his own time. With an aroused cat, the less you interact, the better.

If the behavior is displayed toward a family member or visitor to the house, reexamine how they have interacted with the cat to see if there's a clue. Also, use desensitization and counterconditioning methods to help the cat feel less fearful and more in control. Have the person sit quietly at one end of the room while you offer the cat some treats or a meal. Clicker training would work well here, so you can click and reward any small, positive step in the right direction, such as calm behavior, taking a few steps closer, or even ignoring the person. Any behavior you want to see again can be rewarded. You can also conduct a gentle interactive play session. You don't want the cat going out of control. You want things to remain in check. Allow the cat to stay well within his comfort zone. Gradually, over several training sessions, you can have the person inch closer. Always follow the cat's lead, though. If he shows signs of fear, go back a few steps. As you conduct the gentle play session, instruct the other person to stay quiet and still. This shows the cat that he can shift his focus to something else and not have to worry about that person being a threat. In subsequent sessions you can gradually work up to handing the toy off to the other person so he or she can be included in the game. This also begins to show the cat that the person he viewed as a threat is actually good to have around. Take this step very slowly, though. Let the cat completely set the pace, because you may have to stay at the initial step of having the person remain perfectly still and quiet for longer than you realized.

If the problem is fear aggression due to another cat, help the cats change their association with each other. Feed them, at a very safe distance, in the presence of each other, or offer treats whenever they're in the same room. If using food bowls, keep them on opposite sides of the room, and if the cats eat without a problem, you can inch the bowls a little closer in future sessions. If one cat refuses to eat, you've moved too fast and the bowls are too close together. Work on environmental enrichment aspects that create more security as well, such as more vertical territory and hideaways. Increase resource availability so everyone feels secure.

If the fear aggression is more severe and you can't control stalking or ambushing behavior by the other cat, a reintroduction needs to be done. If a reintroduction doesn't change the fear aggression, contact your veterinarian for a referral to a veterinary behaviorist or certified cat behavior consultant.

Territorial Aggression

This type of aggression may rear its fuzzy little head under several different circumstances, such as the introduction of a new cat, social maturity, or cats roaming freely outdoors. Territorial aggression can be displayed toward a visitor to the home; the cat may growl, stalk, or lunge at the unfamiliar person. It may also be demonstrated toward specific cats in the home but not toward others.

For most cat parents, territorial aggression is most commonly displayed when a new cat is introduced into the home where there is already a resident cat.

Territorial aggression can be exhibited in various subtle ways. It may happen in your home without you even hearing a hiss or seeing a paw raised. For example, a cat may block access to resources. It may look to you as if he's casually lounging in a doorway, but he might be preventing others from entering a key resource area.

Territorial aggression can also be displayed in obvious ways, such as outright fighting, intimidation, or spray-marking.

Addressing territorial aggression—Be observant and watch for hints that territorial aggression is bubbling under the surface. The proper introduction of a new cat, or a reintroduction of current resident cats, if necessary, is the foundation for establishing or reestablishing healthy relationships. Make sure there are enough litter boxes in various areas around the house, as well as multiple feeding stations. Improve vertical territory and establish different levels to help the cats maintain a peaceful coexistence.

Sometimes the behavior is being exhibited toward a visitor in the home. The safest way to deal with this is to keep the cat in a separate room until company has gone. You can also start desensitizing your cat to visitors by making sure the person doesn't make eye contact with the cat and doesn't make any attempt to pet or interact. Have high-value (so tasty they're impossible to resist) treats with you to offer your cat for all desirable behavior and to distract him should he start to get tense. Very often, it's the person who is allergic to cats or who doesn't like cats that the territorial kitty will feel more relaxed around because he can remain in control of how much contact to have. Cat lovers who visit your home can sometimes spark territorial aggression if they move too quickly to interact with the cat or even try to hold him.

Pam's CatWise Tip

Aggression can be overt or covert. With overt aggression, there are obvious signs of fighting and hostile behavior. This type of behavior is easy to recognize through body language and vocalizations. Covert aggression is less obvious to cat parents. It involves behaviors such as blocking access to resources, occupying other cats' preferred spots, and spraying. Just because you don't see actual fighting doesn't mean there isn't aggressive behavior occurring under the radar.

Nonrecognition Aggression

This is a form of territorial aggression and can occur between longtime cat companions when one cat returns from the veterinary clinic, because the unfamiliar and unpopular scents can make him smell like an intruder. Scent is a very important way cats recognize one another. When a cat has been outside for a long time, away at a different house, or at the veterinarian, he doesn't have the familiar group scent.

Addressing nonrecognition aggression—If the problem is triggered by a visit to the veterinarian, put the cat in a separate room when he first comes home so he'll have a chance to groom and smell like himself again. It'll also help him quiet down after the ordeal if he tends to get stressed during veterinary clinic visits. If you repeatedly have a problem with nonrecognition aggression after a veterinary visit, rub the cat who will be going to the clinic with a towel before leaving and then use that same towel again on that cat when he returns home. Don't rub any other cats with the towel, because you'll be spreading the veterinary clinic scent around and you'll end up with a house full of angry cats. This is a mistake some cat parents make to try to reestablish a group scent. This is not the way to do it, because you will be forcing one cat's scent on another cat. When cats create group scent it is done with each cat's permission. If you interfere, your good intentions can backfire.

Pam's CatWise Caution

Sometimes, no matter what you try, there are just some cats who can't coexist peacefully. In that case you must modify the living arrangements so they can remain separated. Before you resign yourself to permanent separation, work with a veterinary behaviorist or certified cat behavior consultant.

Play Aggression

Play aggression tends to be directed toward people. Cats who were taken away from their mothers and littermates too early, or hand-raised orphan cats, may not know how to gauge their play response because they didn't experience social play with littermates as kittens. They may cross the line and play too aggressively with you and may not have learned to keep their claws sheathed during play.

You can also unintentionally bring about this behavior if you used inappropriate play techniques with the cat when he was a kitten. Although it can be tempting to use your wiggling fingers to entice a kitten to play, it sends a bad message that can have serious implications as he grows. If he learns biting the cat parent's hand is acceptable, he'll also think it's okay to bite your young child's hand or that of your elderly grandmother. Hands should never be used as toys.

You also want to avoid wrestling-type play with your cat because it can cause a defensive response.

Addressing play aggression—Watch for signs the cat is moving from play mode into aggression—such as flattening of the ears and growling. Use interactive fishing pole toys when you play with your cat so he gets a clear message concerning what is acceptable to bite. Small toys don't put enough distance between your hand and the cat's teeth. Use treats to reward the cat when he plays correctly. Schedule two or three play sessions a day so the cat doesn't develop pent-up energy, and don't engage in wrestling, roughhousing, or teasing.

If the cat still goes for your hand or ambushes your ankles when you walk into a room, carry a toy with you to divert his attention. Stop walking as well, because it's the moving target that attracts him. Increase environmental enrichment in the form of things like puzzle feeders to keep his mind occupied. The more outlets for his energy made available, the less tempting your ankles will be.

Even though play aggression tends to be directed toward people, be aware of the reaction of other cats in the home. If a cat is being rough with you, it might alarm others, and they may be reluctant to get involved in any group play. Also, if a cat stays revved up from improper play with you, he might be less than amiable to unsuspecting cat companions afterward.

Redirected Aggression

Redirected aggression results from a cat being cut off from the primary source of his agitation or focus, so he turns his aggression on the nearest unsuspecting cat, person, or dog. The aroused cat is in such an agitated state that he doesn't realize at whom he's lashing out. (Humans do this, too!)

The most typical example of redirected aggression happens

when a cat looks out the window and spots an unfamiliar cat in the yard. He becomes agitated and highly frustrated. A cat companion walks by or jumps up on the window to join him, totally unaware of his state of arousal, and instantly becomes the target. A surprise attack like this can damage the close relationship between two cats—especially between close companions. Other situations that are potential triggers include the scent of an unfamiliar cat on your clothes, a sudden loud noise, being in an unfamiliar environment, or a cat parent trying to physically break up a cat fight. Redirected aggression usually doesn't last too long, but it may continue when fueled by the ongoing defensive posture of the attacked cat. Suddenly, the two cats no longer recognize each other as friends because of the antagonistic posturing.

Redirected aggression is often misdiagnosed as unprovoked aggression because a cat parent is unaware of the primary cause. After seeing a cat outdoors, your indoor cat can stay highly reactive for hours, so by the time you come home from work, the outdoor cat is long gone and the only evidence you see is a very aroused cat going after his cat companions.

The best way to determine if the appearance of an outdoor cat is causing any of your indoor cats to get upset is to have outdoor camera surveillance (if you don't witness the event firsthand). This way, you will not only confirm the intruder but also possibly identify the cat and where he came from.

Addressing redirected aggression—Separate the cats immediately. If you can coax the agitated cat into another room safely, then do so without picking him up. Otherwise, remove the other animals, if you can do so safely. The safest way to separate agitated cats is to use something that blocks your body, such as a large piece of cardboard. Never handle an upset cat. The sooner you separate the cats, the quicker things will get back to normal, and the risk of long-term damage to the cats' relationships will be greatly reduced. Even if you only suspect redirected aggression, separate the cats.

Leave the upset cat alone until he calms down and resumes normal activity—eating, using the litter box, normal (not displacement) grooming, or napping. Darken the room and keep it quiet. When you reintroduce the cats again, do it under positive circumstances, such as offering a meal or treats. Don't be in a rush to reintroduce them—make sure everyone is calm and back to normal.

If you can identify the initial stimulus, eliminate or modify it. For instance, if you know the cause to be an outdoor cat, block your cats' view by covering the bottom half of the windows with opaque window paper. The half-blocked windows will allow light to enter and your cats to enjoy watching birds in the trees. The outdoor cat may move on to another yard if he can't see your cats through the blocked windows. If a neighbor owns the cat and you feel you can talk to him or her about keeping the cat indoors, that would be ideal. This can be a very touchy subject for people, and you don't want to ruin neighbor relations. If you know the cat is a stray, try to rescue him so he can have an opportunity for a forever home (not necessarily yours). If you don't think you can do this yourself, contact the local feline rescue organization.

If you have bird feeders outdoors and they attract unwanted cats into the yard, you may have to remove them.

Increase activity for the cats in your indoor environment through interactive play, puzzle feeders, cat enrichment videos on YouTube, and more vertical territory. In general, give your indoor cats activities to keep their minds focused away from the source of any outdoor frustration.

Pain-Induced Aggression

Pain-induced aggression is a defensive reaction that can occur when a cat is handled roughly, or if he has an injury or underlying medical condition, as in the case of an arthritic cat who may experience pain when picked up or brushed.

Sometimes pain-induced aggression can turn into a secondary problem of fear aggression. For example, a cat with a chronic painful ear infection may display pain-induced aggression initially, and then after it's healed the memory of the pain may cause him to display fear aggression when the ear is touched.

Pain-induced aggression may seem to come out of nowhere, from the cat parent's perspective. A cat parent may be unaware that a cat has developed arthritis, or that as the result of a fight with another cat there's an abscess developing in a certain spot. When the cat is petted, brushed, or handled, the sudden pain causes the cat to lash out, leaving the cat parent completely bewildered.

Sometimes cats hurt each other unintentionally. Social play during kittenhood is important because it teaches cats how much pressure to use when biting so as not to inflict pain. The reaction of the kitten he bites becomes a valuable lesson. Cats raised without littermates miss this lesson and, as adults, may bite too hard when playing with a cat companion and end up on the receiving end of pain-induced aggression.

Abuse—either spiteful or unintentional (such as by rough handling by a child)—can also cause pain-induced aggression.

Addressing pain-induced aggression—Obviously, the first course of action is to find the source of the pain, alleviate it as much as possible, and get the cat to the veterinarian. In the case of chronic pain, such as arthritis, teach all family members how to handle the cat carefully so as not to cause further discomfort. Talk to your veterinarian about possible treatments for chronic pain issues, including providing an orthopedic and/or heated bed, and using the Assisi Loop (a noninvasive product that uses electromagnetic pulses to reduce inflammation and lower pain levels) or other treatments that are safe and effective for cats. *Never give aspirin to your cat for* *pain as it is highly toxic.* Never punish a cat who is reacting aggressively due to pain.

Petting-Induced Aggression

Let me set the scene. You're sitting on the sofa, watching your favorite TV show. Your cat is curled up in your lap and you're lovingly petting him. At the end of a long day, this is the perfect way for you to relax. Suddenly, like a bolt of lightning, your cat whips his head around and sinks his teeth into your hand hard enough to draw blood. Then he leaps from your lap and sits on the floor a few feet away, grooming himself as you stare in disbelief at your injured hand and wonder what just happened. The behavior displayed is called petting-induced aggression, and although you may think the attack came out of nowhere, or that your cat became momentarily possessed, he most likely did give warning signs before the attack.

Some cats initially enjoy being petted, but then reach a definite tolerance threshold. The cause of this type of aggression may be overstimulation or temporary contact confusion as the cat gets drowsy. When the cat gets sleepy and then feels something coming in contact with his body, his survival instinct may take over and he might bite or scratch in defense. Some cats are also particular about where on the body they prefer to be petted. Some may not like being stroked down the back, along the sides, or near the tail.

Although you may think this behavior is unprovoked, the cat will give body language signals and sometimes vocalizations as well. Warning signs may include skin rippling, tail lashing or thumping, shifting body position, tense posture, ears rotated backward, low growling, and cessation of purring. From the cat's point of view, he has given plenty of notice that he's no longer enjoying being petted. When he feels he has no choice, that's when he bites.

Addressing petting-induced aggression—The best way to handle this problem is to pet for shorter periods. If you know the cat can tolerate only two or three minutes of petting, stop after one minute. To break the behavior pattern, always leave the cat wanting more. If you don't know the cat's limit, watch for warning signals as you pet him. It's better just to give a quick pet and be content to let him merely sit on your lap. When you do pet him, stick to areas you know he enjoys. This positive experience will help him change his association with the situation. Over time you may be able to gradually increase the length of the petting session, but respect your cat's limit. Keep in mind as well that just because one of your cats enjoys a certain type of petting doesn't mean another likes it the same way. Pay attention to individual preferences.

Status-Related Aggression

A higher-ranking cat can display the same type of behavior toward you that he does toward other cats in the home.

The cat might bite or scratch in order to be in control. He may bite when lifted off a table or moved from a chair, when you try to pet him, or even when you simply walk by. He may exhibit this behavior only to certain members of the family or to visitors in the home.

Other examples of status-related aggression include blocking a cat parent's path and direct stares. The cat may also accept affection only if he is the one to initiate it. Mouthing behavior is also possible, where he puts his teeth on you without actually biting down.

Addressing status-related aggression—Watch for body language signals—flattened ears, direct stare, growling, tense body posture. If the cat is on your lap and starts growling at you, staring you down, or mouthing your arm, stand up so he is released to the floor. Don't place him on the floor with your hands because you'll surely get bitten. Stand up and let him release safely to the floor so he learns his behavior doesn't give him the control he wants. Don't interact with the cat until he has resumed normal behavior. Don't hit or punish him, because it's inhumane and it's also something that will be viewed as a challenge, compounding the problem. If the cat is blocking your path, use an object such as a piece of cardboard to protect your legs, and then walk past him so he knows blocking isn't an acceptable behavior. Make sure you watch for signs that he might lunge at you. When you have a cat who shows this type of unpredictable behavior, have objects nearby that you can use for body blocking.

Use of clicker training is a technique to help the cat learn what type of behavior will earn desirable rewards. Click the instant the cat does what you want and immediately offer a treat. Click for behaviors you want to see again. The clicker helps the cat make the immediate connection between the behavior and the reward. Refer to chapter 5 to learn more about clicker training.

Speaking of food, feed the cat on a schedule rather than using free-choice feeding, so his meals will be earned and he'll make the connection that they come from you.

Environmental enrichment will help, as it does in all other situations. The more you can improve vertical space, offer constructive activities to occupy a cat's mind, and locate resources in all preferred areas, the less threatened a cat will feel. If he doesn't feel threatened, he doesn't have a need to flex his muscles, so to speak, in an aggressive way.

Predatory Aggression

Predatory behavior toward appropriate targets (real prey, toys) is a normal behavior. Predatory aggression simulates a hunt: silent approach, body and head low to the ground, then the swift pounce.

The problem occurs when this behavior is directed toward you instead of a felt mouse. You may be a target as you get out of bed in the morning and the cat pounces on your moving feet. He may also slink around following you, then pounce whenever you make a sudden movement.

Addressing predatory aggression—The cat needs enough outlets to satisfy his prey drive. Conduct interactive play sessions on a minimum twice-daily basis so the cat can appropriately engage his prey drive. The use of an interactive toy is essential because it puts distance between your hands and the cat's teeth. Never play with the cat using a small toy. Incorporate puzzle feeders into the cat's daily routine as well to provide him with the activity of hunt and reward.

Maternal Aggression

Mother cats may show aggression toward people or other animals as they protect their nests. They'll do a lot of warning (growling, posturing) to keep intruders at a very far distance from the babies. Unfamiliar people and cats who pose a potential threat are most often targeted.

Don't underestimate the threat of a queen. She will attack in order to protect her kittens.

In free-roaming situations, there's a risk of infanticide by male cats. Even an indoor queen may become aggressive to any of the male cats in your home, regardless of whether they previously had an unfriendly relationship or not. As the kittens grow, the intensity of the aggression lessens.

Addressing maternal aggression—Keep the nest safe from the other cats in the home. It's often necessary to set up a nursery for them in one room of your home where you can keep the door closed. Provide a litter box in there, a scratching post for the mother, as well as food and water. You can place a box lined with butcher's paper, which is cleaner than newspaper, in the closet or behind a piece of furniture—wherever the mother seems to want her nest. Cut a low entrance on one end of the box so it's easy for the queen to go in and out. If you suspect any of your male cats may try to harm the kittens, be very careful when going in and out of the room to make sure no one sneaks by you.

To reduce the risk of maternal aggression, avoid handling the kittens for the first several days after birth and then handle only on a very limited basis for the first two weeks. Early handling before two weeks should be restricted to family members with whom the mother cat is very comfortable. Begin daily socialization and frequent handling of kittens at two weeks to help them become comfortable with humans and with being touched and held. The crucial socialization period for kittens is between two and seven weeks.

Idiopathic Aggression

This is totally and truly unprovoked aggression that seems to have no known cause.

All other possible causes of aggression must first be ruled out, including those often misdiagnosed, such as redirected aggression. Underlying medical causes must be ruled out. For example, hyperesthesia may be the cause of what seems to be totally unprovoked and unpredictable aggression. Hyperesthesia is often referred to as rolling skin disease. The cat may appear to be fine one minute, but when touched, turns very aggressive. Seizures can be associated with this syndrome as well.

Idiopathic aggression is rare. It's difficult to diagnose and difficult to treat. Almost all aggressive behavior can be traced back to a specific cause.

Addressing idiopathic aggression—This is far too difficult and dangerous for a cat parent to try to correct without professional help. You must work with your veterinarian so an accurate diagnosis can be made and a treatment plan developed. Your veterinarian will refer you to a veterinary behaviorist.

Learned Aggression

Learned aggression is really a subcategory that can apply to any of the aggression types. Learned aggression can occur when the cat parent inadvertently reinforces a cat's aggressive behavior. If you attempt to cuddle a cat displaying aggression, it may reinforce the pattern. It's a common mistake made by cat parents because they want to comfort and calm the cat, but it may send the message to him that his aggressive behavior is good. On the other hand, you never want to punish a cat for displaying aggressive behavior. This is where it's important to be familiar with your cat's body language, anticipate what might be the trigger, and use fitting behavior techniques. If you recognize early warning signs in the cat's body language that tell you he's starting to get tense, that's the time to use distraction to keep him calm or to leave him alone to settle back down.

People can also create learned aggression in cats through teasing, provoking, or physical punishment.

REINTRODUCTIONS

A reintroduction is simply starting from scratch and introducing familiar cats as if they'd never met. The process may not take as long as a true first-time introduction, though in the case of serious aggression between cats it may take as long. Whatever time frame is needed, the technique will basically be the same.

There are a few situations that suggest you need to do a reintroduction. For example, if you incorrectly introduced a new cat into your existing cat family and things have never settled down, it's best to just start all over again. There are circumstances that may come up in which cats who previously got along beautifully may suddenly become archenemies. It can happen, for example, when a severe episode of redirected aggression continues to cycle around because the attacked cat becomes self-protective and cautious.

When dealing with cats who are constantly after each other, the more you keep trudging onward without progress, the more the agonistic relations become cemented. The reintroduction allows the cats to get a much-needed breather from each other so the stress level can go down. Then, once everyone seems back to normal, you can begin the reintro process and help the cats rediscover what they previously liked about each other or get to like each other for the first time. No matter how badly the initial introduction went or how long the cats have been together, the reintro method is your best shot at correctly the problems so the cats can start to live peacefully. How slowly or meticulously you'll have to do each step will vary depending on your situation, but I'd advise you to err on the side of caution. It's always better to go more slowly than you think you need to.

The one major difference between a new cat introduction and a reintroduction is *location*. If one cat is picking on another cat, it's best to separate the cats in a way that gives the victim the choice location of the house. You don't want to isolate the victim in a less-choice area and give the cat displaying the aggression the run of the house, because getting the results he wanted will just reinforce his behavior. He'll think his aggressive display scared off the other cat, and you may end up with even more of a problem on your hands. The victim cat will also benefit from having access to the premium areas because it may boost his confidence and level of security.

Sometimes, though, it just doesn't work out to separate the cat displaying aggression into one area if he gets too worked up or irritated. Also, sometimes the victim is just too terrified and feels more secure in a sanctuary room. You must adapt the separation details to fit your individual cats.

Before beginning the reintroduction, you need to work on a little confidence boosting for the victim and a little anger management for the cat who initiated the aggressive behavior. Interactive play will help the victim start to feel safe and relaxed enough to engage his prey drive. If the aggression repeatedly took place in particular areas of the home, conduct his sessions in those locations to help change his mind-set. You may need to start by allowing him to have some cover during the play sessions by using an open paper bag or box. It takes confidence for a cat to be a predator, so hopefully these play sessions will bring out his more confident side. Playing at the scene of any altercation will also create a new positive association with that area. You can also offer treats there. A pheromone diffuser would be a useful addition to the location. If the victim cat feels more secure in the sanctuary room, then keep the play in there for now. After a little while, you should be able to open the door and entice him out with the toy. Make sure the other cat is safely away in another room; then let the victim cat set the pace of expanding his comfort zone. To avoid unwelcome surprise ambushes, other cats in the home should be kept away from the area as well during individual playtime.

For the cat who initiated the aggressive behavior, his separation into a less-than-premium area of the house shouldn't be a punishment. It's not supposed to be cat jail. Don't banish him to the basement or lock him in a bathroom. His area should be inviting and cozy, but don't give him the prime area that he was fighting for. You don't want him to think his aggressive behavior will get rewarded. Engage him in several daily play sessions to help him learn what are appropriate targets for biting. When both cats seem calm and ready, you can begin the reintroduction described in chapter 4.

Pam's CatWise Tip

Setbacks are bound to happen, so don't panic. Just go back one or two steps to where both cats were comfortable, and then pick up from there.

Before the cats are out of their confined areas and together again, keep an eye out for potential situations in the environment that could trigger another problem, and tweak essential aspects of the environment to provide more security and territorial peace. If you were feeding your cats out of one food bowl, everyone should have their own bowls now, kept at a distance from one another. The two cats with the relationship issue may need to be fed completely separate. Look at other aspects of the environment as well, including the setup and locations of litter boxes, beds, elevated areas, and anything else that might need some modification.

WHAT TO DO IF A CAT BITES YOU

The three most important rules to follow to avoid being on the receiving end of a cat bite:

1. Pay attention to the cat's body language.
2. Don't use your hands as toys.
3. Don't physically punish a cat.

Even if you follow those rules, you still may find yourself with a cat's teeth embedded in your hand. How you handle the situation at that point is essential to minimizing injury to yourself and to preventing the cat from suffering additional stress.

The first mistake is to try to pull away from the cat. It's a natural reaction, but it's a mistake because you then are behaving like prey and the cat may bite down harder. It's his natural response when he feels something tugging to get out of his grasp. Instead of pulling away, gently push *toward* his mouth and this will loosen his grip. This momentarily confuses him, because prey would never voluntarily move in the direction of the predator. When he has loosened his grip, you can quickly remove your hand. At the moment the cat bites, you should also use your voice to startle him. Let out high-pitched "ouch" (the word will come naturally, along with a few other more colorful ones, I'm sure). The sudden high-pitched sound will startle and confuse him.

If the cat was biting in play and got a little carried away, or if he thought he was biting the toy and you moved your hand at the wrong time (and it's a mild nip, not a skin-breaking bite), redirect him toward the toy. Make sure you use only interactive toys and don't get the cat so worked up. Remember, beneficial playtime is as much mental as it is physical. If the cat is doing backflips and bouncing off the wall during playtime, then you're not playing with him in a way that stimulates his mind. If he was biting out of aggression, look for what triggered the behavior. Did you ignore body language signals? Could he be in pain? Was he startled? There's always something that triggered it.

Finally, don't forget to reward the cat for good behavior. You can't just keep training him for what *not* to do—you must let him know what you *do* want as well. During the training process, keep treats in your pocket or wear a trainer's pouch, and reward him when he acts appropriately.

Important note: Cat bites can be serious and can cause infections. A cat's canine teeth are very sharp and can cause deep puncture wounds. These wounds can seal over quickly and leave bacteria trapped. If you're bitten, wash the wound immediately with soap and water but be careful not to scrub hard because you could damage tissue. See your doctor or go to a walk-in urgent care facility immediately. Don't play wait-and-see when it comes to a cat bite.

Pam's CatWise Reminder

GUIDELINES FOR TREATING AGGRESSION

- Your cat must be seen by the veterinarian to rule out underlying medical causes.
- Find the trigger that sets off the behavior.
- Be observant of the cat's body language and watch for warning signs.
- Avoid situations that trigger the behavior.
- Distract the cat's attention to a more appropriate activity.
- Use positive techniques to show the cat what behaviors are desired.
- Reward desirable behavior.
- Make necessary changes to the environment and provide ample territory and safety zones for the cats.
- If the problem continues, ask your veterinarian for a referral to a veterinary behaviorist.
- Remember, don't label the cat as an aggressive cat but rather as a cat displaying aggression under specific circumstances.

DRUG THERAPY

Drug therapy can be very helpful in treating feline aggression. It must be used in conjunction with behavior work or you will merely suppress the behavior, which will likely resurface when the drug is stopped.

Psychopharmacology isn't "one size fits all." It's critical to have an accurate diagnosis of the problem so the appropriate drug is prescribed. Work closely with your veterinarian or veterinary behaviorist when a cat is on behavioral drug therapy.

Managing Stress

You may not think cats have much to get stressed over. After all, they don't have to do out to work, they don't have money problems, and they don't have to put kids through college. As you look at your cats lounging in the sun or playing with their toys, it may be hard to imagine what in their lives could be stressful. Actually, cats are subject to a lot of potential stress. Remember, cats find reassurance in predictability and routine, which can put them at risk for lots of stress. Being territorial means it may be stressful when unfamiliar people come to the house. And we all know how stressed out a cat gets when it's time for a visit to the veterinarian. When you prefer things to be predictable and consistent, imagine how baffling it must be to endure a move to a new home. Look at how stressful new cat introductions are (to both cats and the human family members). If you read chapter 1, you can appreciate what a delicate balance most multicat environments maintain. Just using the litter box can be risky in some multicat homes.

Pam's CatWise Reminder

POTENTIAL STRESSORS

- Addition of a new animal in the home
- A new person entering the family (new baby, new spouse)
- Loss of a family member (death, divorce, going off to college)
- Change in a human family member's schedule
- Appearance of an unfamiliar cat in the yard
- Abrupt change in food or litter
- Chronic pain
- Inconsistent training
- Dirty or poorly located litter box
- Lack of key resource availability
- Poor health
- Moving or renovation
- New or rearranged furniture (especially when it involves cat furniture)
- Overcrowding
- Hospitalization or boarding
- Abuse
- Unpredictable environment
- Confinement
- Denial of human contact
- Inability to groom due to obesity
- Loud noises (fireworks, thunder, construction)
- Isolation
- Lack of choice
- Punishment
- Boredom
- Tension or anger between human family members
- Living with a family member who doesn't like cats
- Agonistic relationship with another cat
- Trauma
- Not feeling safe
- Inability to engage in normal feline behaviors
- Natural disaster, severe weather, fire, or another emergency

As cat parents, however well meaning we may be, we are often the cause of stress. We abruptly switch litter or food brands based on what's on sale; we don't keep the litter box clean enough; we have erratic schedules, so our cats never know when we're coming home; we show up one day with a new feline buddy and expect all the cats to quickly become friends. We may not notice signs of illness, we use punishment, and we misread what cats are trying to tell us by their behaviors. We move, we marry, we have children, we divorce, we remarry, we get a dog . . . You get the picture.

The symptoms of stress can vary but your best diagnostic tool is your power of observation and the fact that cats are creatures of habit. Change in any one of your cats is a potential red flag. However minor a deviation may appear, it's worth further investigation.

Stress can have many symptoms, and unfortunately they can also be associated with underlying medical conditions and other behavioral issues, so it can be difficult to diagnose. Have your cat examined by a veterinarian to rule out a medical condition. Long-term stress may affect a cat's ability to fight disease. It can also cause recurrences of urinary tract problems.

Some common symptoms of stress can include the following:

- Elimination outside the litter box
- Hiding
- Withdrawing from family and other cats in the household
- Becoming more demanding and constantly seeking attention
- Increased scratching behavior
- Excessive vocalization
- Change in appetite
- Aggressive behavior directed at either a family member or another cat
- Avoidance of certain locations

- Overly clingy behavior
- Lack of grooming
- Overgrooming (maybe even to the point of creating bald patches)
- Pulling out hair
- Restlessness
- Diarrhea
- Constipation (often because of accumulated hair from overgrooming)

In multicat environments, each cat will be affected by and handle stress in different ways. If most of your cats adapt easily to change, you may not notice when one or two aren't going with the flow. Keep your powers of surveillance sharp! Look at the relationships your cats have with one another and also relationships between the cats and their human family members. Are you inconsistent or misdirected with your training? Is your schedule unpredictable? Have you kept up your part of the litter box maintenance responsibilities? When you're home, are you interacting with your cats enough? Have there been any changes in the home? Have you noticed one cat has withdrawn from the family recently? Perhaps a cat who is normally very playful now shows a reduced interest. Has a cat suddenly become your shadow, meowing constantly? View any change in behavior as an indication that a cat is trying to tell you something important.

KEEP STRESS LEVELS DOWN

In a multicat home, overcrowding is a real risk. If you're concerned about the welfare of a stray outdoors, the more responsible and humane thing to do might be to find her a home—just not your home. Do you realistically have enough space for another cat? If you don't have enough space to create a sanctuary room for a newcomer, it's probably not a good idea to add another cat to the family.

If you do decide to bring in another cat, take the time to do a proper introduction. Even if your decision to adopt another cat was impulsive, the introduction process should never be. Improper introductions create immense stress for all the cats. Provide sufficient territory for each cat. Don't force cats to share litter boxes, feeding stations, or sleeping areas. There should always be enough resources and locations so cats can have a choice. Maximize vertical space and create hiding places so all cats can find their own comfort zones.

Watch for signs of stress and address behavior problems early. Since cats are creatures of habit, pay attention to deviations from the norm. A potential behavior problem identified and addressed early stands a much better chance of successful correction and is far less traumatic for the cat, her cat companions, and the human family members. Stress is a real enemy of a cat's health and welfare. Notice that stress is an underlying thread throughout all the issues discussed in this book. Keep that in mind as you look for the true cause of a behavior problem, and work on a plan to correct it. Reducing a cat's stress level should be one of the major components of any behavior plan.

It's also very stressful for cats to get mixed messages about behavior from different family members. Get all family members on the same page regarding training and how to interact with the cats.

Ease cats through transitions—whether it's the seemingly minor adjustment of helping them get used to the newly installed carpet or the major trauma of losing a loved one. The end of a traumatic event doesn't mean a cat will be able to bounce back emotionally as quickly as you'd like. When you live with more than one cat, it's easy to miss the fact that one hasn't resumed her normal routine.

OVERGROOMING

Cats can respond to stress in several ways, and one common reaction is overgrooming. Because cats are such meticulous groomers, cat parents may assume the behavior is nothing unusual. Displacement grooming is a normal way for cats to reduce their anxiety and calm themselves during or after a stressful situation, or to release frustration. You may see this after a cat miscalculates a jump and falls to the floor or if she rolls off a surface while sleeping. Although it may look as if she's embarrassed, it has more to do with her need to get her bearings because she was caught off guard. Denied access to something desired can prompt a little displacement grooming, such as wanting to jump onto a counter and being repeatedly scolded or placed back down on the floor.

Sometimes a cat takes grooming to the extreme. She may groom one spot, or as much of her body as she can reach, to the point of baldness. The skin beneath looks normal, but the hair will just be stubble. This excessive grooming is called psychogenic alopecia.

Before determining that the condition is psychological, a veterinarian must rule out other potential conditions such as parasites, allergies, pain, arthritis, or hyperthyroidism, to name a few. A common cause of hair loss can be flea allergy dermatitis. Even though you may not actually see a flea because of the exceptional grooming proficiency of a cat, you may see bumpy skin and hair loss.

If psychogenic alopecia is diagnosed, environmental adjustments and behavior work are needed. Your veterinarian or veterinary behaviorist may also prescribe drug therapy to help break the behavior pattern.

Hairballs are a side effect of excessive grooming. Keep a close eye on the litter box to see if there's much hair in the feces, and be aware of how often your cats throw up hairballs. It's often hard to tell who did what in a multicat home, but if you know what's normal for your family of cats, you should be able to spot changes quickly enough. If a cat swallows too much hair, it can cause a blockage in the intestines, which can require surgical removal. The cat doing the overgrooming may need an oral hairball prevention product on a regular basis while you begin the behavior plan.

Addressing overgrooming—If it's determined that there's no underlying medical cause, it's time to figure out the stress trigger. It's easy to dismiss small stressors, thinking that they don't have an effect on your cats or that they have adjusted to them, but trouble could be simmering until it finally becomes an obvious physical sign—bald patches. By then, though, the cat has been grappling with the stress for a while.

Interactive play comes to the rescue yet again. Use it to boost confidence and help release endorphins. Interactive play on a regular basis gives the cat a job, so to speak. She needs to occupy her mind and do what she is hardwired to do—be a successful hunter. In addition to interactive playtime, provide puzzle feeders, tunnels, and climbing structures. Clicker training will be a beneficial addition here as well. In addition to using it to reward the cat for desirable behavior, consider using it to train simple behaviors such as sit, circle, high-five, or go through a tunnel. Don't make the training frustrating. Keep it fun and you may find that the more the cat learns and successfully performs the behaviors, the more confident she becomes.

If you notice the cat sits or sprawls out in a certain position before she begins a session of compulsive grooming, that's the time to use an extra play session as a diversion so she can work off that stress. The more often you catch the behavior before it actually takes place, the more effective the behavior work will be. Be dedicated about the twice-daily interactive play sessions, and if you can fit in one or two more during the day, all the better.

If drug therapy is prescribed, don't overlook how important environmental adjustment, enrichment activities, and ongoing behavior work are while the cat is on the prescription.

SEPARATION ANXIETY

Many people assume cats can be left alone for long periods of time without any problem. In fact, the reason some people choose cats over dogs is that they believe cats are more convenient. Sadly, it's assumed that cats are solitary, low-maintenance animals, and as a result, people are taken by surprise when a behavior problem such as separation anxiety is displayed.

People typically associate separation anxiety with dogs (and children), but cats can suffer from it as well, although the symptoms may be different. The signs in cats are more subtle than those associated with canine separation anxiety. With dogs, there is frequently household damage and object chewing involved. It's difficult to miss the problem when you come home and find the sofa cushions chewed to shreds.

Pam's CatWise Feline Fact

Orphaned cats are more prone to separation anxiety. Premature weaning may also be a factor.

Cats are social animals and they can suffer from loneliness and lack of human contact. Maybe you've changed from working at home to a full-time job that has you away for long hours. Suddenly your cats have gone from having you at home most of the day to seeing you for only a few hours at night. And just because you have more than one cat doesn't mean a cat who is especially bonded to you isn't at risk for separation anxiety. Cats have relationships with one another and then they have their individual relationships with you. You may not realize at first how much your absence affects the dynamic within the home. Separation anxiety can occur for many reasons: vacations, change in schedule, or increased absence due to a change in your social life.

Symptoms of separation anxiety can include:

Litter box problems—A cat may eliminate on your clothes or on your bed because of the strong presence of your scent. She will try to soothe her anxiety by combining her scent with yours. Elimination outside the litter box is connected with other medical and behavior issues as well, so this can make accurate diagnosis of separation anxiety more difficult.

Withdrawal—The cat may stop interacting with the cat parent and even may avoid other cat companions. It's easy for the cat parent to label this behavior as spitefulness, but it's really just stress overload.

Overgrooming—This displacement behavior can get taken to the extreme, where the cat will groom to the point of creating bald patches. Some cats will even pull out clumps of hair.

Change in appetite—This can range from loss of appetite to eating too fast when the cat parent is not around. Appetite changes can also be associated with medical conditions, so a veterinary exam is needed.

Aggression toward cat companions—Extreme stress can result in changes in the cat's relationship with her cat companions or other pets in the home.

Increased vocalization—A cat experiencing separation anxiety may meow or cry while walking around the house.

Increased clingy behavior—The cat may always be by your side, in your lap, or following you everywhere in the house. Velcro cats, who are very needy and overly attached to the pet parent, are more at risk of separation anxiety, regardless of how many other cats are in the home.

Addressing separation anxiety—The cat needs a faithfully kept schedule of daily interactive play sessions. Do one before leaving in the morning, when you come home, and then again before bed, if possible.

Solo enrichment activities are also a must for cats with separation anxiety. Make the surroundings more interesting and stimulating to provide opportunities for exploration, discovery, and reward. Use puzzle feeders, hide toys in tunnels, trigger the prey drive, and boost confidence.

Increase vertical space. Being elevated creates a feeling of security. Cat trees, elevated walkways, cat skyways, and perches will help expand vertical real estate.

It's important to note that separation anxiety is not the same as loneliness. If a cat is lonely, you may determine the best thing to do is add another cat into the family so she has a feline friend. With separation anxiety, the addition of another cat may not address the fact that the cat is specifically anxious about your absence.

Pam's CatWise Caution

Watch the noise level in your home. Cats have very sensitive hearing. Lower the volume on that great sound system you recently bought. Be aware on a daily basis of how noisy your home can get and how that might affect your cats.

Don't make a big deal about leaving the house. For a cat with separation anxiety, you'll just make it worse if you go overboard on the good-byes. Your cat will think you're leaving forever instead of just for the day. Make good-byes casual and quick. Cats easily pick up on the emotions and stress levels of the human family members. If you're upset, then it can set off alarm bells in a cat's mind.

There's a routine you follow when getting ready to leave and each step can raise the volume of your cat's anxiety. Take the drama out of leaving. Pick up your keys, purse, briefcase, or coat a few times a day without actually leaving. Change the order in which you gather those items as well. Periodically, pick those things up, say a quick good-bye, walk out the door, and then come back in a few seconds. Later in the day, do another quick walk outside. Practice these sessions several times a day and increase the time spent outside the home. When you walk back in the door each time, greet your cat in a casual manner. You can even do a quick play session. Don't overdo the emotion and cuddle your cat. Keep everything light and casual. You can also carry objects around the house that trigger the anxiety, such as your car keys, so they start to lose their stress-inducing power.

Pheromone diffusers that contain synthetic calming pheromones may also be a help in the environment. Calming music can be a possible help as well, in the form of cat-specific bioacoustic music, such as *Through a Cat's Ear* (see the appendix).

STRANGER ANXIETY

Some of your cats may be social butterflies who charm every person who walks through the door. Other cats may dive under the bed at the sound of the doorbell. Cat-loving visitors who insist all cats like them can make the situation worse. These are the people who, despite your requests, are resolved to reach down to pet the cat or try to hold a kitty who is urgently attempting to get away. It takes only a couple of these episodes for a cat to realize it's safer just to hide when the doorbell rings, because whatever is on the other side of the door can't possibly be good.

Cats have their own comfort zones, and some cats can't handle the confusion of strangers suddenly appearing in their territory. Some cats will watch the stranger from a distance. Some may even show aggression if approached, and others just disappear and hide with the dust bunnies under the furniture. It's very dismaying to know the mere act of having a few friends over for dinner will leave one or more of your cats stressed out for the rest of the night.

Pam's CatWise Feline Fact

Ironically, cats often love (and often approach) the visitors to your home who don't like cats or who are allergic, because those guests make no attempt to touch them and they know they'll be safe. Cats can go up to those guests and do a scent investigation without being held, petted, or restrained.

Addressing stranger anxiety—You can help desensitize your cats to visitors with a simple exercise. You'll need the help of a friend. This should be a quiet, calm friend whom most of your cats already like. When the guest enters, if the frightened cat is in the area, your friend should completely ignore her—no eye contact whatsoever. If the cat chooses to disappear into another room, that's fine. Sit and talk to your friend in a calm voice for a while to give the cat time to settle down. After about ten minutes, excuse yourself and go to wherever the cat is hiding. Allowing her to stay in her hiding place, introduce a favorite toy and conduct a very casual, low-key game. Don't dangle the toy in her face, but rather, just try to get her to focus on the toy's movement. Even if she doesn't come out of hiding, if you can at least ignite some degree of interest, you'll lower her stress level. What's key during this exercise is for your frightened cat to take her cue from you. You're sending the signal that you're not troubled by the "intruder" in the territory and that she shouldn't be either.

After a few minutes of playtime (whether or not your cat actively participates), go back to your company. Leave the door to that room open. If the cat doesn't come out of the room, then wait about fifteen minutes and go back in for another low-key play session, then return to your company again. If the cat does start to venture out, your friend should still ignore her. The cat may choose just to sit at the threshold of the room. If so, that's marvelous progress, because she's starting to feel as if she has some control over her environment. Keep the interactive toy with you and use that to entice the cat if she shows an interest. Don't move the toy toward the company, though. Keep the action within the cat's comfort zone. This is a big step for her. If other cats are around and they start playing with the toy, that's okay, provided it doesn't trigger the frightened cat to feel unsettled or alarmed. You must play this by ear based on the relationship between the cats in your home.

After several visits, you may be able to hand the interactive toy to your friend so she can engage in a play session with the cat. Also, you can then start inviting different friends over so your cats get used to various people.

Clicker training can be used as well during this type of training. Familiarize your cat beforehand with clicker training so you can use it during your friend's visit. If the cat enters the room, walks by the guest, or does any other behavior that can be viewed as positive or even neutral, click and reward.

LESS STRESSFUL VISITS TO THE VETERINARIAN

I couldn't write a chapter on stress without covering this topic. I know you wish you could find a way to communicate to your cats how important the veterinarian is in their lives, but to them, a visit to the clinic often prompts sheer terror. It's a shame many pets view the person in the white coat as the enemy. There are some ways to make these visits a bit less stressful. Although the veterinary clinic may never be a place a cat looks forward to visiting, at least you can make it a bit more endurable.

Let's start with what veterinarians are doing on their end. There are more and more cats-only veterinary clinics opening, and that can make a big difference in taking lots of fear out of the visit. Not having to see or hear dogs can really lower the volume on the stress-o-meter. Many mixed-species veterinarians have separate waiting room areas for cats and some even have cat-exclusive exam rooms.

Look for Cat Friendly Practice veterinary clinics or ones that have Fear Free certification. Both are programs designed to educate veterinary professionals and staff on reducing stress and fear for animals in the clinic environment. You can check and see if there's a Cat Friendly Practice clinic or Fear Free clinic in your area by visiting their websites (see the appendix).

Now comes your part. With a kitten, the time to start getting her used to the veterinarian's office is right now. It's also good to get her used to being in her carrier and traveling in the car. Take her to the veterinary clinic just for scheduled social visits. The earlier a cat gets used to carriers, travel, and being handled by veterinary staff, the better.

No matter how calm your cat has been during previous visits to the veterinarian, you must always transport her in a carrier, no matter if you are walking, driving, or going on public transportation. First, it's dangerous to drive with a cat loose in the car because she can easily get wedged under the accelerator or brake pedal. She can also cause a dangerous distraction. In an accident, the cat stands a much better chance of survival if confined in a carrier. Another reason for the carrier is that you never know if this visit is the one that causes your cat's stress-o-meter to go over the top. It might be because of another animal in the waiting room or a painful procedure. Don't risk it—always use a carrier. If you have a cat who gets terrified or fractious, use the type of carrier where the top and bottom unscrew and come apart. Sometimes being able to remain in the bottom half of the familiar carrier will reduce a cat's anxiety. Much of the veterinary exam can be done with the cat resting there.

Pam's CatWise Tip

Leave the carrier out all the time so it becomes a neutral object in the environment. Train your cat to become comfortable with being in the carrier. Offer treats and feed your cat near the carrier and then ultimately inside the carrier so she associates it with positive experiences.

Unless it's an emergency, schedule your veterinary appointment for the least busy time of the day for them. If your veterinarian tends to get behind schedule, make your appointment for early in the morning. That's also a good time if your cats react adversely to other animal scents, because the clinic will have been cleaned the night before or maybe first thing in the morning and the scents of various animal patients will be at a minimum.

Bring a light towel to drape over the carrier if your cat gets excited in the car or while in the waiting room. If your cat is fine in the car but freaks out once you step into the clinic, wait in the car until it's your turn and ask the receptionist to text you when the veterinarian is ready to see you.

You may have a window of opportunity, so to speak, with a cat. Some cats tend to be very fearful at first and then settle down after being in the exam room for a while. With another cat you may have to move quickly because she's okay for the first ten minutes and then at the eleventh minute she turns into a buzz saw. Know your window of opportunity with each cat so you can manage the veterinary exam accordingly.

Pam's CatWise Tip

Desensitize your cat to car travel by building up to a trip slowly. Put the cat in the carrier and then place the carrier in the car for a few minutes. In future sessions work up to starting the engine, then take short drives around the block. Take each phase gradually before moving on to the next step. To help a cat relax during car travel, the trip shouldn't always end at the veterinary clinic.

If any of your cats must be hospitalized, bring a couple of paper bags and T-shirts that contain your scent. The cat will feel more secure if she has a place to hide, so ask the staff to open the paper bag, cuff the end to keep it from collapsing, and place it on its side. Line it with a T-shirt for extra reassurance and scent familiarity. The bag should be placed in the cage at an angle so the cat can feel totally hidden. Having a hiding place in the cage eases stress because it gives the cat the choice of whether to hide or remain visible. As you've learned throughout this book, having *choice* is key to keeping stress under control.

Give your cat time by herself before reintroducing her into the multicat environment. Scent is crucial in cat communication and it's normal for the cats who remained at home to feel threatened by the veterinary clinic scents on the returning feline patient.

PANDORA SYNDROME: THE ROLE OF STRESS IN FELINE URINARY TRACT PROBLEMS

If your cat experiences recurring bouts of urinary tract problems, stress may be the main culprit.

We used to label urinary problems under the umbrella of FLUTD (feline lower urinary tract disease) and FIC (feline idiopathic cystitis). Research has now shown how stress impacts the health of a cat's urinary tract. The term *Pandora syndrome* refers to the myth of Pandora's box, which when opened released all the demons. Even though Pandora syndrome presents as a litter box issue, it has everything to do with stress and how a cat reacts to it. And you know how many things are stress triggers, right?

I've outlined Pandora syndrome in chapter 7, but you'll also need the information in this current chapter to help you with stress reduction guidelines. Chapter 3 and chapter 5 will be part of your overall behavior plan as well. That's how much stress can infiltrate a cat's daily life.

Aging and Illness in a Multicat Home

Life in your multicat household may go along smoothly for years and then a sudden illness can cause a drastic change in the cats' relationships. It may affect the dynamic between a couple of cats, or it may affect everyone. When one cat gets seriously sick, it's not just a crisis for that individual cat—it can be a crisis for everyone in the home. Being prepared will help you handle the emotional aspects of illness as well as the physical. This also applies to aging cats. Changes in relationships may be missed because they creep up subtly and slowly as the cats get older or as illness progresses. You may not notice a distinct change until one cat is no longer able to jump and climb or perhaps becomes grouchy when disturbed while lounging in the sun. Stay observant for potential changes to help your eldercats through the golden years.

THE ILL CAT

Obviously, a cat with a contagious illness should be separated from the rest of the cat family, but a cat with a chronic illness that isn't contagious can still be an active member of the group, with

Pam's CatWise Caution

If your cat has been allowed outside access, it's time to keep him indoors. Any decrease in senses, limited mobility, or the beginning of age-related cognitive dysfunction will leave him at risk of getting lost, injured, or killed.

modifications to the environment made if needed. A cat with chronic problems may need to be separated if the pain or discomfort makes them intolerant, aggressive, or too fearful. He may continue to get along with one or two of his companions, depending on temperaments and ongoing relationships, so you may find those companion cats can move between the sick cat's sanctuary and the main part of the house as well. The main thing you don't want to do with an ill cat is increase his stress. Make sure his surroundings are safe and comfortable—whether that includes all his companions, some of them, or none of them.

Environmental modifications can do wonders for a cat suffering from a long-term illness. The following sections refer to aging cats, but all the basic techniques will apply to cats who are debilitated for other reasons as well.

THE ELDERCATS IN THE FAMILY

If you have older cats in your household, you want to do all you can to make sure their senior and geriatric years are comfortable and happy. That can take some careful planning in a household filled with cats of various ages and temperaments.

Pam's CatWise Feline Fact

A cat is considered a senior between the ages of eleven and fourteen years.

The geriatric years begin at age fifteen.

WORK WITH YOUR VETERINARIAN

Now more than ever, an aging cat needs to be seen by the veterinarian on a regular basis—at least twice a year, and more if needed to monitor a condition. Age-related problems such as renal failure, diabetes, or arthritis, among other conditions, are relatively common, but they can come on quickly, and early diagnosis will enable you and your veterinarian to establish a medical plan and help your cat stay healthy and comfortable for more years. Even though an old cat may naturally slow down and sleep more, some age-related problems aren't immediately obvious. Keep an eye on his physical state, and monitor his food and water intake, litter box habits, and activity level. With older cats, scheduling regular wellness visits will help ensure good health and catch age-related issues early. Accurate diagnosis of underlying medical problems can also explain a senior or geriatric cat's behavior change that could be affecting everyone in the household.

FOOD AND WATER INTAKE

Your older cat may gain weight due to decreased activity or he may lose weight as a result of not having the robust appetite he had in younger years. A decline in appetite might be due to decreased sense of smell, cognitive issues, disease, or dental pain.

Your veterinarian may put your older cat on a senior-formula food, or on a special diet if he has a medical condition. Kidney disease is common in cats, and there are special foods to address this and other ailments. This can be tricky in a multicat home if the cat wants to eat what everyone else is eating. The other cats may also want the senior cat's prescription food instead of their own.

To ensure your older cat gets the appropriate food, use scheduled meals so you can monitor his intake. If having the cats eat in one location no longer works because of the food formula change, create separate feeding stations.

Your older cat, especially if geriatric, may also need to eat smaller meals fed more frequently than the other cats, so you may be cordoning off one or the other for a while.

Cats aren't scavengers, so they use their sense of smell to determine if food is safe to eat. If your cat has a compromised sense of smell due to age or illness and doesn't want to eat what she can't sniff, warm her wet food in the microwave for a few seconds to release a more enticing aroma. Stir after heating to break up any hot spots and feel the food with your finger to make sure it's slightly below body temperature. You can also try putting a few drops of warmed, low-sodium chicken broth over the top of the food. If you have questions or concerns about your cat's appetite, contact your veterinarian. If a cat goes without eating longer than twenty-four hours, it can cause serious health complications.

Keep an eye on water intake as well. If chronic renal failure or diabetes are diagnosed, a cat will drink more water. This may mean you need to have more water bowls available. If the problem is that your older cat isn't drinking enough water, try a pet water fountain. This may create more interest and the freshness of the moving water may be more appealing.

Raise food and water bowls to make it more comfortable for a cat suffering from arthritis in the neck, shoulders, or spine. You can place the bowls on top of a book or other small platform.

DENTAL PROBLEMS

Dental pain from periodontal disease is a common reason an older cat has trouble eating or stops eating altogether. Brush the cat's teeth daily. All cats, young and old, should have their teeth brushed, in fact. If you have trouble doing that, talk to your veterinarian about dental sprays or gels. For the older cat, check his mouth regularly for signs of trouble. Drooling, foul odor, and inflamed or very red gums are just some of the symptoms of periodontal disease. You may also notice a cat pawing at his mouth, chewing only on one side, or gulping food. The cat's coat may also have a bad odor from the saliva deposited during self-grooming. Don't neglect dental issues because they are very painful, and bacteria can travel through the bloodstream to vital organs.

NAIL HEALTH

Help your older cat out by keeping his nails trimmed. The back nails typically get worn down by walking because they don't retract back into a sheath, but your older cat may not be active enough to keep those back nails in shape. To prevent them from growing too long, keep up those regular nail trims.

An eldercat may have more difficulty retracting his front nails back into their sheaths. This can cause nails to get snagged on upholstered furniture, carpet, or bedding. Trim nails regularly but be gentle when handling paws as a cat's joints may have developed arthritis.

GROOMING

An older cat may become less concerned with self-grooming. Lack of mobility may also make grooming certain areas of the body more difficult. The cat's coat may begin to look messy and may even develop an odor. Brush your older cat on a consistent basis to keep the coat in good condition, distribute natural oils, and increase circulation. It's also a time to check for any lumps or bumps that may have recently appeared. If a cat has lost a lot of weight or muscle tone, use a soft brush to make it more comfortable going over bony areas of the body.

Pam's CatWise Tip

With increased age, there is also reduced stress tolerance. Circumstances (such as intercat conflicts or erratic schedules) that a cat tolerated when younger will be more difficult and pose more of a risk to overall health. Watch out that the younger cats don't take advantage of the eldercat's vulnerability, especially around resources.

CHANGES IN VISION

Just as with humans, eyesight gets worse as cats age. Don't move furniture and/or change where you place resources so an older cat with decreased eyesight can still navigate around the environment.

High blood pressure can cause painful changes in eyesight. Your cat's blood pressure should be checked at every veterinary exam. Older cats may also develop a hazy film over their eyes as they age.

CHANGES IN HEARING

A decreased sense of hearing may mean a cat sleeps more soundly, and as a result he might not feel the sensation of a full bladder. Have litter boxes conveniently located. If the cat tends to urinate in his sleep, put absorbent pads over his bedding.

Decreased hearing may mean that the cat is more easily startled. Be aware of how you approach a senior or geriatric cat when he's sleeping.

ENVIRONMENTAL MODIFICATIONS

In his prime, your older cat may have been able to leap from the floor to the top of the dresser in one graceful move. Now, however, he may hardly be able to jump up into a favorite chair. Since cats love elevated places, make adjustments to accommodate him. A cat tree with multiple layers is ideal because it allows a cat to easily climb to the top perch without having to make a giant leap. For some older cats, the perches of some trees may be too far apart. Look for a tree with several closely spaced perches. The perches should be wide for ease when ascending or descending and U-shaped for maximum comfort and safety.

A heated window perch is great for a senior or geriatric cat and allows him to still enjoy the window view and stay comfortable, especially during colder months. If he has trouble reaching it, create a ramp or pet stairs for easy access. Place a ramp or pet stairs next to the bed as well so your older cat can still enjoy sleeping with you if that's what he has been used to all these years.

If your cat enjoys napping on favorite elevated locations, place folded blankets or towels on the floor or carpet below in case he loses his balance and falls. All perches should be wide to make it safe and less likely a cat will roll off.

An orthopedic bed (one with egg crate–type foam to relieve pressure on joints) may be an extra comfort, especially if a cat suffers from arthritis or stiffness. If any of the beds or perches you set up are heated, make sure the cat is mobile enough to be able to move from them should he become too warm. Never put a cat who is unable to stand and walk away on a heated bed.

If an older cat likes hiding places, get him a fleece-lined covered bed or high-sided donut-shaped bed. The high-sided beds help retain body heat. Place beds in several rooms to help him maintain social visibility and continue to be a part of the family. If the cat suffers from cognitive issues or mobility problems and can't climb into a high-sided bed, in addition to offering flatter ones, you can place an open box on its side and line it with a soft towel or small blanket.

Tile, laminate, or hardwood floors can be too slippery for an eldercat, especially if he's trying to play. Cover some of the floor with a low-pile carpet to make it easier for him to get traction and maintain balance. Don't use loop carpet that can catch a cat's nails. Carpet will also make it more comfortable on the cat's joints if he chooses to lie on his side during the game.

Use secure, low-pile carpet runners in hallways that currently have hardwood, tile, or laminate. Prevent runners from sliding around by using nonslip rug pads underneath.

To help with nighttime navigation when the house is dark, place night-lights along frequently used pathways so a cat with limited vision can more easily find his way to the litter box and other needed locations.

THE LITTER BOX

An older cat, especially one with arthritis or other mobility issues, may have difficulty climbing in and out of the litter box. Use a low-sided box or a high-sided one with a low entrance cut out on one end. A cat experiencing stiffness or pain may not be able to fully squat for urination, so a high-sided box may help catch urine from going over the sides. Don't resort to a covered box as it may be uncomfortable to get into and out of, and may cause the cat to feel cramped. If the cat is experiencing cognitive issues (discussed later in this chapter), he may even have trouble getting out of a covered litter box. Some cats with serious mobility limitations can't step into a litter box, even if it has a low entrance on one end. If that's the case, use something like a cookie sheet or other very low-sided pan so he barely has to step in. Place absorbent pads under and around the pan. Scoop the litter frequently and level it as you do to prevent uneven mounds. This will make it easier for the cat to stand and balance. In some cases, a cat can't balance on litter at all, so you'll have to line the pan with an absorbent pad.

Increase the number and locations of litter boxes. Make sure they're sturdy, to prevent tipping if a cat loses his balance during elimination.

Monitor litter box habits so you'll be alerted to any potential underlying medical problem. I know this can be tricky in a multi-cat home, but since cats are creatures of habit, you may notice certain cats tend to frequent specific boxes or consistently use the ones in their preferred areas. Be understanding of litter box mishaps with an aging cat. Decreased bladder control may make it more difficult for him to get to the box in time. A cat with diabetes or in chronic renal failure also may not make it to the box in time, due to increased water intake. You may find a cat has urinated in his sleep. Clean urine off your cat immediately to prevent scalding of the skin, to reduce his stress from having to do extra grooming, and to prevent companion cats from having a negative reaction to him.

Constipation is another common issue with older cats. If the cat associates the box with physical discomfort, it can lead to litter box avoidance. Talk to your veterinarian if constipation is a problem with your older cat.

The scent of an ill cat can create anxiety in some companion cats. A companion may be upset by the strange odor of a medicated or ill cat's urine, so he may start eliminating outside the box. Scoop boxes meticulously. Watch for signs of trouble and increase the number of boxes so the concerned cat has more options. If a companion cat starts showing fear or aggressive behavior toward an ill cat, you may have to separate them to avoid stressing out both cats.

SCRATCHING BEHAVIOR

Make sure scratching posts are conveniently located. Some older cats may use them more just for the good stretch they provide, but others may no longer be able to reach up and stretch. Vertical scratching posts may cause pain when a cat with arthritic joints or spinal pain tries to reach up. Place several wide, horizontal scratching pads around the house, especially near the old post, so a cat always has a comfortable option.

PLAYTIME AND EXERCISE

An older cat may no longer be the athletic predator he once was. He may not pounce on a toy with lightning speed, but he'll still enjoy and need playtime. Encourage your older cat to remain active as an important part of maintaining his health. For a sluggish digestive system, exercise will help improve intestinal motility and improve circulation. From an emotional standpoint, maintaining a play schedule may also keep that spark going so an aging cat doesn't become too sedentary or withdrawn.

The playtime routine will have to be modified to fit an older cat's medical and physical condition. Don't force a cat to do things he can no longer comfortably do. Keep the movements of the toy within the cat's capability, even if that means just wiggling it on the carpet a few inches in front of him. Play sessions may have to be shorter as well. If you match the game to the cat's ability, he'll enjoy it much more and will benefit from the exercise, even if it just involves pawing at the toy. Any amount of activity will benefit a cat in his senior years. Be sensitive to his ability, customize the game, and share these special moments together.

If needed, use different toys that entice the play response. What used to spark a cat into play mode when he was younger may no longer be effective. Do some toy testing to see which ones trigger a positive response. He may now have changed preferences in terms of size, movement, or texture.

Because an older cat may not have the ability to engage in group interactive play sessions with the youngsters in your home, don't forgo individual play sessions with him. If you have a large cat family, it can be hard to find time to make sure everyone gets their fair share of playtime, but for a senior or geriatric cat, this exercise is vital. If you have a couple of older cats who are good friends and play cooperatively, you can do a mini group session with just them.

Even if you have an older cat who acts like a youngster and effortlessly leaps from chair to cat tree, be sensitive to his movements during playtime. Don't stress his joints by encouraging high leaps or have him racing to exhaustion after a toy. Remember, much of a cat's hunting technique involves mental work as he stalks and plans. Older cats need that mental stimulation.

Pam's CatWise Reminders

SENIOR AND GERIATRIC CARE

- Provide easy access to favorite napping places, feeding stations, and litter boxes.
- Monitor relationship with the other cats.
- Monitor food and water intake.
- Maintain top-quality nutrition.
- Monitor litter box habits for change and be understanding of litter box misses.
- Customize interactive playtime to accommodate a cat's physical condition.
- Follow your veterinarian's advice regarding frequency of wellness visits.
- Educate family members on how to handle an eldercat because they may not be as aware of sensitive or painful areas as you are.
- Brush the cat regularly and trim his nails.
- Brush your cat's teeth and routinely check for dental issues.
- Provide a sanctuary area for the senior or geriatric cat as needed.
- Address conflicts between cats to reduce stress.

SLEEPING

An older cat loves his naps now more than ever. Make sure your eldercat has easy access to his favorite spots and can nap undisturbed. If you have feline youngsters in the home who view a napping senior as the perfect target for practicing their pouncing skills, then some periodic separation is needed. Offer the younger cats plenty of opportunities for play in other places and at other times. In addition to their regular interactive play sessions, set out puzzle feeders and fun enrichment activities to keep them occupied.

SOCIAL RELATIONSHIPS WITH COMPANION CATS

With aging comes illness, declining senses, pain, limited mobility, and decreased cognitive function. Whether feline or human, getting old isn't fun, and relationships between your cats can change as they age. This can be due to a decline in cognitive ability, irritability associated with pain, or other elder challenges. Cats who always played together may have some issues now if one tries to wrestle with the other, not knowing the pounce causes pain. A napping cat may now become startled when a companion cat jumps up to cuddle next to him.

A cat with cognitive decline or decreased senses may not respond to a companion cat anymore, and the relationship may grow distant. It can be confusing and stressful for the companion, who doesn't understand why his buddy's behavior has changed.

Watch the relationships between your cats to make sure there are no short-tempered flare-ups. Watch how a cat's deteriorating senses may affect his relationship with the other cats. Make sure he doesn't get startled by revved-up young members of your feline or human family.

Cats who are ill or older ones with decreased senses or mobility may lose status. The stronger, healthier cats may assume higher status in the group. Even though this is a normal aspect of cat life, ensure any older or ill cats don't get pushed out of their favorite areas. Watch the dynamics of the group and use positive techniques to distract potentially agitating cats and do whatever tweaking may be needed to adjust the environment to ensure there are safe places for those who need it.

COGNITIVE DYSFUNCTION SYNDROME

A number of disorders and problems accompany aging in cats, just as they do with humans. As the brain ages, cognitive ability begins to decline.

Cognitive dysfunction syndrome (CDS) is one condition that can affect cats in the geriatric years, and in some cases, it can begin even in the senior years. It's similar to dementia in humans.

The precise cause of CDS is unknown. Diagnosis includes a complete medical exam, behavioral history, history of onset of symptoms, blood tests, and other diagnostics as needed. Other medical conditions such as hypertension, hyperthyroidism, and tumors must be ruled out.

Symptoms of CDS can include the following:

- Disorientation
- Increased vocalization
- Loss of appetite
- Changes in sleep
- Decrease in self-grooming
- Increase in aggression
- Overly clingy behavior
- Litter box issues
- Anxiety
- Pacing or wandering around the house
- Lack of interaction
- Getting stuck in corners
- Losing balance
- Increased attention-seeking behavior

Addressing cognitive dysfunction syndrome—There is no cure, but you and your veterinarian can create a supportive plan to slow the progression of CDS. Your veterinarian may prescribe medication and supplements to support good brain health, and may also recommend some dietary changes, if needed.

On the home front, keep your cat's brain and body active through enrichment activities. Keep that brain exercised through daily interactive play sessions. As I've said in this book, playtime is as much mental as it is physical, and if there was ever a time you need to tailor your play technique to encourage mental stimulation, it's now. In addition to interactive play, set out puzzle feeders that are geared to a level appropriate to your cat's ability. Puzzle feeders must be super easy, perhaps just a water bottle on its side with very large holes so treats easily fall out. The point is to stimulate brain function but not to frustrate the cat. Don't confuse your cat with sudden changes in the environment. Even good changes can be overwhelming for a cat with CDS. Everything needs to be gradual.

Keep up visual enrichment. If you can, place a bird feeder outside a window he can reach, install a cat-proof fish tank, or play a cat-entertainment video on the TV or computer.

Your cat may feel more comfortable if you are nearby during his meals. He may even need a physical connection. Sit nearby and gently stroke him as he eats. Softly speak to him to help add comfort. In some cases, hand-feeding is needed to get a cat to eat.

It's not uncommon for cats with CDS to become lost or disoriented in the house, so set up night-lights to help him. If you hear him howling or crying, he may be stuck in a corner or unable to find his way out of a room. Call to him as you go to locate him to ease his anxiety.

For a cat with severe CDS, changes in the environment or attempts to stimulate the brain may actually create more confusion. As CDS progresses, he may need to be kept in one room to reduce disorientation. Being with you at night will be helpful because the sound of your voice will provide much comfort. Work with your veterinarian as you and your cat go through this journey. Sadly, there is no happy ending with CDS; eventually the cognitive ability becomes too severe.

FACING THE INEVITABLE: DEATH AND MOURNING

The loss of a family member, whether human or companion animal, is always devastating. It turns our lives upside down and it takes all our strength to find a new "normal." Your cats feel that pain as well and grieve the loss of family members. Animals have the added confusion of not understanding where a human family member or companion animal went and why *you* are not acting the way you normally do.

If any of your cats are older, then although this is not a subject anyone wants to think about, it's something that's inevitable. It's also something that will greatly affect the other cats in the home, so it's better to be prepared for how to help everyone through this.

Cats grieve. Some people don't believe that, but animals grieve and feel the pain of loss. In many ways, their grief has added pain because they suddenly lose a companion or family member and don't understand where that person or animal has gone. Then they start to notice their whole world has changed. The cat parent is acting very strangely, and the dynamic of the cat family has changed as well. It's even more painful if the deceased was very bonded to one or more of the cats. Losing a long-time buddy brings an unimaginable pain.

In your effort to provide comfort to your grieving cats, you may hold or cuddle them more. Be careful about how much you do and the way you do it. Cats are emotional sponges and highly sensitive to the emotions you convey. You don't want to set off alarm bells in your cats' heads that this is the end of their world. They may in fact not be grieving as much as you over the recent death; it varies from cat to cat. Balance your cuddling and holding with normal routine, interactive play, and a normal tone of voice. Any cuddling or holding you do should also be in a way that each cat normally prefers. Even though playtime may be the last thing you want to do right now, your cats need the security of their routine. They need to know that although something devastating has happened, most of their world remains intact. Predictability and routine are needed. These are the things that reduce stress and provide comfort. I know these are the first things that get turned upside down in a family crisis, but your cats *need* this. That's why, as hard as it may be, keep your manner and conduct as light and normal as possible, and maintain their expectations of daily life.

Something happens in a multicat home when one of the cats passes away—the social structure may go through some shifting with some renegotiations of territory. You're probably well aware of how *adding* a cat affects the cat family and causes territorial jockeying, but it also occurs when a cat leaves the environment. The entire cat household may go through bumps in the road. The severity of it will depend on the status of the cat as well as how closely bonded he was with other cats. The surviving cats will go through a grieving period, during which some will search for their friend and stay close to his favorite spots. They may vocalize more, and some may stop eating. They may seek out your attention more. Some cats deal with stress by overgrooming. Others may totally withdraw from the rest of the family or become overly clingy. Watch your cats' reactions during this period so you can catch potential problems before they become ongoing. In addition to interactive playtime, tweak aspects of environmental enrichment to keep minds focused on positive activities. This may be the time to install some cat shelving or add a few window perches. If a cat appears to be really struggling with grief or if he stops eating for more than twenty-four hours, consult your veterinarian.

When a cat passes away, wait until everyone (feline and human) has dealt with the grief before adding another cat. The newcomer shouldn't have to endure unfair expectations and comparisons or be seen as a replacement.

Whether adding another cat will be beneficial to your existing cat family is something only you know, based on your specific circumstances. If you are left with just one cat who seems very lonely, then maybe, when the time is right, a companion would be ideal. On the other hand, if the cats had an agonistic relationship and now this cat seems more relaxed, then the addition of another cat might just cause a repeat of stress. A more fearful cat might now come into his own as a solo cat, not having to face daily territorial challenges.

If you're considering adding another cat, make sure the cat(s) who lost the companion cat is emotionally ready for this and not still smack in the middle of overwhelming stress and grief. New cat introductions are delicate enough under the best conditions, so don't set cats up for preventable stress. He should be back to his normal eating, sleeping, and playing routines, as well as other behaviors typical for him.

Although you can't predict how cats may react to the death of a companion animal or family member, do your best to stay alert and provide what they need. I know they will return the favor by being there with the purrs, cat kisses, and affection you need to get yourself through this difficult time.

Professional Help

If you find yourself trying to solve a behavior problem without success, take a deep breath and relax, because there's help out there. Don't feel as if you've failed, because behavior problems can be very complex. Because cats can't tell us what's bothering them in a language we understand, we must use our best detective skills. It's very hard for some cat parents to separate themselves from the emotion of the situation enough to be objective. Some problems are also simply too dangerous to try to handle on your own.

Animal behavior counseling has become a very popular field, and there are now more options available to pet parents than ever before. When it comes to seeking professional help, your first step should always be to talk with your veterinarian. Because cats can't tell us what's wrong, any kind of diagnosis must first rule out underlying medical causes. All too often, behavior is the result of a medical condition.

Your veterinarian may refer you to a certified behavior professional to help you establish an effective behavior plan. The field of animal behavior is science based. A certified, professional expert can explain the *why* behind an animal's behavior. An ethical professional can't guarantee results, because the success of a behavior treatment plan will depend on several things, including genetics, the length of the problem, the compliance of family members, the current environment, and other specifics of an individual case, but you'll get an eye-opening view of the motivation behind a cat's behavior. Animals repeat a behavior because it works. There's no spite, stupidity, or anger behind it. When you begin to see how the animal was using the behavior to solve a problem or cope with a situation, your view changes from being frustrated at her to wanting to provide exactly what she needs. The bond begins to repair itself just by a shift in your mind-set.

There are many people on the internet (or around the neighborhood) claiming to be behavior experts, so it's important to choose someone with the credentials and experience recognized in the field. Ask your veterinarian for a referral to a qualified, certified behavior expert. Certified applied animal behaviorists are certified through the Animal Behavior Society. Veterinary behaviorists are certified through the American College of Veterinary Behaviorists. Certified animal behavior consultants are certified through the International Association of Animal Behavior Consultants (see the appendix).

THE BEHAVIOR CONSULTATION

Before the consultation you'll be given a behavior and medical history form to complete. The more detailed and honest you are in this form, the better. If you have video of the behavior, provide that as well, since the cat may not display the unwanted behavior in front of the behavior expert. Some behavior experts will ask for a floor-plan sketch as well.

For a behavior plan to be successful, it must fit your abilities, schedule, financial limitations, and lifestyle. A qualified professional works to establish a customized plan that is practical, safe, and effective.

The behavior expert should explain why the behavior plan is effective and the science that supports it. Unless the certified expert is also a licensed veterinarian or veterinary behaviorist, no medical diagnosis should be made and no drug recommendations given.

A follow-up appointment with the behavior professional will be scheduled to review ongoing progress. Some experts may have an additional fee for follow-up appointments, but you should be able to contact them with any questions or concerns.

The behavior expert will send a report to the referring veterinarian. This helps the veterinarian follow up on progress made when your cat returns for an exam.

When it comes to a behavior consultation, it's important for you to realize that much of the daily work will need to be done by you. Behavior problems build over time, so they can't be resolved in a one-hour session. Your compliance, as well as that of all family members, will be important. Behavior experts don't have a magic wand they can wave over your cat to instantly correct an unwanted behavior, although we all wish we could. Success will depend on the consistent work you do with your cat and the environmental changes you may need to make. The daily requirement isn't time consuming, but it does require consistency, patience, and love. The cat can't do the behavior work by herself; she needs you to create an environment where she can succeed.

DRUG THERAPY

There are situations where behavior work alone can't change the problem. Incorporating psychopharmacology, though, isn't an answer by itself or an easy fix to avoid doing the work needed. It can only be successful when used along with the correct behavior treatment plan. If you don't change the cat's responses or associations, she might have to stay on medication forever, and if you take the cat off the drug, the undesirable behavior may resurface.

Before drug therapy is prescribed the veterinarian will do a thorough medical exam, including all appropriate diagnostic testing. You will also need to provide details about the behavior problem, including what has been done to try to correct the behavior. If the veterinarian doesn't feel medication is warranted at this time, or thinks you need more in-depth professional guidance, you will receive a referral to a certified behavior professional. Only a veterinarian or a veterinary behaviorist can prescribe medication.

THE RESPONSIBILITY OF THE FAMILY DURING TREATMENT

When starting a behavior plan, whether medication is involved or not, all members of the family must be willing to cooperate. Although one or two adults will be primarily responsible for the specifics of the behavior plan, it's important that everyone remain consistent so the cat doesn't get mixed messages.

It's also important for everyone in the family to understand why the problem occurred in the first place and how to prevent future problems. Education is your best tool, so teach everyone old enough to understand what the cats need and how they communicate. This is the time when you can also make sure family members don't misinterpret the motivation behind a cat's behavior. For example, a family member may feel the cat misbehaves because "she hates me." Warn family members about losing their tempers or getting frustrated. Even though this may be a time of crisis for everyone, if someone shows impatience toward the cat, it can cause an increase in stress and a setback in the progress. Family dynamics will influence the success of the treatment plan. Spouses or family members who yell at one another can keep the home in a constant state of stress. This can keep all the cats in highly aroused states as well. The family needs to stay committed to the treatment plan. Problems aren't corrected overnight. Everyone must understand this is a journey and an investment in future health and happiness. After all, no one adopts or rescues cats in the hope they will pee on the sofa, bite your best friend, be aggressive to the other pets in the home, or hide under the bed every day. We want cats in our lives to establish loving relationships and enjoy close bonds.

REHOMING AND EUTHANASIA

It's not something anyone wants to think about, but some cat parents do sometimes find themselves feeling as if they've reached the end of their rope. Before you decide to place a cat in another home or relinquish her to the shelter, please seek the advice of your veterinarian and a certified behavior professional. Too many cats are sent to shelters or put to death for behavior problems that could have been corrected.

If safety is the issue and you're worried that one of your cats may hurt a family member, keep the cat in a separate area of the home. Your cat will need a veterinary exam, and then you will need to consult a behavior professional for evaluation.

There are times when, yes, a cat may do better in another home. The behavior might be triggered by stimuli in your home that can't be removed or modified. In that case, the cat may thrive in a different environment.

If you do rehome a cat because of a behavior problem, you have a moral obligation to disclose why you are seeking a new home and the specific behaviors that concern you. The cat may do beautifully in the new home, but the prospective cat parents have a right to know the history. It will also be essential for them to have this information in order to do appropriate behavior work themselves.

Sadly, euthanasia is sometimes the quick fix for some cat parents with so-called problem cats who spray, bite, or scratch. How tragic to end a healthy cat's life for a behavior problem that could be corrected. And how especially tragic to end a cat's life for a behavior that is normal and serves a function. If you find yourself at that point where you feel the only option is euthanasia, seek your veterinarian's counsel immediately, and that of a behavior expert. If you can't afford a behavior expert, contact the behavior department of your local shelter. Many shelters have trained behavior personnel working to help keep cats in their homes.

I urge you, though, to not give up on your cat. Learn about behavior and make the investment in figuring out what your cat is trying to tell you. I hope that, having reached the end of this book, you know so much more about cat communication, creating secure territory and environmental enrichment, and looking at behavior from a cat's point of view. These are the valuable tools needed to change unwanted behavior, along with the most important tool of all—your love for your cats.

Appendix

ADDITIONAL READING

Johnson-Bennett, Pam. *CatWise: America's Favorite Cat Expert Answers Your Cat Behavior Questions.* New York: Penguin Books, 2016.

Johnson-Bennett, Pam. *Think Like a Cat: How to Raise a Well-Adjusted Cat—Not a Sour Puss* (updated and expanded edition). New York: Penguin Books, 2011.

VISIT OUR WEBSITE

catbehaviorassociates.com

CONNECT ON SOCIAL MEDIA

Facebook: facebook.com/pam.johnsonbennett
Twitter: twitter.com/thinklikeacat

ADDITIONAL RESOURCES

To Find a Veterinary Behaviorist

American College of Veterinary Behaviorists
  dacvb.org

To Find a Certified Animal Behaviorist

Animal Behavior Society
  animalbehaviorsociety.org

To Find a Certified Cat Behavior Consultant

International Association of Animal Behavior Consultants
   iaabc.org

To Find a Cat Friendly Practice Veterinary Clinic Near You

American Association of Feline Practitioners
   catvets.com

The Cat Friendly Practice program was established by the American Association of Feline Practitioners and the International Society of Feline Medicine as a global initiative to reduce stress in cats, the cat caregiver, and the veterinary staff. You can look for a Cat Friendly Practice on their website.

To Find a Fear Free Veterinary Practice Near You

Fear Free
   fearfreepets.com

Founded by veterinarian Dr. Marty Becker, Fear Free has a Veterinary Professional Certification Program. For veterinary professionals to earn Fear Free certification they must complete the program successfully. Veterinary hospitals may have one certified professional or the entire team may become certified. So much education is provided to help prevent and alleviate stress and fear in pets.

To Learn More About Clicker Training for Cats

Visit Karen Pryor's website on clicker training.
   clickertraining.com

Product Manufacturers

Assisi Loop
   assisianimalhealth.com

The Assisi Loop creates an electromagnetic field that activates nitric oxide to help facilitate the body's natural healing process.

Sticky Paws double-sided tape
pioneerpet.com

Through a Cat's Ear (bioacoustic music for cats)
icalmpet.com
You can choose from several bioacoustically designed CDs or purchase their iCalm player to stream several hours of music that autorepeats.

Toys

Cat Dancer
catdancer.com

Da Bird
dabird.com

Puzzle Feeders

Catit Senses 2.0 Digger
Catit Play Treat Spinner
catit.com

LickiMat Buddy
SloDog Slow Feeder
hyper-pet.com

Egg-Cersizer cat toy
SlimCat interactive feeder cat toy
petsafe.net

Fun Board Strategy Game
Slide & Feed Strategy Game
trixie.de

Index

abscesses, 231
absorbent pads, 269
activity cycle (hunt, feast, groom, sleep), 121–23
affection, communication of, 18–19, 26–27
aggression, 30, 72, 97, 131, 140, 197, 212–43, 252, 283
  catnip in, 128
  countering of, 223, 239, 242
  displays of, 178, 232–33, 241
  by dogs, 93
  fear and, 220–24
  in human-cat interaction, 221, 223–25, 232, 235
  idiopathic, 236–37
  inadvertent reinforcement of, 237
  learned, 237
  maternal, 235–36
  medical issues and, 212–13, 236, 262
  in new cat introductions, 213, 219–20, 224–25
  nonrecognition in, 226–27
  ongoing, 238
  pain and, 132, 230–32
  petting-induced, 232–33
  physical signs of, 220–21
  in play, 10, 215–18, 227–28
  play-diversion techniques for, 119–20
  play vs., 215–18
  predatory, 234–35
  reasons for, 212–15
  redirected, *see* redirected aggression
  spray-marking and, 187
  sudden onset of, 90
  territorial, *see* territorial aggression
  threat and, 3, 212, 233–34
  types of, 219–37
  warning signs of, 21–25, 38, 232–33, 241
aging:
  care guidelines for, 272
  changes and problems of, 263, 267–70, 273
  diet for, 263–64
  mobility loss in, 212–13, 236, 262
  in multicat homes, 261–78
  vet visits in, 263–64, 266–67, 274–76
  vocalization and, 35
  see also geriatric cats; senior cats
air diffusers, 127
air fresheners, avoidance of, 171
air hunters, 114
airplane ears, 28
allergies, 80, 225, 249, 255
allogrooming, 3, 16
aluminum foil, 206

Amazon, toy reviews on, 107
American College of Veterinary
        Behaviorists, 280
anal glands, 14–15
animal abuse, 90–91, 193, 231
Animal Behavior Society, 280
animal shelters, 284
anticipation quiver, 31–32
anti-inflammatory medication, 192
anxiety, 5, 54, 55, 80, 86, 275
    among multiple cats, 86
    scratching and, 206
    status and, 7
    in vet visits, 221–22
    see also separation anxiety;
        stranger anxiety
appetite, changes in, 97, 191, 252, 277
arched tail, 31
arching, 23–24
arthritis, 231, 249, 263, 265, 268,
        269, 270
aspirin, danger of, 231–32
Assisi Loop, 231
attention-seeking behaviors, 19, 97
automatic smart feeders, 150
avert aggression, 226

babies, cat introduction to, 86–90
baby gates, 76, 92–93, 94–95, 150
baby toys, 88
back-turning behavior, 25
balance, 28, 29
bald spots, 249–50, 252
beauty products, 127
beds, 65
    for aging cats, 267–68
    elimination on, 194
    orthopedic or heated, 231
behavioral changes, 86–87
behavioral professionals:
    certification for, 280

when to consult, 80, 94, 95–96,
        100, 199, 214, 224, 243, 279–84
behavior reinforcement, 34–35
belly-up position, 22–23
binocular vision, 26
bioaccoustic music, 254
birdbaths, 131
bird feeders, 131, 186, 230, 275
birds, 96
bird-watcher toys, 105
birth, purring in, 35–37
biting, 9, 13, 23, 101, 227–28, 231–34, 284
    infections caused by, 242
    response to, 240–42
black lights, 181–82, 186, 189
blending, of feline families, 83–84
blockades:
    physical, 76–77, 79, 92
    visual, 78
blocking, 234
body language, 90, 221
    in biting, 241
    in communication, 21–33
    signs of aggression in, 216, 220,
        232–33, 237, 241
bonding, 40, 69, 79, 251
    brushing in, 132
    of cats and dogs, 91
    cat-to-human, 86, 140
    death and, 276
    in kittens, 9
    rubbing in, 17
    scent and, 15–16
bone strength, 36
brushing, 132–33, 266
Buffington, Tony, 191
bunting, 15–16, 18–19

calming, 223, 254
camera surveillance, 175, 180–81,
        222, 229

cancers, xiii
carpal whiskers, 33
carpet-covered posts, 202
carpet protectors, plastic, 156–57
carpets, 268
cleaning and neutralizing of, 183
scratching of, 207
cat behavior, misinterpretation of, 1
cat carriers, 137
desensitization to, 124, 222, 257–59
importance of using, 258
cat condos, 46
cat count, 51, 59
Cat Dancer (toy), 106, 119
cat-dog interaction, obstacles to,
95–96
cat-dog training sessions, 92–95
cat enrichment videos, 131, 230, 275
Cat Friendly Practice clinics,
221–22, 257
cat furniture, 89, 125–26
catios, 57–59, 134
Catit Senses 2.0 Digger, 154
cat kiss, 27
catnip, 23, 46, 67, 127–30, 204, 207, 208
catnip-filled toys, 129
cat-proofing, 65–66
cat rescues, 61
cat shelves, 47–49, 56, 58, 81, 85,
157, 277
cats-only veterinary clinics,
221–22, 257
cat-to-cat social relationships, with
aging cats, 273
cat trees, 44–46, 47, 54, 56, 81, 95, 111,
125–26, 130, 157, 253
for aging cats, 267
positioning of, 45–46, 87
types of, 44–45
cat tunnels, 51–53, 65, 123, 124,
250, 253

cat walkways and skyways, 47–49,
56, 58, 95, 253
ceramic bowls, 142
chasing, 216
chattering, 39
cheek rubbing, 126
children, cat introduction to, 86,
90–91
chirping, 37
chronic illness, 261–62
citrus scents, 171
classical music, 131–32
cleanliness:
of environment, 49, 99
of litter boxes, 126–27, 162–63,
188, 199
of puzzle feeders, 154
urine neutralization in, 182–83
cleansers, 126–27
clicker training, 79, 137–40, 256–57
for aggression, 223, 234
for countering spray-marking,
184–85
for dogs, 93
in overgrooming, 250
climbing structures, 250
see also cat trees
clingy behavior, 253
closed-door mealtime, 72–73
dogs in, 92
cognitive dysfunction syndrome
(CDS), 274–76
strategies for managing, 274–75
symptoms and diagnosis of, 274
cognitive issues, 264, 268, 269, 273,
274–76
collars, 136–37, 150
communal scent, 16
communication, feline, xi–xii, 13–39
of affection, 18–19, 26–27
body language in, 21–33

communication, feline (*cont.*)
  human interpretation of, xii,
    13–14
  spray-marking as, 16, 177–80
  of status, 5–6, 27
compatibility, 62–63
competition, in group play, 118
compulsive behaviors, 97
confidence, 29, 239, 250, 253
confinement, for cat
    identification, 175
conflict avoidance, 3
confrontation, 5, 7
constipation, in aging cats, 270
corrugated cardboard scratchers,
    203, 204
couch potato cats, 104, 128
countertops, keeping cats off,
    156–58
covered litter boxes, 186, 269
  disadvantages of, 164–66
covert aggression, 226
crayon shavings, 175
cribs, keeping cats out of, 87–88
crib tents, 88
cricket nabbers, 105
crouching, 22
crying, 275

Da Bird (toy), 106
death, 276–78
declawing, 209–11
defecation, 15
  covering in, 20–21
  identifying problem cats in, 175
  litter preferences for, 197–99
  medical issues and, 161
  outside of litter box, 196–99
  separate boxes for, 197
defensiveness, 31, 37
defensive posturing, 22–23

dementia, 274
dental pain, 264–65
dependence, of indoor cats, 2
depression, 97
desensitization, 79
  to cat carriers, 124, 222, 258–59
  in stranger anxiety, 255–56
deterrent sprays, 206
deworming, 68
diabetes, 161, 263, 264, 269
diaphragmatic muscles, 35
diarrhea, 191
diet:
  for aging cats, 263–64
  managing, *see* mealtime
    management
  specialized, 149–50
disorientation, 275
displacement grooming, 249
distraction, 77–78, 90, 250
  for aggression, 187, 230, 234, 237
  for countering spray-
    marking, 184
  from food, 146
  for play aggression, 228
  play as, 119–21, 250
  from rough play, 218
diversion, *see* distraction
dogs, 123
  in cat mealtime management,
    92, 155
  cats compared to, 1, 14, 23, 37,
    60–61, 91–92, 251
  new, introduction of cats to,
    91–96
  training of, 93, 139
do-it-yourself projects, 52, 110,
    124, 151–54, 203
double-sided tape, 156–57
drooling, 26, 265
drug therapy, 243, 249, 250

dry food:
    in free-choice feeding, 144
    puzzle feeders for, 152–54
dual wrap (entwining) tails, 32
durability, in toy selection, 106–7

ear infections, 28–29, 231
electronic litter boxes, 166, 199
elevated spaces, 85, 87, 89, 95, 230,
        234, 248, 268
    access to, 6
    benefits of, 49
    in feeding location, 147
    as hiding places, 50–51
    increasing, 125
    off-limit areas in, 156–58
    in sanctuary rooms, 67
    in territoriality, 41–49
    see also cat trees; cat walkways
        and skyways
elevator butt, 24
endorphins, 35, 36, 103, 250
energy levels, 62
enrichment activities, 253, 273, 275
environmental adjustments, 94,
        250, 273
    for aging cats, 267–68, 275–76
    for chronic illness, 262
    for fighting, 281
environmental enrichment, 97–140,
        220, 228, 250
    for aggression, 234
    basics of, 98–100
    in grieving, 277
    outdoor enrichment in, 134–37
    scent enrichment in, 126–30
    sound enrichment in, 131–32
    touch enrichment in, 132–34
    toy selection for, 105–10
    in transition from outdoors, 56–57
    visual enrichment in, 130–31

escape potential, 188
    aggression and, 220–21
essential oils, toxicity of, 127
estrus, 24
euthanasia, 214, 283–84
exploration, in new cat
        introductions, 73–74
extinction burst, 121
eyes, 26–27
eye whiskers, 33

facial pheromones, 187
family, behavioral modification
        role of, 282–83
fear aggression, 220–24
Fear Free, 221–22
Fear Free certification, 257
fearfulness, 28, 30–31, 33, 37, 50, 51–
        52, 66, 68–69, 71, 74, 140, 278
    body language for, 221
    of humans, 217
    in outdoor environment, 135
    playtime techniques for, 113
    punishment and, 203–6
    signs of, 90
    of toys, 108–9
    in travel, 222
    triggers for, 222–23
    in undesirable urination, 195
    in veterinary visits, 221–22,
        258–59
feces, 15, 20–21
feeding, scheduling of, see
        scheduled feeding
feeding stations, dog-proofing of, 95
feline acne, 142
female cats:
    bonding of, 2–3
    unspayed, xiii
feral cats, 2–3
    rehabbing of, 44

FIC (feline idiopathic cystitis),
    191, 260
fighting, xiii
    breaking-up techniques for, 77
    play vs., 215–18
    safe separation in, 216–18
fight-or-flight, 3, 30, 40
fishing pole–type (wand) toys,
    102–3, 228
fish tanks, 96, 275
flea allergy dermatitis, 249
flea and tick preventative, 137
fleas, 58
flehmen response, 17
floor plan, for resource availability,
    53–54
floors, traction on, 268
fluorescein ophthalmic dye, 175
FLUTD (feline lower urinary tract
    disease), 191, 260
food bowls, 65, 73, 78
    cat's preference in, 148
    divided, 143–44
    individual, 240
    litter boxes and, 171, 185
    positioning of, 54–55, 144–48, 159,
        171, 185, 224, 225, 264–65
    types and choices of, 142
food-dispensing toys, 67, 123
food enrichment, 123
food thieves, 156–58
free-choice feeding, 62, 144, 234
    transitioning away from,
        145–46
free-roaming cats, 2–3
furniture, 54
    cat, 89, 125–26
    comfort in, 85
    for elevation levels, 41–42
    rearrangement of, 213
    scratching of, 202, 204, 205–7, 209

gerbils, 96
geriatric cats, 62–63, 161
glass bowls, 142
greeting:
    behavior, 25
    human response to, 30
    of unfamiliar cat, 18
grieving, in cats, 276–78
grooming, 19, 249, 265
    aging in decline of, 266
    displacement, 249
    overgrooming, 206, 247–48, 252
    self-, 265–66
    for touch enrichment, 132–33
ground hunters, playtime
        techniques for, 113
group play, 77, 118–19
group scent, 16–17, 227
growling, 34, 37–38, 75, 233
grunting, 37
guarding behavior, 196
gums, inflammation of, 265

hairballs, 37, 49, 182, 249–50
hair loss, 249–50, 252
hair spray, warning about, 127
"Halloween cat" posture, 23
hand-feeding, 275
harnesses, 136
healing, purring in, 36
hearing:
    age-related changes in, 267
    sense of, 28–29, 253
heartworm, 137
heated beds, 231, 268
heated perches, 267–68
heatstroke, 58
hidden areas, elimination in, 195
hideaways, 55, 81, 124
hiding, as coping mechanism, 124
hiding places, 50–51, 65, 268

high blood pressure, 266–67
hissing, 34, 37–38, 75
homemade toys, 110, 124, 151–54
home range, 40
hospitalizations, 259–60
houseplants, toxicity of, 130
howling, 34
human-cat interaction, 8, 34–35, 76
  aggression in, 221, 223–25, 232, 235
  in behavioral modification,
    282–83
  with children, 90–91
  fear in, 217
  greeting in, 18
  injury in, 214–17, 219, 233–34
  in new cat introductions, 66, 68–
    69, 80–91
  picking up and holding a cat in, 38
  in play aggression, 227–28
  scratching in, 209
  separation anxiety in, 251–54
  sleeping arrangements in, 81
  as source of stress, 193, 246
  stranger anxiety in, 254–57
  in undesirable urination, 194
hunting, 26–28, 30, 32, 39, 96
  in activity cycle, 122
  biting in, 241
  play as simulation of, 101–6, 108,
    110–16, 151, 184, 234–35, 250,
    253
  providing alternatives for, 57
  whisker function in, 33
hyperesthesia, 236
hyperthyroidism, 249

identification:
  scent in, 15–17, 226–27
  spray-marking in, 19
idiopathic aggression, 236–37
ID tags, 136

illness:
  and aggression, 212–13, 236, 262
  in multicat homes, 261–78
  signs of, 27
  status and, 10
  vocalization in, 35
indoor cats, 2
  adjustment to, 120
  environment for, 56–59
  ID for, 136–37
  spray-marking by, 20
indoor/outdoor cats, 17, 56
infanticide, 235–36
infections, from cat bites, 242
inflammation, 231
injury:
  in human-cat interaction, 214–17,
    219, 233–34
  signs of, 27, 29
intact females, in estrus, 24
intact males, 17, 40
  aggression in, 213, 219
  behavior of, xii–xiii
  spraying by, 178
interactive play, 51–52, 57, 66, 69, 76,
    77, 82–83, 88, 89, 102–16, 230,
    256, 277
  for aging cats, 271, 275
  to counter aggression, 223–24
  for countering spray-marking, 184
  in energy release, 218
  maintenance sessions for, 102–3
  in response to overgrooming, 250
  for separation anxiety, 253–54
  specific techniques for, 111–16
  toy selection for, 102–10, 132, 184,
    203, 228, 241
internal clocks, shifting of, 122
International Association of
    Animal Behavior
    Consultants, 280

intestinal motility, exercise for, 271
introductions:
    to babies and children, 86–91
    challenges of, 1–3
    of new cats, see new cat
        introductions
    of new dogs, 91–96
    to new homes, 80, 84–86
    to new spouse or partner, 80–83
    see also reintroductions

jealousy, 86

kidney disease, 161, 264
killing bite, 101
kitchen counters, elimination on, 195
kittens:
    adoption of, 62–63, 66, 68, 69
    avoiding catnip for, 128
    body language of, 23–24
    cat trees for, 46
    early separation of, 227
    grooming of, 132
    kneading in, 25
    lack of stimuli for, 221
    locating of, 28
    maternal relationship with, 2–3
    maturing of, 10
    play benefits for, 104, 231
    in response to purring, 36
    security for, 235
    socialization of, 8–10, 236
    specialized diets for, 149–50
    in veterinarian visits, 257
    vocalization in, 34
kneading (milk tread), 25–26

labeling, 214
ladder analogy, 5–7
language, feline, 14
lap cats, 86

laryngeal muscles, 35
laser-light toys, problems with, 117
lashing (thumping) tail, 32
learned aggression, 237
leashes, 219
    for dogs, 92–93
leash training, 135–37
leg position, 22, 31
LickiMat, 153
licking, 3–4
lightweight formula litter, 170
lip rubbing, 126
litter, 109, 167–71
    making a change of, 167–70
    preferences in, 168, 197–99
    scoopable (clumping), 162–63, 169
    sufficient levels of, 170
    texture of, 133, 169, 198
litter additives, scented, 170–71
litter aversion, 168, 170, 188
litter box environment, 160–99
litter boxes, 52, 54, 65, 100, 186
    age-related modifications of,
        269–70
    avoidance of, 270
    cleanliness of, 126–27, 162–63,
        188, 199
    condition of, 21
    covered, 94, 164–66, 186, 269
    dog-proofing of, 94–95
    escape potential for, 172–74
    food bowl placement and, 145, 159
    guarding, patrolling, and
        controlling of, 196
    number of, 78, 163
    positioning of, 54–55, 65, 80, 89,
        171–74, 195, 197, 225, 235
    posture in, 177
    setup arrangements for, 162–74
    size of, 163–64, 165–66
    in spray-marking, 186

types of, 164–67
usage of, 56
washing of, 163, 196
when to dispose of, 172
litter box problems, 61, 97, 175–88,
198, 252
elimination outside of box, 86–87,
161, 193, 196–99
identifying perpetrators in, 175
odor control for, 126–27
litter box rooms, 172
litter receptacles, 162
litter scatter, 165–67, 170
location aversion, 188
loneliness, 278
separation anxiety vs., 253
lordosis, 24
lowered tail, 30
low-light vision, 26–27
lumps, checking for, 266

male cats:
infanticide by, 235–36
unneutered, see intact males
manual self-cleaning boxes, 166–67
marking:
rubbing in, 17–18
scent in, see scent-marking, spray-
marking
scratching in, 200–202, 204
maternal aggression, 235–36
mating, xiii, 19, 24, 40, 178
matting, 132–33
mealtime management, 100, 141–59
for aging cats, 264, 275
closed-door, 72–73, 92
customized for cat's needs, 149–50
multiple cat challenges in, 141
in new cat introductions, 72–73,
74, 76
in Pandora syndrome, 192

scheduled feeding in, 62, 145–46,
149, 234, 264
supplies for, 142–44
see also diet
meat-loaf position, 25, 31
medical issues, 176, 177, 252
aggression and, 212–13, 236
litter box problems and, 16,
161–62, 167–68, 269
in stress, 246
see also illness; specific conditions
meowing, 34–39, 57, 68
directed toward humans, 34–35
at night, 121
in pain, 231
mice, 96
microchips, 136
middening, 20–21
mimicry, 38–39
mites, 29
mixed-species veterinarians, 257
moaning, 37
mobility, age-related changes in,
267–68, 269
mood indicators, 29
motherhood, 2–3, 28
bonding in, 9
protective aggression in, 235–36
motion-activated water
sprinklers, 186
motorized toys, 108–9
mousers, 105
mouthfeel preferences, 133
mouthing behavior, 233
murmuring, 38
music, 67, 254
as sound enrichment, 131–32
muzzle whiskers, 32–33

nail caps, disadvantages of, 208–9
nail health, 265

nail sheaths, 200, 202, 209
napping, 54
nepetalactone, 127–28
nesting, 235–36
neutering:
  to control aggression, 220
  importance of, xii–xiii, 19
  for spraying, 178
new cat introductions, 60–96, 180
  aggression in, 213, 219–20, 224–25
  beginning the process of, 68–71
  in blending of feline families, 83–84
  compatibility in, 62–63
  considerations for, 61–62
  after death of cat, 278
  to dogs, 91–96
  involving declawed cats, 211
  leashes in, 135
  litter use in, 169–70
  mealtime management in, 72–73, 74, 76, 147–48
  need to redo, see reintroductions
  to new spouse or partner, 80–83
  overcoming obstacles in, 78–80
  preparation for, 63
  resident cats in, 69–70
  sanctuary rooms in, 64–67, 74–77
  seven-step process in, 71–78
  spray-marking in, 187
  for stress management, 248
  supervised visitation in, 77–78
  visual contact in, 75–77, 78
new home introductions, 80, 84–86
night-lights, 66, 268, 275
nighttime activity, curbing of, 121–23
nonrecognition aggression, 226–27
nonscoopable litter, 162–63, 169
nose color, 15
nose sniffing, 25
nurseries, 87–88

nursing, 25–26
nutrition, 99

OCD-type behavior, 117
odor neutralizers, 182–83
open areas, elimination in, 195
oral hairball prevention products, 250
orphan cats, 227, 251
orthopedic beds, 231, 268
outdoor cats, 224
  dangers for, 56, 58, 134, 219, 262
  as source of redirected aggression, 229–30
  territoriality of, 40–59
  in transitioning to indoor environment, 56–57
  see also feral cats; stray cats
outdoor enclosures, see catios
outdoor enrichment, 134–37
outdoor intruders, 180, 186
overcrowding, stress and, xii, 247–48
overgrooming, 206, 249–50, 252
overstimulation, 232
overweight cats, 33, 113, 144, 147, 149

pain:
  aggression and, 213, 223, 230–32
  in aging cats, 273
pain-induced aggression, 230–32
pain relief medication, 192
painter's tape, 182
Pandora syndrome, 191–96
  addressing stress in, 192–93, 260
  diagnosis of, 191–92
parallel play, 77
parasites, 58, 137, 249
pariah cats, 7–8, 195
paw pad scent glands, 16, 21, 26, 201
peek-a-boo hunters, playtime techniques for, 114

perches, 54, 56, 81, 95, 253
  window, 47, 130, 157, 267, 277
periodontal disease, 265
personal (critical) space, 40
pet doors, 174
pets, incompatible with cats, 96
pet stairs, 267
petting, 24, 133
  tolerance threshold for, 232–33
petting-induced aggression,
  232–33
pheromone diffusers, 239, 254
pheromone products, 67
pheromones, 15–16, 17, 18, 21, 67,
  71, 126
pheromone therapy, 186
pill bottles, dangers of, 155
piloerection, 23–24, 220
plastic, chewing on, 155
plastic bowls, 142
play, playtime, 56, 87
  avoiding mixed messages in, 111
  benefits of, 100–101
  biting in, 241
  cat vs. dog, 91
  customized for cat's preference,
    112–16
  as distraction technique, 119–21
  ending techniques for, 116
  in energy release, 228
  environmental enrichment
    techniques for, 100–110
  fighting vs., 215–18
  with grieving cats, 277
  group, 77, 118–19
  health benefits of, 104
  inappropriate, 227–28
  interactive, see interactive play
  in kittens, 31
  lack of interest in, 115
  pre-bedtime, 122–23

predatory simulation in, 101–6, 108,
  110–16, 151, 184, 234–35, 250, 253
  in reintroductions, 239–40
  solicitation of, 23–24
  for stress reduction, 85
  tailored for aging cats, 270–71, 275
play aggression, 10, 215–18, 227–28
plug-in room fresheners, warnings
  about, 126–27, 171
positioning, control and, 6–7
posture, 21–25
  aggressive, 220
posturing, 7, 10
  defensive, 21–23
potpourri, warnings about, 127
predatory aggression, 234–35
premature weaning, 251
prescription foods, 264
primary reinforcer, 138
psychogenic alopecia, 249
psychopharmacology, 281
puffed-up (bristled) tail, 30–31
punishment:
  avoidance of, 83, 215, 232, 234, 237,
    239, 241
  fear and, 203–6
  inappropriate and cruel, 177
  for undesirable urination, 195
pupil size, 27
purring, 26, 34–37
puzzle feeders, 57, 67, 90, 107, 123,
  149, 157–58, 218, 228, 230, 235,
  250, 253, 273, 275
  benefits and fun of, 151–55

question mark tail, 30
quivering, 31–32

redirected aggression, 73–74, 214,
  228–30, 236, 238
  definition and example of, 228–29

rehoming, 283–84
reintroductions, 220, 222, 224, 225,
        237–40
    after aggression, 230
    location for, 238–40
    after veterinary visit, 260
relaxation, 23, 27, 28, 30, 33
renal failure, 263, 264, 269
reproductive availability, 19, 178
rescue cats, 61, 64, 230
resident cats, in new cat
        introductions, 69–70
resource availability, 2–3, 53–55, 213
rewards, 241–42, 257
    in clicker training, 138–40, 184–85
RFID (radio-frequency
        identification) collars, 150
roaming, xiii
rolling, 23
room fresheners, 126–27, 171
room swapping, 74–75
    dogs in, 92
roughhousing, 228, 231
rubbing, 3, 15–16, 17–18, 25, 126

safety, 8
    in catios, 58–59
    cat-proofing for, 65–66
    in environmental enrichment, 98
    in outdoor enclosures, 134
    in toy selection, 106–7
sanctuary rooms, 47, 52, 68, 70, 74, 77,
        79, 84, 92, 169–70, 171, 187, 239
    in new cat introductions, 64–67,
        74–77
    for new dogs, 92
    in new homes, 85
    preparation of, 64–65
scent, 26, 66, 73, 75
    comfort from, 46

    in identification, 15–17, 92, 226–27
    of illness or aging, 270
    information gathering
        through, 194
    in new cat introductions, 70, 71–72
    security and, 259
    in soothing, 252
scent communication, 14–20
scent enrichment, 126–30
scent glands, 14–16, 21, 26, 201
scent investigation, dogs in, 92
scent-marking, 74, 179, 186–87, 201
    spraying in, see spray-marking
scent receptors, 14
scents:
    of baby, 88
    in cat furniture, 125–26
    comfort in, 85
    in toy selection, 110
    unfamiliar, 135
scheduled feeding, 62, 145–46, 149,
        234, 264
schedules, minimal disruptions
        of, 80
scratching, 23, 200–211, 233, 284
    aggressive, 13
    benefits of, 202
    communication functions of, 21
    in confrontations, 209–10
    correction techniques for, 206–8
    emotions conveyed through, 201
    purposes of, 200–202
scratching pads, 207
scratching posts, 54, 65, 66, 100, 111,
        139, 201, 202–5, 235
    for aging cats, 270
    cat trees as, 45
    choosing of, 202–4
    homemade, 203
    positioning of, 204–7

when to replace, 208
screen doors, 79
scruffing, 38
secondary reinforcer, 138
security:
  in defecation, 197
  of elevated spaces, 45
  hiding places as, 50–51
  in litter box use, 164–65
  in mealtime management,
    147–48, 154–55
  scent and, 259
  sense of, 51–52, 64–66, 76, 88
security cameras, 59
seizures, 236
self-cleaning boxes, 199
  disadvantages of, 166–67
self-grooming, 265–66
senior cats, 62–63
  age range for, 263
  toy selection for, 110
  see also aging; geriatric cats
senior-formula diet, 264
separation:
  in aggression, 217, 220, 227,
    229–30, 238–39
  for aging cats, 272–73
  in fighting, 217
separation anxiety, 194, 251–54
sexual maturity, 10
shake cans, 88
sharing, discomfort with, 54
shelters, 284
shovels, for litter, 162
shrieking, 34, 38
significant others, cat introduction
    to, 80–83
silver vine, 129–30
sisal-covered posts, 45, 202–3
sleep, sleeping, 3, 100, 232

in aging cats, 272–73
  urination in, 267, 269
sleeping arrangements, 80–81, 100
slight horizontal (half-mast) tail, 30
slow blink, 27
slow-feeding bowl, 148–49
smell:
  sense of, 69, 71–72, 155, 259, 264
  see also scent
snakes, 96
snarling, 38
sniffing, 4, 25
sociability, misinterpretation of, 1–2
socialization, early, 8–10
social maturity, 10, 224
  aggression in, 219
social structure, feline, xi, 1–12
  hierarchy in, see status
sock exchange, 71–72, 74
"soliciting purr," 36
solo (object) playtime, 67, 102,
    106–7, 132
sound enrichment, 131–32
spaying:
  to control aggression, 220
  importance of, xii–xiii, 19, 24
speed barfing, 148–49
spider snatchers, 105
spitting, 37
spray bottle, avoidance of, 217
spray-marking, 19–20, 31, 140,
    176–88, 284
  changing cat's behavior patterns
    in, 183–88
  communication through, 16,
    177–80
  diversion for, 120–21
  gender in, 179
  identifying perpetrator in, 180–81
  management of, 20, 180–88

spray-marking (*cont.*)
  reasons for, 178
  scratching as alternative to, 205
  target areas for, 180–83
  triggers for, 180–83, 186–87
  undesirable urination vs., 176–77
spray quiver, 31
"spray reaction," 180
squeaking, 38
stainless steel bowls, 142
stalking, 78, 119, 224
staring, 27, 83, 233
startle reflex, 191, 223, 241, 273
status, xi, 2–8, 174, 178–79, 195–96
  age-related changes in, 273
  behavioral conveyance of, 5–6, 27
  elevation levels in, 42
  and environment, 6–8
  maturing and, 10
  pecking order in, 1, 4–8
  rubbing in, 17
  shifting of, 273, 277
  timidity and, 50
status-related aggression, 213,
    233–34
Sterilite containers, 165
Sticky Paws (double-sided tape),
    206–7
storage containers, as litter boxes,
    165–66
stranger anxiety, 254–57
strangulation, risk of, 52
stray cats, 186, 230, 247
stress, 50, 81, 180, 181, 278
  aggression and, 213
  in aging, 266
  behavioral changes and, 247
  in cat videos, 131
  change and, 84–85, 86
  early responses to, 248

family as source of, 283
illness and, 262
in new cat introductions, 79–80
physical responses to, 75
scratching and, 201
sources of, 244–46
spray-marking and, 187
symptoms of, 246–47
in transitions, 248
triggers for, 250
in urinary tract problems,
    191–96, 260
in veterinary visits, 226–27, 244
whiskers in, 143
stress reduction, 67, 95, 99–100, 140,
    195, 244–60
  catnip in, 128–29
  outdoor enclosures for, 134
  techniques for, 192–93
stress response (fight/flight), 3, 30, 40
stretching, 24, 201, 205, 270
sudden infant death syndrome
    (SIDS), 87
sunburn, 58

tail lashing, 75
tail position, communication
    through, 24, 29–32
tail twitching, 32, 39
teasing, 90, 228, 237
teeth brushing, 265
televisions, as enrichment, 131
tensions, 10, 57
territorial aggression, 2, 212, 220,
    224–25
  nonrecognition in, 226–27
territoriality, 13, 19, 20, 40–59, 89,
    181, 213–14
  aggression and, *see* territorial
    aggression

cat preference in, 53–55
fearfulness and, 135
increasing vertical space in, 43–49
in mealtime management, 144
stress and, 244
time-sharing in, 41
in transitioning to indoor
    environment, 56
urination and, 197
territorial markers, 178–79
territorial negotiations, 6–7
texture, cat response to, 109, 133
Think Like a Cat (Johnson-
    Bennett), xii
threat, 37, 178, 179
aggression and, 3, 212, 234
humans as, 217
response to, 30–31
Through a Cat's Ear, 132, 254
ticks, 58
timidity, 50, 55, 62, 66
catnip for, 128
distraction for, 120
hiding places for, 124
playtime techniques for, 113, 118
top-entry boxes, 167
touch enrichment, 132–34
touch receptors, 32–33
towels, for panic control, 137
towel swap, 72, 74
toxicity, 127, 232
toys, 65, 66–67, 73–74, 76, 77, 218,
    253, 256
for aging cats, 270–71
catnip-filled, 129
customized for cat's preference,
    108–10
for distraction, 119–21
food-dispensing, *see* puzzle
    feeders

homemade, 110, 124, 151–54
inappropriate choice of, 227–28
for interactive playtime, 102–10,
    118–19, 132, 184, 203, 228, 241
movement techniques for,
    113–14
rotation of, 109
safe storage of, 105
for sound enrichment, 132
testing of, 109
tips for choosing, 105–10
trainer's pouch, 184, 242
training:
leash, 135–37
spray bottle use in, 217
see also clicker training
travel, 135
acclimation to, 222, 257, 259
treasure hunts, 155
treats, 73–74, 88, 138–39, 155, 158, 184,
    228, 242, 258, 275
tricks, clicker training for, 139
trilling, 37
trust, 4, 18, 25, 64, 69
tucked tail, 30
twitching tail, 32, 39

uncovered litter boxes, 164
undesirable urination, 176–77, 283
causes of, 188–90
identifying areas of, 193–96
spray-marking vs., 179
unscented scoopable litter, 169–70
unsociable cats, 61–62
upright tail, 29–30
urinary tract problems, 161, 177,
    195, 246
Pandora syndrome in, 191–96
signs of, 189–90
stress and, 191–96, 260

urination:
  age-related changes in, 267,
      269–70
  identifying and cleaning areas of,
      181–82, 193–96
  identifying problem cats in, 175
  medical issues and, 161–62, 167–68
  outside the litter box, 175–77
  poor aim in, 165–68
  see also undesirable urination
urine-marking, 15, 17, 19

vaccinations, 68, 137
velcro cats, 253
vertical life, see elevated spaces
veterinarians:
  for aging cats, 263–64, 266–67,
      274–76
  cat aggression at, 221
  fear in visits to, 221–22
  in scent recognition, 226–27
  as source of stress, 226–27, 244,
      257–60
  when to consult, see specific issues
veterinary expenses, 11–12
videos, 131, 230, 275
  for behavioral consultation, 280
vision, 26–27, 33
  age-related changes in,
      266–67, 268
  in low light, 66
visual blocking, 185–86
visual enrichment, 130–31, 275
vocalizations, 34–39, 139, 252, 277

aggression and, 232
  in play vs. aggression, 216
vomeronasal organ (Jacobson's
      organ), 17
vomiting, 37, 97, 148–49, 191
vulnerability, 23
  in feeding, 146–47
  in litter box use, 164–65, 167,
      172–74

walking jackets, 136
warmth, 47
water bowls, 65, 143–44
water enrichment, 123
water fountains, 123, 143, 264
water intake, 269
  for aging cats, 264–65
weaning, 9, 25, 251
weight control, 144, 147
  in aging cats, 263–66
  food management in, 149–50
  playtime in, 104
wet food, puzzle feeders for, 153
whiskers:
  in food bowl choice, 143
  function of, 32–33
window perches, 47, 130–31, 157,
      267, 277
wounds, from cat bites, 242
wrapped tail, 31
wrestling, 216, 228

yawning, 24
YouTube videos, 131